THE DUKE OF NORFOLK'S DEEDS
AT ARUNDEL CASTLE

CATALOGUE 1

Dacre Estates in Northern Counties

THE DUKE OF NORFOLK'S DEEDS AT ARUNDEL CASTLE

CATALOGUE 1

Dacre Estates in Northern Counties

Edited by

Heather Warne

Phillimore

2006

Published by
PHILLIMORE & CO. LTD
Shopwyke Manor Barn, Chichester, West Sussex, England
www.phillimore.co.uk

ISBN 1-86077-377-X
ISBN 13 978-1-86077-377-8

Printed and bound in Great Britain by
4EDGE LTD
Hockley, Essex

Contents

Foreword by the Duke of Norfolk

The task of preserving and cataloguing the archives of the Dukes of Norfolk, storing and keeping them in good order as tools in the management of the estates, and also to enable their historical content to be understood, has occupied the family archivists throughout the centuries. Old reference and location notes dating from the 16th century onwards can be found written on the backs or fronts of most rolls, bundles and volumes.

One of the final goals has been to bring to the light of day the many details contained in the twelve thousand or more title deeds that have accumulated in the archives as the ducal estates grew through the centuries. This had been done in the past for small groups and collections of the deeds, and scholarship has benefited from the efforts involved. But the project embarked upon in 1994 was a greater one. All the collections of deeds would be looked at as a whole, enabling their inter-relationships, and therefore their context and their significance to the Norfolk family and local history, to be better understood.

My late father gave enormous encouragement to this work and was always delighted to learn of some new nuance of Howard family history that the cataloguing had revealed. He would have found great satisfaction, as I do, in supporting this publication, for its scholarly content and for the benefit to historical research that it will provide.

Acknowledgements

The following persons are warmly thanked for the various ways in which they have helped in the completion of this stage of the Arundel Castle deeds catalogues: Dr John Martin Robinson, Librarian to the Duke of Norfolk, for his ongoing support; my colleagues Pamela Taylor and Sara Rodger for dealing with the day-to-day tasks in the office on those many occasions when I was too deep into my texts to answer the phone. I would especially like to thank my recently deceased, dearly missed, husband George: for the hours he initially spent in devising computer styles for cataloguing the medieval deeds; and for the patient hours he would spend in front of the computer screen, sorting me out when things had gone wrong.

I would like to thank Mr Neville Howard of Greystoke Castle for the image of the castle on the front cover of the dustjacket. I am grateful for the encouraging response given to me by the archivists at the Cumbria record offices at Carlisle and Kendal when I deposited my draft texts with them in Summer 2001. I am also especially grateful to Brian Dyson, then archivist at the University of Hull, and Judith Smeaton, Acting Archivist at the North Yorkshire Record Office, for the care they took in reading the Yorkshire section of this catalogue and for their corrections and suggestions. Finally, the interest and help given by Dr John Todd and other members of the Cumberland and Westmorland Antiquarian and Archaeological Society has been much appreciated and a warm thanks goes to Mary Atkin for the time she spent in identifying modern locations for the more obscure place names.

Finally, and most importantly, I remember with great affection the interest, support and the steady encouragement of Miles, late Duke of Norfolk; and I thank the present Duke, Edward, for his continuing support to this work.

Heather Warne, June 2005

1. General Introduction to this Catalogue

When Anne Dacre married Philip Howard in 1571, she brought half the estates of her forbears in Cumberland and Westmorland into the Norfolk Howard family. The other half went to her sister and co-heiress Elizabeth and formed the basis of the inheritance of the Earls of Carlisle. In Anne's portion was the Dacre family seat of Greystoke Castle, together with a significant surrounding estate known as the Barony of Greystoke. Broadly this lay in Cumberland, north of the eastern reaches of Lake Ullswater. Its homelands were the fertile meadowy plains around the settlement of Greystoke, originally 'Craystock' or 'settlement at the confluence of streams'. There were outlying villages such as Stainton and Watermillock and there were high fells south towards Ullswater, with higher mountains to the west.

The southern shore of Lake Ullswater, in Westmorland, was occupied by an estate described by the Howard family as 'the Barony of Barton'. Following the old county boundary, this estate cut across the Lake to encompass the Lake head, Glenridding and Patterdale. Anne Dacre's ancestors had acquired a stake in this territory by 1319 following the marriage of Ranulf, Lord Dacre and Joan of Multon. This was the first hold that the Dacres acquired on the shores of the Lake. Dacre, their ancestral seat, lay a little way beyond the north-east shore. However, with the acquisition of the Greystoke estate by marriage in 1488, their hold on Lake Ullswater was complete.

Other significant lands were acquired by the Dacres in the beginning of the 14th century or a little earlier, probably also as a result of the marriage of Joan Multon with Ranulf Dacre. For she had inherited the Barony of Burgh, comprising almost the entire peninsula running from Burgh on Sands west to Bowness on Solway. Title deeds generated by transactions within this estate form a significant part of Catalogue 1, part I.

Deeds relating to the family estates in Yorkshire and elsewhere are in section i of this catalogue, while the Yorkshire deeds in section x of this catalogue do not represent the mainstream estates. Their place in the archives is discussed below in the introduction to that section.

Anne Dacre's Cumbrian inheritance remained with the Howard family estates with Greystoke Castle at its centre until the 18th century, although it was not in the main ducal line until the succession of the 10th Duke of Norfolk in 1777. The estate passed out of ducal hands after the death of Charles, 11th Duke of Norfolk, in 1815. He had felt very engaged with his northern inheritance and he made his mark by rebuilding farmhouses idiosyncratically, and by erecting Lyulph's Tower on the shores of Lake Ullswater in romantic memory of his earliest ancestors there.[*]

---

[*] See J.M. Robinson, 'The follies of Solomon', *Country Life*, 30 June 1985.

Being in hand until 1815, the estate generated records of various kinds which have found their way into the archives at Arundel, while others have passed to the Cumbria Record Office at Carlisle.* Greystoke Castle remained in the Howard family, descending through a younger brother of the 12th Duke of Norfolk to its present owner, Mr Neville Howard.

Apart from those in sections i-ii below, the medieval deeds in this catalogue do not, in the main, relate to the home estate. Instead they relate to small plots and holdings *within* the main estates of Greystoke, Barton and Burgh and in various satellite estates that came in with one marriage or another. The disjointed nature of these deeds collections, and the fact that they are generally early, with no follow-through of title, heavily implies, as observed elsewhere, that they were selected for survival for their antique value. A similar story is true for the North and East Yorkshire deeds, section *x* below. The dorse side of the deeds have collected several sets of cataloguing memoranda over the years. The earliest of these are in a 16th-century hand.

There are a few post-medieval deeds in Part 1 of this catalogue, but most are presented in PART II. There is some overlap in dates. They mainly concern the chief family estates, picking up from section i, '*Greystoke family inheritance*', below. These were numbered by Dr Francis Steer, former archivist at Arundel, but were only bundle listed. I have since catalogued the property clauses in full, which has brought to light some interesting topographical details. For instance, Gowbarrow, near Ullswater, was styled a 'park' by 1668 whereas in 1647 it was simply described as an outpasture of the Greystoke estate (D7123, D7129).

Part II of this catalogue has been arranged so that the family deeds and settlements relating to the Cumberland and Westmorland estates are separate from other evidences of title. This will enable easy comparison with Howard family deeds and settlements to be catalogued in Catalogue 6 and elsewhere (see 2 ii, below, '*The current cataloguing scheme*'). The arrangements of both PART I and PART II of Catalogue 1 can be seen in their separate lists of *Contents*. In the case of Catalogue 1, the brief introduction to subject matter that has been given in this general introduction is amplified by further, more detailed introductions at the start of each new section, in which the rationale for the deeds being in the Howard family archives is explained, as far as possible. It is hoped that local historians, reading content about their home area, may be able to supply further details as to the provenance of some of the material, where these facts have eluded my best endeavours to tease them out.

The value of the Cumberland, Westmorland and North Yorkshire deeds to historians and local historians is not only as a source for Howard family history. They indeed contain many inferences and implications for the early history of the Dacres and their antecedents which may not have been known before. These nuances are interesting, although peripheral to the main history of the Dukes of Norfolk.

---

* The Howard family records at Cumbria Record Office are mainly under the prefix D/HG. For the holdings at Arundel, there are four printed catalogues of the Castle archives, F.W.Steer (ed.) Arundel Castle Archives: a catalogue, vols. I-IV (West Sussex County Council, 1968-1980). Court rolls of various manors within the Greystoke estate are listed in vols. II and IV. Ongoing cataloguing lists are available at the Castle. For information concerning these and concerning access for research, please enquire to The Archivist, Arundel Castle, Arundel, West Sussex, BN18 9AB. Details of the catalogued material are currently also available through the web site of the Historical Manuscripts Commission, now part of the National Archives, at http://www.nationalarchives.gov.uk

Perhaps the greater value of this catalogue lies in the wealth of details it contains to aid our understanding of the medieval north of England - its local place-names, its people and their interactions one with another. For medieval Carlisle, for instance, or Appleby, the interlocking patterns of back lanes and house plots will be better understood, now that the topographical descriptions in these deeds are known. In Barton circa 1250, for instance, we learn of 'the great stone called Greyostan' (CW 281). In the barony of Brough, a 13th-century landscape is graphically illuminated by boundary information given in CW 74 below: ... *into the lake of Glassan ... and thus along the deep marsh as far as Glassan Quitholm ... ascending by the great stone before the fishery of Bochenes* [Bowness on Solway].

Features of the common fields of various communities are frequently given in the conveyance of arable and meadow strips, as, for instance, around the year 1300 at Carlton near Penrith (CW 192) or at Skelton in Cleveland (section x, North Yorks, YK 23). In Hunmanby in the East Riding of Yorkshire in 1225 there is the rarer survival of a conveyance of arable land together with its 23 named tied tenants; while further 'tofts' in the village have the names of former tenants against them. The personal names themselves are an interesting mix of English and Norman, providing us with a glimpse of social integration in the post-Conquest years. And, finally, nearly all the medieval deeds contain, in their list of witnesses, at least one toponymic surname. While most of these can be identified with known parishes, hamlets and farms, others represent 'lost' localities yet to be discovered through research and field work.

It is hoped, therefore, that the work that has gone into this catalogue, and its dissemination, will aid historians in a multitude of different ways as the content of the deeds is examined and re-examined according to each different line of enquiry to which students of today, and of the future, may be drawn.

Heather Warne, June 2005

2. The deeds collections and their previous catalogues

i. History

The largest series of deeds at Arundel is known at Arundel as the '*the post-medieval deeds*'. It is composed of three elements: a) actual title to Howard family properties, b) earlier title to constituent parts of those properties and c) internal family settlements and trusts relating to one or more of those properties. The entire series consists of around 8,500 deeds and documents and relates to many counties of England. They were administered as a collection by the family's 19th-century archivists when the Howard family archives were stored at Norfolk House in London. The deeds were bundled and referenced by their locations in the muniment room there. Although these 'cage' and shelf numbers appear on the outside of many of the deeds, they are no longer relevant. A beautifully-bound catalogue, with a fine illuminated frontispiece and plan of the Norfolk House muniment room, was produced in 1889 in the handwriting of Charles Kent, the Duke's then archivist (ref. MD 1412). This remains in the archives at Arundel as an antiquarian piece, rather than an active finding aid.

The entire series was referenced afresh by Dr Steer as **D/-** (for '**deeds**') in which each document was allocated a unit number in a series 1-*c*.8500. A handwritten 'catalogue' or bundle list was produced in two volumes, one for Sussex and one for other counties, available in his lifetime, in the search room at Arundel, as it still is. Although most of the material in this collection is post-medieval, there are several items which are earlier. Dr Steer's **D/-** references have not been changed for the new catalogues currently in progress.

The generic title of the above series distinguishes it from '*the medieval deeds*' series of around 3000 deeds and documents. These had been separated out in the 19th-century, or earlier, as of 'antiquarian' value. With the benefit of modern professional expertise we may criticise the early archivists' methods, but it is wise to remember that these early deeds might not have survived at all, had their antiquarian value not been recognised at that time. There is even some evidence (see '*HMC deeds*' below) that some deeds were bought in as historic pieces.

Unlike the '*HMC deeds*', virtually no attempt had been made to produce an itemised catalogue of these before 1992 when I arrived at Arundel, although the old Norfolk House cage and shelf numbers and brief bundle details existed, and were noted in the contemporary catalogue (MD 1412) as for the post-medieval series. A few had been boxed up separately and some repairs had been done, including restoration of their seals. The boxes and a pencil hand list proclaimed them as *special charters*. In tackling the main run of medieval material, I chose an alpha-numeric referencing system, in which the prefix indicates the county or area (eg., MX/- for Middlesex or NR/- for Norfolk) and in which each piece has its own separate number. As with the 'post-medieval' deeds, there is some overlap in date, with items from the 16th and, occasionally, the 17th centuries being included in the series. The *special charters* and a group of medieval deeds that do not fit into the main estate categories were taken into the family deeds collection under the reference GD/-, which is explained more fully below.

The collection known as the '*HMC deeds*' is a further artificiality, introduced in the early part of the 20th century when the Historical Manuscripts Commission (HMC) selected out and listed a cross-section of the same 'medieval deeds' series. The catalogued items were physically separated out and boxed as a 'collection'. The published HMC lists, together with additional manuscript lists and notes at Arundel have reinforced the tendency to treat these deeds as a proper collection, which they are not. They are known as '*the HMC deeds*' at Arundel, a habit which will no doubt continue. They were numbered by box/item. (For example, the 12th document in the third box would be HMC III/12.) These are now being incorporated in the alpha-numeric reference system applied to the rest of the medieval series, but the old HMC number is noted in the catalogue.

A further group of around 350 post-medieval deeds is known as the '*STD deeds*'. For reasons that are not clear, these were formerly separated out as being the earlier or 'more-interesting' items in the post-medieval deeds series. These were referenced by Dr Steer as **STD/-** , for '**supplementary title deeds**' and they are still known at Arundel as '*the STD deeds*'. Nos. 1-86 of these were individually catalogued by a volunteer, Mr. A.B. Bartlett (died c. 1982). PhD student Lucy Moye, who was using these deeds for her research, made further notes, and also catalogued nos. 87-110. All these notes have since been typed up by a volunteer, Sheila Neil. The deeds themselves have been further investigated by myself. Unlike the D/- series, the STD/- numbers related indiscriminately either to single documents or to bundles. For itemised catalogue entries, therefore, I have sometimes had to introduce subnumbers. The *STD deeds* are being re-merged into the appropriate post-medieval deeds catalogue, but their reference numbers are left unchanged.

A further series of title deeds which were still being used for estate purposes during Dr. Steer's lifetime and which were referred to as '*current deeds*' have since been referenced as CD/-. These too have been incorporated into the relevant post-medieval deeds catalogues.

ii. The current cataloguing programme

As well as the fresh cataloguing that has been done in all of the five 'classes' of deeds and the re-marrying of divorced parts of series as explained above, two important new initiatives have been undertaken. Firstly, it is intended that the entire collections will be published over a broad time scale. Six volumes are planned, of which this is the first. Catalogue 2 will relate to estates of the Dukes of Norfolk in London, including the important development, from 1672 onwards, of the Strand Estate in St Clement Danes. The estate centred on Worksop manor in north Notts., with lands in Sheffield, south Yorkshire and Derbyshire will follow; and later volumes will cover East Anglia, Sussex and Surrey.

For counties or regions for which a reasonable series of medieval deeds exists, the *medieval deeds* and the *HMC deeds* have been integrated as Part I, while the D/-, STD/- and CD/- collections have been integrated as Part II. It is hoped that this arrangement will aid the majority of those researchers using title deeds, who tend to concentrate on one area or another.

The family deeds catalogue will cover perhaps the most frequent research subject at Arundel, the Norfolk Howard family itself, together with its many, often important, related branches. Up till now, the earlier deeds of title which concern family matters have been little used by our researchers, mainly because their existence is not clear. I have therefore separated out, and thus hope to enhance the researcher's view of, those deeds that spring from the action taken by the Howard family and their agents in harnessing their existing fortunes at any given time. They are the royal patents, the family trusts, marriage settlements, mortgages, bonds and other such instruments whereby the family fortunes were secured, or lost, for future generations. This catalogue will include the **special charters**, mentioned above, and relevant post-medieval deeds which, until now, have languished under a heading of 'various counties' as part of the main D/- or STD/- series. However, they do not sit comfortably in the county series. By bringing them together as a class, it is possible to see what individual heads of family were doing to help or hinder family fortunes.

Deeds in this series which I have newly catalogued have the prefix GD/- (for 'general family deeds'), while the post-medieval items retain their D/- or STD/- references. This catalogue is in progress.

iii. Storage and conservation

Time has been spent during the cataloguing process to improve the storage of the deeds. The medieval deeds had generally been well wrapped and labelled by (I think) Charles Kent the archivist at Norfolk House in the late 19th century. However, his packaging had become dirty and I am replacing it with modern archival packaging, though most of his old labelling has been kept, as, for example, CW 361 on p. 183 below. The post-medieval deeds were mostly in huge and heavy bundles and were very dirty indeed. For further on these, see pp 259-260 below. All deeds are being re-boxed in archival boxes.

iv. Access

All the Duke of Norfolk's deeds, medieval or post-medieval, are available during the cataloguing process for researchers visiting Arundel in person or making enquiry by post, email or by phone. Those wishing to enquire further should contact the Archivist at Arundel Castle, West Sussex, BN18 9AB.

3. The medieval deeds: editorial practice

The medieval deeds at Arundel Castle are catalogued using a specially-designed computer style. In this, the words property, witnesses and seal are always present in bold text, to aid researchers who may only be interested in those aspects of each document. Further details on the format and editorial practice are as follows.

Reference:

an alpha-numeric reference has been designed for the entire collection of medieval deeds, which relates in total to 22 counties of England. For the larger family estates the county to which any sub-series relates is identifiable by the first two characters of the reference.

Document description:

nearly all the documents in the series are deeds of one sort or another. Where the text reinforces the transaction with near synonyms, eg 'given, granted and confirmed', this catalogue simply gives the first word used. Prior to around 1375 the word *concessi* - *I have granted* - is generally the first word but after that *dedi* - *I have given* is more common.

Date:

the earlier items, prior to around 1300, tend to be undated. For these the year date in the right-hand column is a guestimate, based mainly on handwriting style and cross referencing names of parties and witnesses. I am open to informed criticism of my guessed dates. Once a formula of dating by feast and regnal year has come in, this is copied in full into the catalogue and the calendar date of the actual feast day is added. The year date in the right-hand margin is then an accurate *anno domini* in modern reckoning.

Parties:

These follow immediately after the date. In this section are to be found not only the active parties to the transaction but also significant other persons, such as earlier tenants or ancestors of current landholders. Their names are brought in here for clarity, rather than being buried in the explanation section. The parties are designated as a), b) c), etc., for clarity in the explanation section. Otherwise, clarity can often only be achieved by long-winded lists of names or explanations of relationships. See also: *Readings of personal names*, below.

Property:

As one who is personally involved in medieval landscape research, I have felt it important to extract everything from the original text of each deed that has any bearing on the broad locality of that land grant. All local place-names, be they parish, township, field, furlong, croft, wood or way, etc. have been extracted into the catalogue and the spellings have been retained as in the original. The researcher may feel assured, therefore, that if the catalogue contains no details of local and minor names, then neither does the original deed. See also: *Readings of place names*, below.

Matters appurtenant to the property:

The longer lists of appurtenants to a property have been condensed in places, but without, I hope, losing vital distinctions, such as types of commons. The assiduous researcher will, of course, want to check such clauses for himself. Annual rents have been carefully noted but not the intermediate feast days on which quarterly, third- or half-annual rents were due. I omitted these because I did not believe they had anything to add to our understanding of medieval rural life. However, as I went through, I began to realise that Martinmas was a very common payment day in these deeds, perhaps relating to the pastoral nature of the agriculture in the north and to the return of outpastured stock from the hills. The topic therefore awaits its researcher.

Explanation:

This follows from the property section and explains the legal transaction of the deed, noting any monies that have already exchanged hands, or which will change hands in the form of rent; and also noting the conditions of tenure. A variety of feudal conditions of tenure (possibly meaningful) are still being expressed up to the last quarter of the 14th century; but after that a single formula is used, as feudal ties gradually became nominal rather than active. This formula is translated as '... to hold of the chief lords of the fee *by the usual services*' [literally usually *per servitia inde debita et consueta*].

The warranty clause: is not noted, but it is always present in the text.

Witnesses:

Prior to 1500 the witnesses' names are usually part of the text of the deed. After that they may be either absent or endorsed. See also *Personal names*, below.

Seal:

This catalogue gives basic information on seals as follows:
none - there was never a seal on the document; *absent* - a seal was once appended but has since gone; *impression* - the seal is present and has an image; *legend* - it has an inscription around the image.

I did not spend time measuring each seal. The deeds generally have small seals, around half an inch in diameter and the impressions are not very big or clear. Any divergence from this norm is noted by a few extra words in the text.

Seals appended to the very earliest deeds of the late 12th and early 13th centuries are often an inch or more in diameter and the word *fine* may be used to convey their quality. The word *small* means 'smaller than the norm', while *blob* means unformed wax with no impression. Occasionally, where a well-formed crest or coat of arms are impressed this is noted. To summarise, this catalogue should be regarded as a starting point for those who wish to make a study of seals.

Signatures: are unusual in this catalogue and are always noted.

Language:

The text of the majority of these deeds is Latin. Where English or French is used this is noted in a separate line after the seal clause. I have transcribed some of the English clauses as samples of the whole (eg, CW 117), to alert scholars of Middle English to the source.

Medium:

The universal medium of these deeds is ink on parchment. Where paper rarely occurs, this is noted immediately after the seal clause. If the document is in a poor state, or has physical defects, this is also noted here.

Readings of personal names:

Christian names have been rendered into modern form. Occupational surnames have been translated from the Latin or French, usually with the textual reading in square brackets. Filial and toponymic surnames have either been copied in the exact spelling of the original, or, in some circumstances, have been translated.

Readings of place names:

Many family names are effectively minor place-names. These are rendered, it seems, arbitrarily, in either English or Latin in the text of the deeds. The Latin ones are generally translated, but the Latin is quoted in italics in square brackets. See, for example, CW 213, '... John of the Castle [*de Castr'*]'. All other place-names, from parish down to minor local features, are in English in the original. These have been rendered in the catalogue in exactly the same spelling as in the deed. Relevant modern parish spellings are given at the start of each section of the catalogue.

Unclear and interesting readings:

A question mark, followed by my judgement as to meaning, is used where a reading is too faint, etc., or where I genuinely cannot construe the Latin. In the latter instance I have added the actual untranslated text in square brackets, in italics. I have also given the Latin in brackets where I think it is an unusual or interesting usage. Oddities, eg *haliud* for *aliud*, are also noted as they may have a bearing on the history of dialect.

Heather Warne, June 2005

THE DUKE OF NORFOLK'S DEEDS AT ARUNDEL CASTLE

DEEDS CATALOGUE 1   PART I

THE MEDIEVAL SERIES OF DEEDS

Dacre Estates in Northern Counties

Contents: Part I

THE DUKE OF NORFOLK'S DEEDS
AT ARUNDEL CASTLE

CATALOGUE 1   PART I

Dacre Estates in Northern Counties

i

The Greystoke family estates

i Greystoke family inheritance

INTRODUCTION*

CW 1-44 relate principally to the estates of the Fitzwilliam family as lords of Greystoke. They acceded in 1306 at the death of Sir John of Greystoke, 1st Baron Greystoke, whose unfortunate marriage had effectively ceased with his wife's desertion around 1297 and had left him with no children. On his death in 1306, his first cousin Ralph Fitzwilliam inherited the Greystoke estates. As well as Greystoke itself, these included the manors of Dufton in Westmorland (see section vi, Appleby and area, below) and Morpeth in Northumberland which John had inherited through his mother Mary de Merlay. He had acceded to all these estates in 1289 when his father William of Greystoke died.

Although the greater part of this section relates to the Greystoke ('Craystok') inheritance in northern counties, there are also some premises in southern counties (see gazetteer below). These are the earliest of a genre of deeds to be found throughout the Dukes of Norfolk's archives - deeds and settlements relating to clumps of properties in various counties. Most of the later series will be dealt with in Catalogue 6.

CW 1-3 at the start of this series relate to premises in Northumberland and elsewhere belonging, in 1285, to Ralph's grandfather, Ralph Fitzwilliam in the right of his wife, Margery Corbet. The grandfather's chief manors, Henderskelf and Grimethorp in Yorkshire are not mentioned at this stage, presumably because they were entailed differently as hereditaments in the male line. By 1301 the Northumberland premises were settled upon son Robert and Elizabeth his wife, to secure the inheritance. None of these lands seem to have descended through to the Dacre family.

Ralph Fitzwilliam inherited the Greystoke properties in 1306 aged about seven but he did not become the feudal lord of Greystoke until 1317 when his father Robert died. The inheritance clauses in CW 20 below indicate that Robert and Elizabeth had had at least four other children, a son John, and three daughters. Ralph, aged eighteen in 1317, also obtained seisin of (?his father's) manors of Grimethorp, Croft in Teesdale (Croftethwaite)† and Thorpe Bassett in Yorkshire and Neasham in county Durham by writ from the King. After this his title was officially 'lord of Greystoke and lord Fitzwilliam', but the 'lord Fitzwilliam' was later generally dropped. As his eighteenth birthday and the day of his inheritance was approaching he married. His wife was Alice, daughter of Hugh, lord Audley and sister of the Earl of Gloucester. He died

---

* The main sources for this and the other introductions throughout this catalogue are: the deeds themselves; Complete Peerage (entries for Dacre, Greystoke and allied families); Henry Howard, Memorials of the Howard Family, XI and appendices to that chapter (Corby Castle, 1834).
† The *Complete Peerage* cites this manor as 'Crossethwaite'.

only a few years later, in 1324, but the marriage had produced a son and heir, William. Alice, who later married Sir Ralph de Nevill of Raby, county Durham, outlived her first husband by 43 years, dying finally in 1367. This husband, Sir Ralph, had been Keeper of the Realm and Overseer of the Keepers of the Temporalities of the See of Durham in the Bishop of Durham's absence on King's service. His grandson was Ralph, 4th lord Neville of Raby, created Earl of Northumberland in 1397.

It is with the era of William of Greystoke, Alice's son by her first marriage, that this series really begins. A grand sweep of deeds relate to his entailment of estates in 1344 before going abroad. Not only was his clear possession hampered by the long dowry years of his mother Alice, but his grandmother Elizabeth had also outlived her late husband by about 30 years. William's settlement of the key family estates in the north of England is evidenced not only by CW 5-22 below, but also by GD 4/1-2 (Family Deeds Catalogue, in preparation). The latter were separated out by earlier cataloguing systems of the Duke of Norfolk's archives, designated as 'select charters'. Although they remain stored and referenced in that series, they properly belong here with the main series and should be consulted along with these deeds.

The Greystoke line descended through Ralph (suc. 1359) to his son John, who succeeded in 1418. It was John who, through his marriage with Elizabeth de Ferrers, brought the lordship of Wem in Shropshire into the Greystoke possessions. In the deeds of this catalogue, Wem is no more than a lordly title, appended first to the Greystoke surname and later assumed by the Dacres. However, title deeds and other papers relating to the Wem estates survive elsewhere in the Duke of Norfolk's archives.

Ralph of Greystoke succeeded to the family estates in 1456 as John's son, but his own son, Robert, died during his lifetime, leaving a grand daughter, Elizabeth (born 1471), as his heir. Following her marriage, around 1488, to Thomas Dacre, second lord Dacre of Gilsland, the Dacres added Greystoke and Wem to their titles and to their inheritance. In 1571 an account shows that the Dacres in fact held lands in eleven counties. The entire Dacre estates at that time were worth over £1748, of which the Cumbrian portion was worth £670.[*]

The key constituents of the 'de Craystok' family estates were Greystoke itself, Morpeth in Northumberland and Henderskelf (where 'Castle Howard' was later built) in north-east Yorkshire. In Cumberland and Westmorland it was only Greystoke and its ancillary estates that descended to the Dukes of Norfolk after partition between the two heiresses, Ann and Elizabeth, in 1571. The rest, together with the Dacre possession of Gilsland and its seat, Naworth Castle, devolved to the Earls of Carlisle and to the Howards of Corby Castle, as set out more fully in the introduction to Part II, the Post-medieval Deeds, below. Further 'Greystoke estate' deeds, from 1486 on, will be found in Part II.

Finally, it should be mentioned that many of the deeds that constitute CW1-44 are severely damaged by past exposure to mould. Some have crude paper repairs which themselves are fairly old and moth-eaten and which were probably done before the archive was transferred to Arundel Castle.

---

[*] Arundel Castle Archives: A 1053

A gazetteer of places mentioned in CW 1-44

The place-names in this catalogue are rendered in the same spelling as in the original deed (see Introduction, 3, *Notes on editorial practice*). The following gazetteer is intended to provide an overview of the places mentioned in the deeds. However, some minor locations remain dubious. These are shown in italics, as are some of the 'interesting' original spellings of identifiable places. This gazetteer is not an index to specific pages, because the reader is encouraged to look holistically at the entire group of deeds in each section. This approach enables an appreciation of the range of the family's possessions; and also of the ways in which they are parcelling them up in various types of settlements. This gazetteer should be compared with the place-names that occur in the same estates in the post-medieval period, on pp. 265-6.

County	Place
Bedfordshire*	Wyboston
Cumberland	Greystoke
	Stainton
Durham	Brierton (*Brereton*)
	Cocken
	Coniscliffe, High
	Coniscliffe, Low
	Neasham
Essex	East Ham
	West Ham
Hertfordshire	Ayot
Lincolnshire	Northope
Northants.	Finedon (*Thingeden*)
Northumberland	Angerton
	Birkenside
	Blakesdale [suggested by M. Atkin as possibly Blaggdon]
	Broomhaugh
	Doddington
	Hartburn
	Hedon on the Wall
	Hepscott
	Horsley
	Hugham (?variant of Ulgham below)

---

* Wrestlingworth, Co. Beds. see CW 200 below.

Northumberland, cont.	*Merthenlye/Mithingley*
	Middleton
	Morpeth
	Nesbit
	Newbiggin
	Newton
	Riding
	Scheldeford/Shelford
	Shotley
	Spirindone/Spiridene
	Stannington
	Styford
	Thornbrough
	Ulgham
	Warskerley
Westmorland	Dufton
Yorkshire	Belby (near Howden)
	Brunnum (and variants: Nonneburnholm. See footnote)*
	Butterwick in Grindale (*Butterwick in Crendale*)
	Croft (in Teesdale) (*Croftethwaite*)
	Folkton near Scarborough (*Folketon*)
	Ganthorpe (*Galmnethorpe*), near Malton
	Grimthorpe (near Wakefield)
	Henderskelf (Castle Howard)
	Hutton (?same as Sheriff Hutton. see CW 10 etc.)
	Malton
	Meltonby (near Pocklington)
	Moreton upon Swale
	Nidd
	Nonneburneholme
	Osmotherley (*Osmunderlay*)
	Scagglethorpe (*Skakilthorpe/ Skakenthorpe*), near Malton
	Sheriff Hutton
	Terrington (near Malton)

---

* This difficult place-name reading consisted of the letters Br-, followed by eleven identical strokes. Some appeared to be grouped as Brun-, others as Brim-, and an earlier archivist had endorsed the deed as 'Brimham'(near Ripon). However, I preferred to assume that the place was the same as 'Burnholme' or 'Brounom' in the post-medieval deeds (see D7113, 7114, pp 270-2 below). Mary Atkin has further clarified it as Nonneburnholm(e) in post-medieval forms.

Thrintoft (*Thirnetoft*) near
Northallerton
Thornton le Moor (near Thirsk)
Thorpe Basset (near Malton)
Willebiry (held with Henderskelf –
?Welburn near
Malton; or ?Welbury near
Northallerton)
Yapham (near Pocklington)

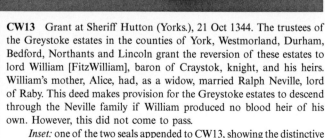

CW13 Grant at Sheriff Hutton (Yorks.), 21 Oct 1344. The trustees of the Greystoke estates in the counties of York, Westmorland, Durham, Bedford, Northants and Lincoln grant the reversion of these estates to lord William [FitzWilliam], baron of Craystok, knight, and his heirs. William's mother, Alice, had, as a widow, married Ralph Neville, lord of Raby. This deed makes provision for the Greystoke estates to descend through the Neville family if William produced no blood heir of his own. However, this did not come to pass.

Inset: one of the two seals appended to CW13, showing the distinctive cross saltire of the Neville arms.

ia Greystoke family inheritance, 1285-1344

CW 1   **Final concord:** at Westminster before the King's Justiciars
[names given], Michaelmas term, 13 Ed. I   **1285**

a) John of Melaund, plaintiff, by his attorney Henry Drinkalup
b) Ralph son of William [or expressed as 'Fitzwilliam']
c) Margery his wife
d) Walter of Undercumbe [also spelt Huntercumbe]
e) Hugh of Vale

Property: i) manor of Ayete [Ayot] and advowson of the church
there in Hertfordshire
ii) 8 acres of wood and appurts. in Westhammes and one
third part of the manor of Esthammes, and appurts.,
in Essex
iii) 10s. rent in Middeltone [?in Teesdale, co.
Durham]
iv) one quarter part of the manors of Angertone,
Hertborn, Dodingtone, Nesbit, Hedun, Stiford,
Spirindone, Nethone [later spelt *Neutone*], Rydingge,
Merthenleye, Bromhal, Shelford, Thornburghe, Sotle,
Blakedesle, Berkenside, Warskerley and Neubigg' in
Northumberland

Parties b) and c) acknowledge that the premises belong as of right
to a) who holds them to himself and his heirs by gift from b); that
d) holds property iv) for life, that e) holds a different ¼ part of the
same for life and that d) and e)'s quarters will come to b) and c)
at the respective deaths of d) and e). The deed was drawn in the
presence of d) and e) who each swear their fealty to a)
Witnesses: none
Seal: none

CW 2   **Gift:**   at Sadberg, the morrow of the Ascension in the
year of grace   **1301**

a) Ralph son of William [ie., 'Fitzwilliam'] of Grymethorpe
b) Robert son of a), and Elizabeth his wife

c) Margerie nee Corbet, wife of a)

d) Lord Walter of Huntercombe and Lord Hugh of the Vale

Property: all the lands and tenements, rents and posessions of a) both in demesne and in lordship and service in Angerton, Herteburne, Mithingley, Schoteley, Byrkenside, Neubiginge, Hedon on the Wall, Neutone, Spiridene, Thornburge, Stifford, Scheldefelde, Brumhalghe, Riding and Dodington in co. Northumberland; with all appurts., homage, services, and the '*villani*' [customary tenants] and their dues in moors marshes, woods, waters, ways, paths and mills; except 100 acres of the demesne land of Dodington which Robert of Wodeford once held and his proportion of the services and escheats

Recites that a) holds the land in reversion by hereditary right of c) and that d) hold a life interest in the property. Now a) grants to b) and his heirs to hold of the chief lords of the fee by the usual services.

Witnesses: lord John, son of William of Greystokes, Hugh Gubyoun, Walter of Huntercombe, Hugh of the Vale, Walter of Binghdon, knights; John of Dodon, Adam of Jenemylle, John of Denum

Seal: two, each with impression (coats of arms) and legend; slight damage

CW 3   Copy of CW 1, undated   *c.*1308

CW 4   **Copy Royal writ: 25 May 1 Ed. I**   **1308**

Citing CW 1 above the King instructs the sheriff of Northumberland to enquire and report by the morrow of midsummer next as to what claim John of Lancaster, kinsman and heir of Marjorie nee Corbet, may have to the properties cited in CW 1-2. John of Melaunde, kinsman and heir of a), is also to be instructed by the sheriff's attornies Robert of Rithille and Robert son of Ralph to appear on that date

Witnesses: none

Seal: none

This deed is attached to CW 3 above. For further Lancaster family properties, see section vii below.

CW 5   **Declaration:** at Craystok, 16 December 16 Ed. III   **1342**

a) William of Dacre, John of Derwentwater, knights, William of Hoton, Giles of Horeton and Thomas of Laton   b) William of Craystok, lord of Craystok   c) John of Blebury, parson of the church of Eure and Walter of Langchestre, clerk

> **Property:**   manor of Craistok in Cumberland, manor of Morpath co. Northumberland and manor of Brunom co. York (*Everwyk*)

Recites that b) has granted the properties to c) together with all his other lands and tenements in the same counties, in demesne, in services and in reversions. a) now declare that they have sworn fealty to c) as overlords of the land they themselves hold at Craystok; and this deed witnesses that they have handed over one penny to c) in lieu of all other services

> **Witnesses:**   none
> **Seal:**   five fragments, each with well defined impressions, including Dacre and Lancaster
> Text is in Anglo-Norman French

CW 6   **Grant:**   undated   *c.* **1344**

a) John of Blebury, parson of the church of Eure and Walter of Langcestre, clerk   b) William of Craystok, knight
c) Elizabeth who was formerly the wife of Robert le Fitz Rauf
d) Ralph of Neville   e) Alice [*Alesia*] his wife
f) Robert of Craystok, brother of b), William and Robert, sons of d)

> **Property:**   i) two parts of two parts [one quarter] of the manors of Brunnum in Yorkshire, Craystok in Cumberland and Morpathe in Northumberland
>   ii) one third part of the same properties
>   iii) manor of Ulgham, Northumberland

a) grants property i) to b) and his heirs, with contingent remainders, in default of such heirs, to f). He also grants property ii), which is currently held by c) as her dower, but which is a)'s inheritance, to b) and his heirs; and the other ⅓ part of the same, which d) and e) hold, are also now granted by a) to b) with the same contingent remainders.

> **Witnesses:**   Thomas of Lucy, William of Dacre, Thomas Ughtred, Ralph of Hastynges, Hugh of Louthre, Peter Tyllioll,

9

Gerard of Wytheryngtone, knights; Thomas of Fencotes, Thomas of Setone, Peter of Rychmond, Clement of Skeltone

Seal: oval with fine impression

This deed is backed with early repair paper

CW 7   **Grant**:   at Hylderskelf, 15 October in the year of our Lord   **1344**

a) William of Craystok, knight, baron and lord of Craystok
b) Thomas of Neville, Archdeacon of Durham
c) Lord John Baron, parson of the church of Thorpebasset
d) Elizabeth, widow of lord Robert, son of Ralph (of Craystock)
e) lord Ralph of Neville, lord of Raby and Alice his wife, formerly wife of Ralph of Craystock who was father of a)

Property: i) manors of Hilderskef, Ga[lme]thorpe, Stakilthorpe, and Willebiry with all lands, tenements, rents, fees, services and reversions; and in the manors and vills following: Thorpebasset, Folketone, Beleby, Yapom and Croftethwayt in Teesdale; Nidde in Yorkshire; Dufton in Westmorland; Wybaldeston, Beds., Thyngden, Northants. and Northorpe, Lincs., with all appurts.
ii) advowsons of the churches in the said counties; manor of Brunnum co. York, held in chief from the King
iii) manors of Butterwyk in Crendale, Moreton upon Swale with Thirnetoft with all appurts., rents, fees, etc. in Thorneton in the More and Osmunderlay (north Yorks.)
iv) manor of Grymethorpe in Yorks. and all its appurts.

a) grants property i) to b) and their heirs but reserves property ii) to himself. He holds the reversion expectant upon properties iii) and iv) expectant on the deaths of d) and e) respectively

Witnesses: lord Richard [of Bury], Bishop of Durham, lords John of Fauconberge, Ralph of Bulmer, Thomas Ughtred, Robert the constable of Flaynburghe, Ralph of Hastynges, Gerard Salvayn of Hersewell, Thomas of Mecham and Thomas of Rokeby, knights

Seal: absent

Deed torn at the bottom

CW 8 **Power of attorney:** at Hylderskelf, 15 October   **1344**

a) William of Craystok, knight, known as [*dictus*] Baron and Lord of Craystok b) Richard of Seteryngton and Thomas Barnard c) Master Thomas of Neville, Archdeacon of Durham and lord John Baron, parson of the church of Thorpebasset

Property: manors of Hylderskelf, Galvethorpe, Skakilthorpe and the other lands, etc. a) in the manors and vills of Thorpbasset, Beleby, Yapoum and Nydde, co. Yorks.

a) appoints b) as his attorneys to deliver seisin to c)

Witnesses: none
Seal: fine impression (Greystoke arms)

CW 9 **Gift**:   at [?Durham] 15th October in
        our 11th year as Bishop   **1344**

a) Richard [of Bury], Bishop of Durham b) Ralph of Nevill c) William of Graystok d) Master Thomas of Nevill, Archdeacon of Durham e) John Baroun, parson of the church of Thorpebasset

Property: i) Manor of Breretone; two parts of two parts [ie., a quarter] of the manors of Nesham, Overconesclif and Netherconesclif
    ii) reversion of three parts [ie. three quarters] of the same manors

a), at the special request of b), conveys property i) to c) for c) to hold of him in chief in order that c) may be able to enfeoff d) in the property. **Property** ii), the reversion of the rest of it, which are currently held in their dotage by Elizabeth and Alice (as in CW 6 above) is hereby conveyed by a) to d). Contingent remainders are detailed to persons as in CW 6 above.
Witnesses: none
Seal: absent
Very damaged parchment mounted on early repair paper, also damaged

CW 10 **Grant and confirmation:** at Sherefhotone, 16 October **1344**

William of Craystock, baron and lord of Craystock, grants to parties d) and e) of CW 9 above all the manors and lands in the Bishopric of Durham and in co. York, Westmorland, Bedford, Northampton and Lincoln which are held in dower by Lord Ralph

of Neville lord of Raby and Lady Alice his wife, once wife of lord
Ralph of Craystok who was father of c)
Witnesses:　none
Seal:　　absent
Deed torn

CW 11　**Power of attorney**: at Nesham, 19 October 18 Ed. III　　　　**1344**

a) Master Thomas of Neville and John Baron, parson of the church
of Thorp Bassett　b) Clement of Skeltone and John Gardiner of
Rabi c) William of Craistok, knight, known as [*dictus*] baron and
lord of Craistok

　　Property:　manors of Dufton in Westmorland and Croftethwayte
　　　　　　　in Yorkshire

a) appoint b) to enter and take seisin of the property on their
behalf, according to the tenor of a deed made by c)
Witnesses:　none
Seal:　　two, with impressions; one of which is a fine impression
　　　　　of arms (Neville) in decorative surround

CW 12　**Power of attorney**: at Schirrefhotone, 20 October　　　　**1344**

a) Ralph of Neville, lord of Raby and ... b) Alice his wife c) Master
Thomas of Neville, Archdeacon of Durham
d) Lord John Baron, parson of the church of Thorpebasset

　　Property:　all the manors and lands of a) in the Bishoprick of
　　　　　　　Durham and in cos. York, Westmorland, Bedford,
　　　　　　　Northants and Lincoln which b) holds as her dower

a) authorises c) to enter and to receive rents, etc.
Witnesses:　none
Seal:　　fine impression of Neville arms.

CW 13　**Grant**: at Shirrefhoton, 21 October　　　　**1344**

a) Thomas of Neville and John Baron, as in CW 12 above
b) Lord William of Craystok, knight, baron and lord of
Craystok
c) Alice, wife of Ralph Nevill, lord of Raby

a) grant b) and his heirs the reversions of all the properties as in
CW 12 above, which they hold during the life of c); specifying

contingent remainders conferring the right to the Greystoke arms
in default of heirs male of b)

Witnesses: none
Seal: two, each with small but fine impression of arms

CW 14   **Grant of seisin**: At Schirref[hoton] 21 October   **1344**

Reciting CW 13 above, Ralph Neville of Raby and Alice his wife
acknowledge receipt of a penny from lord William of Craystok and
they confer on him full seisin of the reversions in question

Witnesses: none
Seal: fine impression of Neville arms in decorative border

CW 15   **Grant**: At Schirefhotone, 24 October   **1344**

a) Master Thomas of Nevile, Archdeacon of Durham and lord
John Barone, rector of the church of Thorpe Basset
b) Elizabeth, wife of lord Robert, who was son of ... c) lord William
of Grymethorpe   d) lord William of Craystock, son of lord Ralph
of Craystock who was son of b) and c)

Property: i) all those lands and tenements, rents and services
which a) held, in lordship as well as in demesne, in the
vills of Angretone, Hertburne, Mithingley, Schotteley,
Birkynside, Hedone on the Wall, Neutone, Spiridene,
Thorneburghe, Stifford, Scheldford, Brumhalghe,
Ridyng and Dudyngton in co. Northumberland, as
in CW 2 above

ii) all the lands, tenements, rents and services which
a) held in the vills and territories of Mortone upon
Swale, in co. York; all the lands and tenements which
a) held in the vill of Thirentoft, with the homage and
service both of the free men and of the villeins and all
appurts.; all the lands and tenements of a), in lordship
as well as in demesne and in service in Thingeden co.
Northants.

Recites former gift by c) to b) and her husband of all the properties,
to hold to them and their heirs and that d) has since granted to
a) the reversion expectant on the death of b); b), by deed dated at
?Beverl' [Beverley, East Yorkshire] on the 20th of the same month,
had 'attorned herself' to a). Now a) concede that b) may have and
enjoy all the premises, despite the 'attornatione'.

Witnesses: none

Seal: fine impression of lady flanked by two shields

CW 16   **Indenture of gift:** at Hilderscelf, Wednesday after
Ss. Simon and Jude (28 October)   **1344**

a) Master Thomas of Nevill, archdeacon of Durham and lord John
Baron, parson of the church of Thorpebasset
b) William of Craystok, knight, Baron and Lord of Craystok
c) Robert, son of lord Ralph of Nevill

Property: i) manors of Hilderskelf with Galmethorp, Scakilthorpe
and Wellebiry, in co. York
ii) manors of Thorpebasset, Folketon, Beleby, Yapum,
Croftethwayte in Teesdale, and Nidde, all in co.
York
iii) manor of Dufton in co. Westmorland
iv) manors of Wybaldeston, co. Bedford, Thyngden
co. Northants and Northorp in co. Lincs
v) manors of Butterwick in Crendale and Moreton
upon Swale with Thirntoft and all other tenements
and rents, etc. which Elizabeth, widow of lord Robert
son of Ralph, holds as her dowry, in Thornton in the
More and Osmunderlaye
vi) manor of Grymthorpe in co. York which Alice, wife
of lord Ralph of Nevill, lord of Raby and widow of
lord Ralph of Craystock, holds as her dowry

a) convey properties i)-iv) and the reversions expectant on v) and
vi) to b) and the legitimate heirs male of his body. If there are no
heirs male then the premises all pass to c) and his heirs male, with
the condition that he takes the name and arms of b) for evermore
[*cognomen et propria arma predict domini Willelmi de Craystok
in perpetuite*]. Further remainders to the youngers brother of c),
Ralph and William, but finally if none of them have heirs male,
it all reverts to the rightful heirs of b).

Witnesses: as in CW 7 above, and also Alan of Claveryngg, knight
and Thomas of Meteham
Seal: two large seals on fine cord, deeply impressed, one
with Neville arms; all in the same style as catalogue
8: GD 4/1-2 (see Introduction to this section, above)
This document is in very poor condition, needing repair. The script
has a coloured illuminated intial letter encompassing the Greystock
arms.

CW 17 **Indenture of gift:** at Nosham [sic], Friday after Ss. Simon and Jude
(28 October) **1344**

Parties as in CW 16 above

Property: manors of Nosham, Overcunisclif, Nethercunisclif and
Brereton within the Bishoprick of Durham

a) grant to b) the reversion expectant on the deaths of Alice and
Elizabeth, as in CW 16, with contingent remainders to c), etc. on
the same conditions as in CW 16

Witnesses: lord Richard [of Bury], bishop of Durham, lord John
of Faucomberge, Ralph of Bulmere, Thomas Ughtred,
Thomas Surtays, Gerard Salvayn of Hersewelle,
Bartholomew of Fanacourt, Thomas of Rokeby, Jordan
of Daldene, knights; Roger of Bla[?yke]stone, Thomas
of Seton, Adam del Boghes
Seal: as in CW 16
This document is in a poor condition. The initial letter is illuminated
in colour with Greystoke arms in a decorative surround sporting
eccesiastical emblems, as in CW 16 and Catalogue 8: GD/4/1-2

CW 18 **Declaration:** at Beverlacu' [Beverley], Thursday after All
Saints (1 November) **1344**
Parties and content as in CW 15 above.
Document and seal in very poor condition

CW 19 **Copy Petition:** undated *c.* **1344**
a) William of Graystock, 'bacheler' b) Father John of Blebyri
[Bleaberry], parson and father Thomas of Pardeshau c) Elizabeth,
widow of Robert fitz Rauf d) Aleyse [Alice], widow of Rauf of
Greystok, mother of a), and former wife of Rauf of Nevill
e) John of Greystok

Property: manors of Brunnom in Yorkshire, Greystok in
Cumberland and Morpethe in Northumberland

Recites that the properties are held in chief from the King and they
were granted by a) to b), subject to separate life interests held in
dower by c) and d); and b) have regranted them to a) and his heirs
male, with contingent remainders to Robert son of Rauf of Nevill,
and his heirs, or in default of heirs male, successively to younger
bros. Ralph and William. Now a) petitions the King that, if these
lines fail, the properties may pass to one John of Graystok, uncle
of a), who is ?around 30 years of age and his heirs, or, if he has
no heirs, to his three sisters, aunts of a)

Witnesses: none
Seal: none
This document is in Anglo-Norman French

CW 20   **Copy conveyance and declaration:** undated   *c.*1344

a) William of Craystok, knight and lord of Craystok
b) John of Blebury, parson of the church of Eure, and Walter
of Langchestre
c) John of Graystock, uncle of a)

Property: i) two parts of the manors of Brunnum, Graystok and
        Morepeth as in CW 19 above
        ii) one third part of the same manors
        iii) the manor of Ulgham in Northumberland
        iv) the third part of the two parts, as in i)

a), by licence from the King, grants the property to b).
Notwithstanding the various life interests [as specified in previous
deeds], the properties will remain to a) and his heirs; and, in default
of heirs of his body, they will descend to c) who is now 30 years
of age, and his heirs; and, in default of his heirs, to his aunts, the
three sisiters of a) who are also of full age.

Witnesses: Thomas of Lucy, William of Dacre, Thomas Ughtred,
        Ralph of Hastynges, Hugh of Louthre, Peter Tylliolle
        and Gerard of Wevryngton, knights, Thomas of
        Fencotes, Thomas of Seton, Peter of Richemond
Seal: none

CW 21   **Letters of attorney:** at London, Sunday after St Martin
            (11 November) 18 Ed. III   1344

a) John of Blebiri, parson of the church of Eure and Walter
of Langchester, clerk b) Sampson of Mulfen and Raufe of
Brantingham

Property: manors of Craystock, Morepeethe and Brun'm

a) appoint b) to receive rents, etc. of all manner of tenants, dower,
farm, free and bond, in the manors.

Witnesses: none
Seal: ecclesiastical; impression

CW 22   **Copy grants (two on one sheet):** undated   **1344**

a) William of Craystock b) John of Blebury, parson of the church of Eure and Walter of Lanchestre, clerk

> i) Two parts of two parts of the manors of Brunnum co. York, Craystok in Cumberland and Morpathe, Northumberland, with all appurts. except advowsons
> ii) The third part of the same manors
> iii) The third part of two parts of the same manors
> iv) Manor of Ulgham, Northumberland

a) grants to b) and their heirs, notwithstanding the life and reversionary interests already specified in this series

Witnesses: Thomas of Lucy, William of Oake, Thomas Ughtred, Ralph of Hastynges, Hugh of Louthre, Peter Tillioll, Gerard of Wedryngton, knights, Thomas of Fencotes, Thomas of Seton, Peter of Rychmond

The second copy:

Confirmation: at Shirefhoton, Sunday after St Martin, 11 November, 18 Ed. III   **1344**

a) William of Craystok, lord of Craystock
b) John of Blebury, parson of the church of Eure

Property: manors of Craystok in Cumberland, Br'mum in Yorks. and Morpathe in Northumberland with all their members and reversions except advowsons

a) confirms the grant to b)

Witnesses: Thomas Ughtred, knight
Seal: none

-oOo-

CW44 An example of an early signature: *John, lorde of Graystok.* 10 August 1499, with a fragment of seal. Earlier medieval deeds relied only on the parties' seals, and the presence of several witnesses, for authenticity. In this deed John 'lorde of Graystok' (elsewhere described as 'esquire') conveys his estates at Morpeth in Northumberland and at *Hynderskelff* in Yorkshire to trustees. The Greystoke estates had, by then, fragmented into parts, the lion's share being in the hands of Elizabeth Greystoke and her husband Thomas Dacre, 2nd lord Dacre of Gilsland. By 1508 all the Greystoke inheritance was firmly in the hands of the Dacres. Neither the Morpeth estate, nor Hynderskelff (later Castle Howard) descended to the Dukes of Norfolk.

ib Greystoke family inheritance 1382-1499

CW 31 **Gift:** at Coken, Tuesday in Pentecost week in
the year of the Lord 1382 and 5 Ric. II **1382**

a) Richard of Cramlyngton [co. Northumb.] and Alianora his
wife
 b) John of Cramlyngton, son of a)

Property: all the lands, tenements, rents and services of a) in Coken
[co. Durham]; and the services of the free tenants and
the neifs there, with the suits of court of them and
their undertenants [sequeli]; and with the meadows,
woods, mines, fisheries. pastures, commons and all
other profits pertaining to the properties.

a) grant to b) and his heirs to hold of the chief lords of the fee
by the usual services

Witnesses: William of Wessyngton and John Darcy del Parke,
knights, John Scrotville, John of Kirkby, Alan of
Ravensworthe
Seal: formerly two, both absent

CW 32 **Marriage settlement:** 12 May 5 Hen. IV **1404**

a) Robert of Ogle, knight of the county of Northumberland
b) William the scrivener of the said county
c) Robert Bristowe
d) Margaret, daughter and heir of John of Croftone

Property: lands and tenements of c) (details not given)

Recites that d) is a ward of a) and that a) and b) are bound to
c) in 100 marks by a statute staple for the payment of £20 on
the feast of the nativity of Our Lady next (8 Sep.) at Kardoil
[?Carlisle] in Cumberland and another £20 at Christmas next and

to deliver d) in person, together with her lands and tenements, to c) in marriage.

Witnesses: none
Seal: absent

CW 33   **Gift**:   22 August 22 Hen. VI   **1444**

a) Ralph [Dacre], baron of Graistok and Wemme   b) John, cardinal and archbishop of York, William bishop of Lincoln, Richard Neville, earl of ?Salisbury [Sar'], George Neville, lord of Latymer, William lord fitz Hugh, Ralph Graistok, knight, Robert Ogle, knight, William Bobbes, knight, Roger Thornton, esq., Raph Bigod, esq., Henry Thwaites, William Hoton, Robert Rides, Thomas Aukland, clerk, Edmund Pole

Property: manor and town of Nethirconscliff within the Bishopric of Durham and all other manors, vills, lands, tenements, rents, reversions, knights' fees, advowsons, possessions and services whatsoever which a) owns in the said episcopacy

a) grants to b) to hold to the uses of his Will which will be written by his hand and sealed with his armorial seal

Witnesses: none
Seal: fragment but with armorial seal intact

CW 34   Counterpart indenture of CW 33 above, identical but with additional parts of the seal surviving

CW 35   **Power of attorney**: date as in CW 33-34 above

a) Ralph, baron of Graistok and Wemme
b) William Wilome and John Robynson

a) appoints b) his attornies to deliver seisin of property as in 33 above to the grantees of that deed.
Seal: as in CW 33

CW 36   A second copy of CW 35 above, identical in all respects

CW 37 **Gift:** 22 August 22 Hen. VI **1444**

a) Ralph [Dacre], baron of Graistok and Wemme
b) As in CW 33 above

Property: manor and castle of Morpath in Northumberland with its members and appurtenances and all other manors, vills, lands, tenements, rents, reversions, knights fees, advowsions, possessions and services in Northumberland

a) grants to b) to hold to the uses of his will, as in CW 33 above

Witnesses: none
Seal: as in 34 above

CW 38 **Power of attorney:** date as in 33-37

a) Ralph, baron of Graistok and Wemme
b) James Buk and John Clapham

a) empowers b) to deliver seisin of the manor of Morpath and appurts. to the grantees of CW 37 above

Seal: as in 34 above

CW 39 **Power of attorney:** date as in 33-38

a) Ralph, baron of Graistock and Wemme
b) James Buk and William Wilome

a) empowers b) to deliver seisin of the manor of Staynton in Cumberland to the same grantees as in previous deeds [mentioning an actual deed of gift, ?33 above, or ?one which has not survived in the series]
Seal: as in 34

CW 40 **Power of attorney**

a) Parties as in 35; date as in 33-39
a) appoints b) to deliver seisin of the manor of Brereton in Durham Episcopacy to the same grantees as in previous deeds (mentioning an actual deed of gift, ?33 above)
Seal: as in 34

CW 41   **Power of attorney:** date as in 33-40

a) Ralph [Dacre], baron of Graistock and Wemme
b) James Buk and John Clapham

a) appoints b) to deliver seisin of the manor of Hepscotes in Northumberland to the same grantees as in previous deeds (mentioning an actual deed of gift, 33 above)
Seal: as in 34

CW 42   **Gift:**   26 March 2 Ric. III   **1485**

a) Randolph, Lord of Graystok and Wemme   b) William Potman, clerk, Edmund Hastynges, knight, Robert Sheffeld, Thomas Pole and Edmund Thwaytes c) Robert Peke and John Todd

Property: manor of Grymthorp co. Yorks., now in the tenure of Thomas Richardson, with the water mill there; the demesnes and manors of Thornton and Thirntoft and all their lands in Thornton, Thirntoft, Hoton and Teryngton co. York

a) grants to b) and appoints c) as his attornies to deliver seisin to b)

Witnesses: none
Seal: fragment but good impression

CW 43   Counterpart of CW 42

Seal: same impression as in CW 42

[CW 42-43 were found with Yorkshire deeds and were first given the reference YK 92 and YK 93, which is now obsolete.]

CW 44   **Gift and Confirmation:** 10 August 14 Hen. VII   **1499**

a) John Grastoke, lord of Grastoke, son and heir male of Ralph of Grastok and Wem
b) Richard, by God's grace Bishop of Durham, Ralph Bowes and Richard Eure, knights, Robert Constable, serjeant at law, Thomas Gray of Horton, Richard Danby esq., John Laynge and Richard Weloughby, clerks, William Longcastre and John Tode, gents

Property: i) the castle and manor of Morpethe in Northumberland; manors of Hugham Stanengton and Horsley with their appurts. in the same county; with all lands, tenements, rents, reversions, services and hereditaments of a) in Hugham, Stanengton and Horsley.

ii) manors of Hynderskelff, Galmnethorpe, Meltenby, Butterwyk and Thorpebasset in co. York, with lands, tenements, rents, services and hereditaments of a) in Skakenthorpe, Malton, and Hynderskelff, Galmnethorpe, Meltenby, Butterwik and Thorpebasset.

a) grants to b) to hold to themselves and their heirs

Witnesses: none
Seal: fragment; and signature 'John lorde of Graystok'

-oOo-

THE DUKE OF NORFOLK'S DEEDS
AT ARUNDEL CASTLE

CATALOGUE 1   PART I

Dacre Estates in Northern Counties

ii

Barony of Greystoke, co. Cumberland

ii Barony of Greystoke, c.1300-1605

INTRODUCTION

The eleven medieval deeds in this section are mere fag ends representing a once-important feudal estate. The 'Barony' was created in the mid-12th century along with that of Gilsland, north-east of Carlisle, to reinforce the power of the English kings in troubled border lands.[*] Both estates probably already existed. By 1289 Greystoke itself was a borough and presumably a market town, while the Castle had acquired its own deer park. By 1472, however, the Borough had declined, for a rental shows that only one 'burgage' property remained in Greystoke by that date.[†] It is suggested by Angus Winchester (see note below) that Greystoke and other small boroughs in the general area had been outstripped by Penrith with its convenient through routes for trade.

None of the deeds that remain in this collection relate to Greystoke itself, but to outlying settlements in the Barony. There is no direct evidence that Lamonby (see CW 51) was in fact a part of the estate, but the deed has been placed here for want of any other 'home'. The rental of 1472 mentions numerous tenements in Grisedale, Sowterfell, Motherby, Stainton, Berrier, Matterdale, Watermillock and Sparkhead Row as well as Greystoke itself. It was an area of contrasting territories, from the water meadows at Greystoke to the low fells abutting Ullswater and rugged mountains to the west. Other areas, such as Hutton Roof and Newbiggin, are mentioned in a rental of 1661 when the Barony was in the possession of Elizabeth (née Stuart), Dowager Countess of Arundel and Surrey mother of Thomas, 5th Duke of Norfolk. This very full rental provides us with the general overview of the extent of the Barony, which these deeds, sadly, do not.[‡] The Barony of Greystoke passed to Elizabeth Arundel's third son, Charles and, by descent, to the Dukes of Norfolk. Further references to the estate while it was in the Dukes' possession can be found in the printed catalogues of the Arundel Castle archives.

---

[*] For further reading, see: N. McCord and R. Thompson, *The Northern Counties from AD 1000* (Longman, 1998); A. Winchester, *Landscape and Society in Medieval Cumbria* (Edinburgh, 1987)
[†] Cumbria Record Office: DHG 6/16
[‡] Arundel Castle: A 538

Contents

ii Barony of Greystoke

CW 51   **Gift:**   at Lamanby, Wednesday before St Cuthbert
                                  (20 March) 14 Ed. III   **1340**

a) Adam of Hoton of Alaynby the elder   b) Thomas his son

Property: one messuage and four acres of land with appurts.
                 in Lamanby, that is the messuage and three acres
                 which Robert Goldyng holds and one acre in Le
                 Burghaues

a) grants to b) to hold to b) and the heirs of his body and to
the heirs of a) by the service [sic] of 1d. each year at Christmas.
The property will revert to a) and his heirs if b) should die before
producing any heir of his body

Witnesses: Clement of S[-?*celton* - faded], John of Hotonrofe,
                  John of [?*Qw*]-ytebergh, John of [?]-ynperon, Thomas
                  [sic, though there is an overlarge gap between the T
                  and the h of Thomas] of Hoton of Alaynby
Seal: oval with indistinct impression and legend
This deed was formerly referenced as HMC Box V, 68

CW 52   Copies made *c.*1450 of:

1   **Gift:**   at Motherby, midsummer 2 Ed. III   **1328**

a) William of Suttone of Motherby
b) Adam son of Katherine of Motherby and Anota [sic] his wife

Property: all the lands and tensements of a) in the vill' of
                 Motherby, with all appurts., easements, commons and
                 liberties

a) grants to b) and the heirs of their bodies to hold of a) and his
heirs and of the chief lords of the fee by the usual services.

Witnesses: lord William Threlkeld, knight, John of Rysoptone, William of Latone, William of Hotone, Richard of Latone, Adam Blenkowe

Seal: none

2   **Gift:**   at Motherby, feast of Ss. Peter and Paul,
                       29 June, 10 Hen. IV   **1409**

a) John Thomson Emmotson of Unthanke
b) Edmund Slee of Motherby

Property: messuage and three acres of land with appurts. in the vill' of Motherby

a) grants to b) and his heirs to hold of the chief lords of the fee by the usual services

Witnesses: Richard Berwyss, Henry Hotone, Thomas Blencowe, esqs., Nicholas Suttone, John Gyll

Seal: none

The copy is endorsed with contemporary note of the descent of title from William of Sutton and from his three daughters Anota, Emmota and Alicia.

CW 53   **Gift:**   undated   **circa 1300**

a) Thomas Follard of Newbigging b) Lord William, son of Thomas of Craystok

Property: all the land of Newbigging belonging to a) with the capital messuage and croft, with the homage and service of all the free tenants and all manner of escheats; and with all appurts., liberties and easements

In return for a certain sum of money given to him in his great need by b), a) grants to b) and his heirs to hold in perpetuity.

Witnesses: lord Robert of Hamptone, Henry of Redmane, Richard of Latone, knights, William of Treelkeld, Thomas of Hotunruf, Gilbert Holeye, Robert of Louther

Seal: absent

CW 54 **Grant:** at Newebyggynge, Sunday after the commemoration
of Ss. Peter and Paul, 29 June, beginning
of 8 Richard II   **1384**

a) Robert of Swynborne, knight   b) Gilbert of Whelpdale

Property: all the lands, tenements, rents and services belonging
to a) in Newebyggynge in Cumberland

a) grants to b) and his heirs to hold of the chief lords of the fee
by the usual services.

Witnesses: none
Seal: impression (arms) and legend

CW 55 **Gift:** 29 April 23 Hen. VIII   **1532**

a) Richard Suthayke, chaplain
b) William Dacre, Lord of Dacre and Graystoke c) Thomas Talantire,
John Allenson, chaplain

Property: one messuage in the vill' and fields of Newbigging
within the Barony of Graystoke, now in the occ. of
Christopher Heremyt; one messuage in the occ. of
Robert Nelson; ½ messuage in the occ. of Thomas
Harskew; one messuage in the occ. of the wife of John
Sympson; one parcel of meadow called Canounyng in
the occ. of Thomas Todd, Robert Nelson and the wife
of John Sympson; with all lands, tenements, meadows,
feedings and pastures, woods, underwoods, hedges,
ditches, ways, paths, services and all other emoluments
pertaining to the said messuages

a) grants to b) and his heirs to hold of the chief lords of the fee
by the usual services and he appoints c) to enter the property and
deliver the seisin to b)

Witnesses: none
Seal: impression; and signature of a)

CW 56 **Bond:** 24 July 31 Hen. VIII   **1539**

a) John Whyte of Sowerby, Edward Abbott of the same and Nicholas
Relfe of the same   b) William Brysbye

Property: messuages, lands and tenements in Sandwyk in
Westmorland and in Newbiging in Cumberland

33

a) is bound in £20 to b) to allow him peaceable possession of the property, according to a deed between them of the same day's date.

Witnesses: none
Seal: two small fragments

CW 57   **Exchange**:   9 February, 4 & 5 Philip and Mary   **1558**

a) Lancelot Penryth of Staynton co. Cumberland, carpenter
b) William Lord Dacre, Graistocke and Gilesland and Lord Warden of the Western Borders [*Westmerchiae*] between England and Scotland

Property: i) 2½ acres of land lying in the field of Newbiging at a place called Pallet Feld; one rood of land at a place called Pallet Buttes; one rood of land at a place called Hoggonie Dores or Gowldye Rood; ½ rood of land abutting on Cowpland Streat; 2½ roods of land at a place called Alme Cayne; all parcels lying between land of Richard Salkeld on one side and of the Chantry of Hotten on the other. ii) ½ acre of land lying in the field of Staynton at a place called Kyrkerydge between land of Thomas Layton on either side; one rood of land at a place called Baston Croftes between land of b) on one side and of said Thomas Layton on the other; one rood of land at a place called ?Sirkelle, between as previous; 1½ roods of land at a place called ?Hughtergyllhow between land of said Thomas Layton on both sides; 1½ rood of land at a place called Crukyth Raynes between as previous; ½ rood of land at Crukyth Raynes between as previous

a) owns i) and b) owns ii) and they freely exchange to hold to themselves and their heirs.

Witnesses: Master John Dacre, parson of Graistocke, Lancelot Lancaster, esq., William Myddelton, the receiver [ie., chief accountant] of Graistocke, Henry Smallman the bailiff of Dacre, William Myllner, Christopher Matheson, John Whitelocke of Staynton.
Seal: impression; and signature of a)

CW 58   **Gift:**   28 December, 4 Eliz.   **1561**

      a) Richard Salkelde of Rosgill in Westmorland
      b) William Lord Dacres [of] Graistock and Gilselande

Property: four tenements with appurts. in Thakthwate in the
              Barony of Graistock in Cumberland, in the separate
              occs. of Richard Nicolson, William Burton, William
              Dawson and the wife of Richard Merten

      In return for a money payment a) grants to b) and his heirs

Witnesses: none
Seal: impression

CW 59   Bond of same day's date in £300 from a) to b), for performance
      of covenants
      Seal: impression of horses head

CW 60   **Letters of attorney:**   24 April 4 Eliz.   **1562**

      a) Richard Salkeld of Rossegille in Westmorland, esq. b) John
      Salkelde, bro. of a)   c) William Herreson of Gilcamon
      d) William Lord Dacre

      Property: as in CW 58

      a) appoints b) and c) his attorneys for entering and taking possession
      of the property in his place.

      Witnesses: none
      Seal: one, small; signature of a)

CW 61   **Lease:**   18 November 3 Jas. I   **1605**

      a) Sir Edward Carill, knight, John Holland, John Cornwalleis,
      Robert Cansfeild, esqs.
      b) Anthony Romney of Golborowe Park in the Barony of
      Graystock
      c) Henry Curwen, gent.

      Property: messuage or tenement within the manor or lordship of
              Wethermelock in Cumberland, now or late in the occ.
              of Edward Wilson, yeoman; with all lands, meadows,
              feedings, pastures, profits and commodities

a) lease to b) for 4 years beginning Michaelmas last to hold at 10s. annual rent

Witnesses: names endorsed, with note of delivery of seisin by c), attorney for b)

Seal: two with impressions, slightly damaged

-oOo-

THE DUKE OF NORFOLK'S DEEDS
AT ARUNDEL CASTLE

CATALOGUE 1   PART I

Dacre Estates in Northern Counties

iii

The Barony of Burgh

iii Barony of Burgh, Cumberland c.*1275-1632*

The Barony of Burgh (pronounced 'Bruff') came into the Dacre family by marriage in the mid-13th century as part of the inheritance of Joan of Multon. Joan married Randolf Dacre, who died in 1286. She had inherited Burgh, among other properties, from her mother Aude, wife of Richard of Lucy of Egremont. The main title to the estate is not part of this collection.

The deeds in this group relate to Burgh, Bowness on Solway and other parishes on the Bowness peninsula as well as a few inland areas such as Bothell near Aspatria and Dalston. They form the most coherent group of all the Dacre family (northern) estates deeds in the Duke of Norfolk's archives. They were mainly found in four separate packets, chronologically, but otherwise indiscriminately arranged within the packets. In addition, several items formerly catalogued at Norfolk House by Mr. Frederick Wood in 1926 have been added to this series, to which they intrinsically belong. Finally, a handful of items among the *HMC deeds boxes* [see *Introduction*, above, for explanation of term] were found to relate to the Barony of Burgh and have been catalogued and added to this list; retaining the old HMC box number as a cross-reference.

The importance of the peninsula as a front line in England's defence against the Scots is witnessed not only by the visible parts of Hadrian's Wall, running from Carlisle to Bowness on Solway, but also by the massive proportions of the defensive tower attached to Burgh parish church. Indeed, the Barony of Burgh was created around 1106 by Henry I, along with the barony of Liddel, north-east of Longtown in Liddesdale. They were adjuncts to the lordship of Carlisle and their specific purpose was to protect it from raids from the west and the north (see H. Summerson, *Medieval Carlisle*, Carlisle 1993).

Another important aspect of the peninsula was its role in the pastoral economy. The tidal marshes on its Solway shores still provide seasonal pasturage for livestock today, providing a direct and powerful link with the place-names of the local settlements - '*Bowness*' and '*Drumbough*'; in which -*bow* and -*bough*, meaning 'cattle', indicate pastoral custom. If the peninsula's early use was as an outpasture for inland settlements, this may be echoed in the similarity of some local names, eg., '*Whitrigg*' and *Fingland* near Wigton, and *Whitrigglees*, *Finglandrigg* in the peninsula. It is not exactly clear which of the two Whitriggs is the subject of the deeds in this group.

A key person in the Multon/ Dacre hierarchy was Hugh of Multon (fl. c.1290-1300). He provides the link between at least three of the sections of this catalogue. For in 1302 (CW 80) he made a transaction relating to Burgh, while being described as 'of Hoff' (near Appleby in Westmorland). Hoff manor was in Lady Margaret Dacre's hands by 1341 (see CW 257); and it was from him that the Glenridding estate at the head of Ullswater passed to the Dacres (see section vii, introduction).

As in other sections of Deeds Catalogue 1, Part I, the Barony of Burgh deeds generally do not relate to the head manor of the estate, but to minor land holding in the estate. Therefore we do not have the early title deeds to Burgh itself.

The series begins with some stray early deeds relating to individual parishes within the estate, or to nearby possessions of related families; and continues in two parts. The Whitrigg land descends through the Whitfeld family to one Clement Skelton, while Drumburgh, Bowness etc. pass from the Brun family to the Haveryngtons. Both were purchased by Thomas, Lord Dacre at the beginning of the 16th century, after which the land passed to the Howard family of Greystoke. The Barony as a whole was sold out of the Howard family in 1685. There are references to the sale and to various constituent parts of the Barony in Deeds Catalogue 1, Part II, below. His family's connection with the estate was commemorated in 1685, at the time of the sale, by Henry, 7th duke of Norfolk with the erection of an obelisk out on the Solway marshes, inscribed - *to the eternal memory of Edward I the most famous King of England, who died here in camp whilst preparing for war against the Scots, July 7 1307. The Most Noble Prince, Henry Howard, Duke of Norfolk, Earl Marshal of England, Earl of Arundel, etc., descended from Edward I, king of England, placed this monument, 1685. John Alionby, a lawyer by trade, caused it to be made.* In 1803 the monument was rebuilt by the Earl of Lonsdale, whose family had purchased the estate in 1685, and it was restored in 1876.

A gazetteer of places mentioned in the Barony of Burgh deeds

As with CW 1-44 above, where the modern location is dubious, the spelling as cited in the documents is given below in italics. As for CW 1-44 above, Mary Atkin of the Cumberland and Westmorland Antiquarian and Archaeological Society has provided help with some lost or minor locations. Not all the places named in these deeds are on the peninsula itself but many are to the south.

Many of the places mentioned here occur again in the post-medieval deeds in Part II of this catalogue. See p. 255 below.

Aikton
Anthorn
Bassenthwaite
Bothel
Beaumont
Bowness on Solway
Boydon
Brunscath, Brunscarr (see *Langbrunscath*)
Burgh by Sands
Caldbeck
Cardurnock
Cwitrig, see Whitrigg
Dalston
Drumburgh
Drumleaning (*Drumlynyn*)
Easton
Fingland and Finglandrigg

Gaitsgill
Glasson
Glassonby (Glassyngby)
Grenerig (?in Westward, or possibly Caldbeck)
Hakehewyd (?Aikhead in Woodside)
Langbrunschaythe (and variants, ?a lost name for a locality in Burgh by Sands)
Mursthwayt (?Mousthwaite comb in Threlkeld)
Partene (?Parton)
Quitrig (= Whitrigg)
Raughton
Stubhill, Stuble
Thakyngecruk
Threlkeld, see *Mursthwayt*
Thursby
Westward see *Grenerig*
Whitrigg
Wormanby in Burgh by Sands (*Wilmorby*)
Woodside, see *Hakehewyd*

iii Barony of Burgh, Cumberland
a) deeds 1275-1375

CW 71 **Grant:** undated **?circa 1275**

a) Robert Iveison b) Ralph son of Ralph

Property: two bovates of land in the vill' of Fyngelan and 1a. more ? of assart [*de incremendo*], viz. ½a. at Laithyld and ½a. next to Hungerstain; with all liberties and easements pertaining

Reciting that b) is already in possession of the land a) grants to b) and his heirs to hold from a) in fee and by hereditary right, paying a) one pair of white gloves each year at Carlisle fair. If b) or his heirs should wish to sell the land b) and his heirs ?would like first refusal [*erimus propinquiorespre omnibus aliis ad eam habendam*]

Witnesses: lord Richard of Levi'cdona, Ralph Feritate, Gilbert of Feritate, Robert of Wahelpol, Robert of Wyterig, Ralph of Feritae of Kyrkebride, Adam of the same, Walter son of David

Seal: absent

CW 72 was formerly HMC, Box X, no. 81

CW 72 **Lease for 20 years:** undated *c.1262*

a) William Pinel of Langberthe   b) lord Thomas of Multon
c) Ralph Walens of Burgh   d) Lady Joan of Morevylle

Property: a meadow in the east marsh of Burgh, with all its appurts. and divisions

Recites that the premises were given to a) as his share of the marsh, which was enclosed with a sea dyke [*fossatum maris*]. He now leases to c) in return for 'a certain sum of money' (not specified), to hold from the middle quarter of the year of Our Lord 1262 for 20 years ensuing at a rent of 1lb of cumin or 2d; payable annually at the feast of the Assumption of the Blessed Virgin (15 August) in lieu of all customs, services or demands. The premises will revert to a) and his heirs at the end of the term.

Witnesses: Robert of Wardwyk, then steward of John of Teriby, Simon of the Sands, Adam of the Foss [or 'Dyke'], Robert of Langberthe, Adam of Thurstanfield, Adam Kocket, Robert son of Ely of Langberthe, Ralph Walens the clerk

Seal: absent

CW 73   **Agreement:** undated   **circa 1280**

a) Ralph of the Ferte of Glasson   b) Lord Robert of Dumbredon c)Robert of Wiltona the parson of Dalastona

Property: land in Quiterig [ie., Whitrigg]

A dispute between a) and b) concerning the property has come to court, involving out-of-county expenses for a). Now a) agrees with c) that, if at the 'Great assize' he is able to recover his costs, c) shall have half what he recovers.

Witnesses: none
Seal: absent

CW 74   **copy (?16thc.) grant:** undated   **original circa 1280**

a) Ralph of Laferce   b) William of Laferce   c) Robert of Laferce

Property: one carucate of land called Glassan along these bounds, viz. it goes down into LeLake of Glassan and ascending up to the small wall [or could be moor] and thus along the deep marsh [or boggy marsh *profundum mariscum*] as far as Glassan Qwitholm then as far as the bounds of Hwiterig; on the other side LeLake of Glassan falls into ?a hollow [*adene*] and thus ascending by the great stone before the fishery of Bochenes; and from that stone as far as Waterscait which is the nearest to the said fishery except one other [? -*scanchum*] and thus ascending the great marsh as far as Dikescache; and two crofts in one [? -*gradium* -or could be a place name, "Mungradium"] in Drumbo, with messuages; and with free and peaceable enjoyment of all meadows, feedings, turbaries and ?sands.

Reciting that his grandfather gave the land to c), who was his father, a) now grants it to b) and his heirs to hold of a) by homage and service and by hereditary right

Witnesses:	Peter of Celleit, John of Raucheclive, Reginald his son, David son of Terri, Nicholas and ?Wilbert his son, Anketon son of Udard and Richard his son, Richard son of ?Fautte, Norman ?the innkeeper [*ostagium*], Richard ?the pack man [*malator*], Henry of Bochenes, Heremund ?the free serf [*burus*], Ralph of the Sands

Seal:	none
NB.	Some of the above readings may have been copied wrongly from the original. This is a paper copy (?15th c.) of a ?13th-century deed

CW 75 was formerly HMC Box I, no. 27

CW 75   **Quitclaim:** undated   *?c.1300*

a) Richard of Stokis   b) lord Robert of La Ferte, chief lord of a)
c) Geoffrey of Hode

Property:	messuage and one bovate of land which c) formerly held from a) in the vill' of Bouness

a) quitclaims to b) any rights he or his heirs may hold in the property, or in mulcts (amercements), the fisheries, the turbaries or in any other easements in the vill of Bounes.

Witnesses:	lord John of ?Teriby, Richard of Kyrcbride, Richard of Boyville, Robert of Quiteric, Walter of Bamtone, William of La Ferte
Seal:	absent

CW 76 was formerly HMC box I, no. 26

CW 76   **Quitclaim:** undated   *?c.1300*

Parties as in CW 76 above

Property:	all the land which a) held or was entitled to hold in Kardrunnok, with all appurts., liberties, muclts, fisheries, saltings, turbaries, and all other easements in the said land and vill'

Recites that b) originally granted the land to a) in return for a certain (unspecified) sum of money. Now a) quitclaims all back to b), including the King's service that pertains to the premises.

Witnesses: Thomas of Neutona and John of Terriby, knights; Walter of Bantona, Robert Quiterig, Richard of Boyville, William of La Ferte

Seal: chipped; impression partly erased

CW 77 **Quitclaim:** undated circa 1290

a) Peter son of Serle of Drumbok'   b) Lord Robert of Feritate

Property: rights of common pasture in the demesne lands and pastures of b) at Drumbok'

The rights of common pasture which a) has been enjoying at Drumbok' he now releases back to b) and his heirs so that in future a) and his heirs can claim no common there

Witnesses: lord Richard of Feritate, lord William then chaplain of Bouness', lord Simon then chaplain of Drumbok', William of Glassan, Robert of Wythryg, Adam his brother of the same, Richard of Stokys, Adam Grosse of Bouness'

Seal: impression erased

CW 78 **Final concord:** undated circa 1290

a) Lord David le Brun, plaintiff
b) Patrick le Brun, tenant of the Manor

Property: i) Manor of Bothil' with its appurts. and liberties
ii) all the land of Haykehewyd with all its appurts.

Recites that a plea between a) and b) concerning property i) was heard in the King's court at Westminster and as a result a) agreed to quitclaim it to b) and his heirs; and, in exchange, b) gave a) property ii) and the sum of 115 marks sterling, to hold from b) at annual rent of 1d. This deed now ratifies that decision.

Witnesses: William of Warthecop then sheriff of Cumberland, Lord Robert of Mulcaster, Lord Alan of Orretone, Lord Richard of Latone, lord Ranulph of Daker, Lord Robert of Feritate, Thomas of Neutone, Robert Wigtherig, Richard of Kyrkebride

Seal: absent

CW 79 **Copy (? 14thc.) gift and quitclaim:** undated   **?circa 1250**

a) Roger Mowebray, Lord of Boltone in Allerdale   b) Alexander of Bastenthwayt and … c) Agnes his wife   d) Robert, son of Lord Richard Brune

Property: the entire waste ground [*totum solum vasti*] of Bastenthwayt, with its wood and with all other profits of the said ground, waste and wood, with all other liberties, rights and claims pertaining.

a) grants to b) and c) and the heirs of b)'s body and he releases to them any claims that a) or his heirs may have on the property; for b) and c) to hold of a) at 14s. annual rent; reserving to a) one mark, one pound of pepper and one pound of cummin out of his old farm [*antiqua firma*] of Bastenthwayt together with the wild pig and the sparrow hawk [*salvagio porco et aucipite*] and the advowson of the church of St Bege of Behekkyrk.
Contingent remainder to d) and the heirs of his body, in default of heirs of b).

Witnesses: none (ie., omitted in copy)
Seal: none
NB. The tenor of this land grant suggests mid 13thc. or earlier. The main Mowbray barony was not created until 1295, so this must be an earlier line.

CW 80 **Gift:** at Hoff, on a Thursday in 31 Ed. I   **1302-3**

a) Hugh of Multone of Hoff'   b) Henry of Lamplow

Property: lands and rents in various fields and places in the vill' of Burgh upon Sands except a ?furlong which Gilbert Col-[illegible] once held and a [word missing] once of Robert son of Elyas and except 3 acres on Estavenham and except 5 acres of the land which Robert [word missing] held and [word missing] roods which lie next to the Manor in a croft near against John Jalpe

a) grants to b) and his heirs in fee in perpetuity to hold of the chief Lords by the usual services

Witnesses: [Illegible] le Brun, lord Richard of Kyrkebryde, Robert of Langeberge, Robert of the Dykes, John Batemane, William of the monks, lord Richard the parson of Ayketon
Seal: absent
A stained and damaged doc.

CW 81   **Grant:**   at Cardoille, 12 August, 16 Ed. II   **1322**

a) Robert le Brune, esq.   b) Richard, son and heir of a)
c) Joan, wife of b)   d) Mons. Michel of Haveryngtone and
Mathilda [*Mauld*] his wife e) Mons. Richard le Brun, father of a)
f) Margaret le Brun, wife of a)
g) the Earl of Cardoille [?Carlisle], a)'s Lord

Property: i) Manor of Beaumound with its appurts. and advowson of the church of the same; two messuages,
38 acres of land and 2 acres of meadow in the vill'
of Langbrunschaythe
ii) 10 messuages and 10 bovates of land and 10
acres of meadow with appurts. in the same vill' of
Langbrunschaythe

Reciting that d) hold property i) as Mathilda's dower a) now grants
the reversion, following her death, to b) and c); and reciting that he
received ii) from e) when he married f), he also grants the reversion
expectant on the property to b) and c); remainder to the joint heirs
of their bodies, or, if there are none, to the rightful heirs of a).
and a) will ratify this grant in the court of Kings bench between
now and Christmas next and levy a fine in the same court, the
costs to be paid by g)

Witnesses: none
Seal: absent
This document is in French

CW 82   **Gift:**   at Bowneys, 6 November 6 Ed. III   **1332**

a) Henry of Raghtone
b) Walter the rector of the church of Bowneys

Property: the land of a) in Bowneys and Aynthorn

a) grants to b) and his heirs to hold of the chief lords by the
usual services

Witnesses: Ranulph of Dacr' then sheriff of Cumberland, Robert le
Brun and John Dorretone, knights, Richard of Berewys,
John of Warthole, Richard of the Sandes
Seal: absent

CW 83   Abbreviated copy of CW 82

48

CW 84   **Letters of attorney:** at Kardoille, 30 July 7 Ed. III   **1333**

a) Robert of Mulcastre, esq. b) Hugh of Levyngton
c) John of Mulcastre

Property: one of the ?60 [*sesant*] acres of land of a), with appurts., in Eston

Recites that a) has recovered the property from c) in the King's court

Witnesses: none
Seal: fine small seal with shield impression and legend

CW 85   **Gift:**   at Drumboughe 20 April 19 Ed. III   **1345**

a) Richard Brun, Lord of Drumboughe b) William of Kirkeby, parson of the church of Bonnesse c) Lord Adam of Bamptone, chaplain

Property: manors of Drumboughe, Beawmond and Bothel and moiety of the Manor of Bounesse, with all the meadow of a) in the hamlet of Cardrunnok; with the feudal services of the free villeins and all their men [*sequela*], together with the advowson of the churches of all the said manors.

a) grants to b) and c) and their heirs

Witnesses: lord William of Dacre, lord Alexander of Moubray, lord Peter of Tilliol, lord Robert of Mulcaster, lord John of Orretone and lord Henry of Maltone, knights
Seal: shield impression, rather faint

CW 86 was formerly HMC Box X, no. 77
CW 86   **Memorandum of gift:**   **c.1345**

a) William of Kyrkeby, parson of Bowness
b) Adam of Bamptone, chaplain
c) Richard Brun, late lord of the manor of Drombughe

Property: all the goods and moveable chattels of a) and b) in their manors of Drumbughe, Bowmond and Bothel; and in the moiety of the manor of Bowness; and in all their parts of the hamlet of Cardrunnock

Memorandum that a) and b) grant to c). No warranty or other clauses.

Witnesses: none
Seal: two small seals (one broken), with impressions, on one tag

CW 87 **Gift:** at Bownes, 3 June 20 Ed. III **1346**

a) Henry of Raghtone of Aynthorn and Idonya his wife
b) Richard Brun, Lord of Dromboghe

Property: the eigth part of the Manor of Bownes with its appurts. and the feudal service of the free men that pertain to that eigth part

a) grants to b) and his heirs to hold of the chief lords by the usual services

Witnesses: lord Thomas of Lucy then sheriff of Cumberland, Peter of Tyllioll, Henry of Maltone, knights, Richard of Kirkebryd, Richard of Berwys, John of Croftone, John of Iwhynnehow
Seal: formerly two, both absent

CW 88 **Grant for lives:** at Karl'e (Carlisle), 11 August 20 Ed. III **1346**

a) Richard Bruyn, Lord of Dromboughe
b) Henry of Raughtone of Aynthorn and Idonea his wife

Property: the eighth part of the manor of Bowenes

a) grants to b) to hold for life from a) and his heirs at annual rent of one rose at midsummer in lieu of all services

Witnesses: Thomas of Lucy then sheriff, Richard of Dentone, John of Orton, knight
Seal:
impression and legend

CW 89 **Gift:** at Dromboghe, Thursday the Nativity of St John the Baptist, 24 June, 35 Ed. III **1361**

a) Robert Bruyne, Lord of Dromboghe   b) Lord William of the Hall, rector of the church of Bownes and Lord Thomas, rector of

the church of Beaumont c) Richard Bruyne, father of a)
d) Henry of Raghtone and Idonea his wife

Property: i) Manors of Dromboghe, Beaumont, Botell and
Langbronchat with the moiety of the vill' of Bownes
and eighth part of the same vill'
ii) the part of the hamlet of Cardronnok that belongs
to a); with all appurts. and with advowson of the
churches of the said manors

Recites that c) purchased the property i) from d). Now a) grants
both properties to b) and his heirs together with the feudal services
of all the free villeins and their men.

Witnesses: William of Daker, Alexander of Moubray, Adam
Parnynk, John Orretone, Henry of Malton, knights,
William of Stapulton, John Bruyne, Thomas of
Skelton
Seal: absent

CW 90 **Confirmation and quitclaim:** at [word missing] castle of Naward
in Gillisland, 30 December 37 Ed. III   **1363**

a) Ranulph, Lord Dacre, Lord of Gillisland   b) John of Raghtone
c) Lady Margaret of Dacre, mother of a)

Property: i) all lands, tenements, fees, services, mills, suits and
dues in Raghton and Gaitscalis ii) all lands and tens.
in Le Sandis in the vill' of Burghe next the Sands;
and b)'s part of the manor of Glassyngby with all its
appurts. in lands, tens., mills, woods, wastes, moors,
fees and services in the vill' of Glassyngby.

Recites a previous deed of exchange between b) and c) whereby c)
gave i) to b) and he in turn gave ii) to her. a) and b) now reaffirm
the exchange and quitclaim to each other and their heirs their
respective rights in their former properties.

Witnesses: none
Seal: clear impression and legend
Document damaged in centre and at left hand side

CW 91 **Gift:** at Drombughe, 22 September 38 Ed. III   **1364**

a) William of the Hall and Thomas of Soureby, clerks
b) Robert Bruyne   c) John Bruyne of Glassene

Property: all the Manor of Dromeboughe with all its. appurts. in co. Cumberland viz. the hamlets of Estone and Fyngelawe with the services of the free tenants as well as the neifs, and all their men, and with mills, fisheries and all other appurts.; and advowson of the church of Bowenesse

a) grant to b) and his heirs to hold of the chief Lords of the fee by the usual services; remainder to c) and his heirs male, if it happens that b) has no heirs of his body but if c) has no heirs male than the property shall revert to the rightful heirs of b)

Witnesses: lord Robert of Tilliolle, lord John of Orretone, knights, Christopher of Moriceby then sheriff of Cumberland, John of Dentone, William of Stapletone, Thomas of Skelton

Seal: formerly three, all absent

CW 92 was formerly HMC, Box V, no. 69

CW 92   Counterpart of CW 91 above
Seal: two, with impressions, one a shield

CW 93   **Gift:**   at Drumboughe, Monday after the Exaltation of the Holy Cross, 14 September   **1364**
Parties as in CW 112 above

Property: Manor of Drumboughe with appurts. and moiety of the manor of Boughnesse

a) grant to c) and the heirs male of his body with remainder to the rightful heirs of b) if c) should die without heirs male

Witnesses: Thomas of Lucy, knight, Ranulph of Dacre, clerk, Robert Tyllioll, knight, Adam Parnyng, knight, John of Ortone, knight, Christopher of Monceby then sheriff of Cumberland, William of Stapiltone and Thomas of Skelton

Seal: one of two remains, with impression

CW 94   **letters of attorney:** at Beaumond, Sunday after the Exaltation of the Holy Cross, 14 September,   **1364**

a) William of the Hall and Thomas of Soureby, clerks
b) Matthew of Whitfeld and Thomas of Skeltone   c) John Bruyne

Property: manor of Drumboughe and moiety of the manor of Boughnesse

a) appoint b) their attornies to deliver seisin to c)
Witnesses: none
Seal: impression as in CW 114

CW 95   **Letters of attorney:** undated   **?circa 1365-1375**

a) John Broyne of Glassane
b) Lord Thomas of Sunderland, Lord John Laveroke, John of Ellerington, Adam of Drumboughe, Geoffrey ?Rory and John Watson

Property: manor of Drumboughe

a) appoints b) as his attorneys to enter and take seisin of the property following the death of Robert Broyn

Witnesses: none
Seal: none

-oOo-

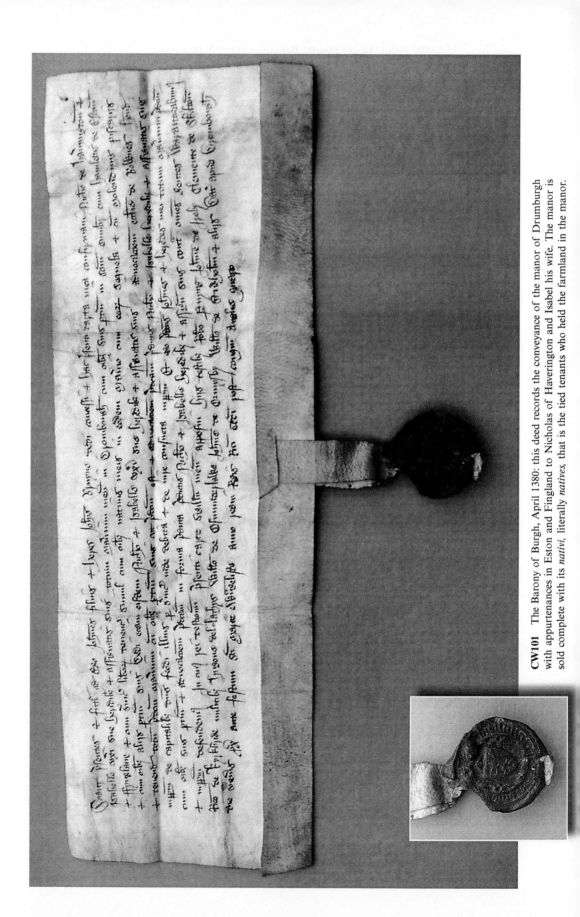

CW101 The Barony of Burgh, April 1380: this deed records the conveyance of the manor of Drumburgh with appurtenances in Eston and Fingland to Nicholas of Haverington and Isabel his wife. The manor is sold complete with its *nativi*, literally *natives*, that is the tied tenants who held the farmland in the manor.

iii Barony of Burgh, Cumberland
b) deeds 1380-1482

CW 101 **Gift:** at Dromboughe, Wednesday before St Mark the
Evangelist, 25 April, 4 Richard II   **1380**

a) John son and heir of John Bruyne
b) Nicholas of Haveryngton and Isabel his wife

Property: manor of Dromboughe and all its. appurts. and the
hamlets of Estone and Fynglane, with the services of
the free tenants as well as the neifs and all their men
and with the mills, fisheries and all other appurts., and
the advowson of the church of Bownes

a) grants to b) and their heirs to hold of the chief lords of the fee
by the usual services

Witnesses: John Parnyng, John of Ireby, Clement of Skelton,
Richard of Kyrkbride, knights, Hugh of the Lachys,
William Osmunderlawe, John of Ormysby, William of
Studholm
Seal: shield impression with legend, slightly damaged at the
rim

CW 102 **Letters of attorney:** at Bothell, the conversion of St Paul, 25
Jan., 7 Richard II   **1384**

a) Nicholas of Haveryngton, knight and Isabel his wife
b) Matthew of Camicefeld, Walter of the Grene and Thomas
Ellisson of Bothell   c) Robert Broune

Property: manors of Bothell, Bemund and Drumbogh and all
their messuages, lands, rents and services in Baunes,
Cardronnok, Langbrunscayth and Stubhill

a) appoints b) to receive seisin of the properties on his behalf,
which formerly belonged to c)

Witnesses: none
Seal: shield impression, with legend

CW 103 **Letters of attorney:** at Dromboughe Thursday before
               St Mark the Evangelist, 25 April, 8 Richard II   **1385**
a) Nich. Haveryngton esq. and Isabel his wife
b) Master William of Boweness, clerk or Thomas of Sunderland,
chaplain   c) John son of John Bruyne

Property: the Manor of Dromboughe etc. and the advowson of
           the church of Bowenesse, as in CW 101 above

a) appoint either of b) to receive seisin of the property on their
behalf which they have received from c)

Witnesses: none
Seal: two on one tag: one fragment and one with shield
           impression

CW 104 **Gift:**   at Carliell, Monday before Ss. Philip and James,
            1 May, 13 Richard II   **1390**

a) Nicholas of Haveryngton, knight and Isabel his wife
b) Thomas of the Grene, parson of the church of Whyttryngton
        and Robert Avenalle, chaplain

Property: manor of Drumboghe and all its appurts. and all
           messuages, lands, tenements rents and services in
           Bownes, Cardrunok and Stubhill together with the
           advowson of the church of Bownes; third part of the
           manors of Bothell, Bemond, Langbrunskath with all
           appurts. (etc.) and advowsons of their churches

a) grant to b) and their heirs to hold of the chief lords of the fee
by the usual services.

Witnesses: lord Peter Tylliolf, lord John of Ireby, lord Clement
           of Skelton, lord Robert of Parnyng, knights, Alan of
           Blonderhasset.
Seal: two: one with shield and legend; one a simple
           letter 'I'

CW 105 **Letters of attorney:** at Farltone in Lonsdale, Sunday after the
Invention of the Holy Cross, 3 May, 13 Richard II   **1390**

a) Nicholas and Isabel Haveryngton   b) Thomas of Sunderland,
chaplain   c) Thomas of the Grene and Robert Avenell

Property: as in CW 104 above

a) appoint b) to deliver seisin to c)
Witnesses: none
Seal: two: one with impression partly erased, the other with
shield impression and legend

CW 106 **Gift:**   at Carliell in the feast of St John the Baptist,
24 June, 13 Richard II   **1390**

a) Thomas of the Grene, parson of the church of Whityngtone
and Robert Avenell, chaplain   b) Nicholas of Haveryngton and
Isabel his wife   c) James, eldest son of b)

Property: messuages, lands, tenements, meadows, rents and services
in the vills of Bawnes, Cardrunok and Stubhill, with
the advowson of the Church of Bawnes

Recites that a) have received the property from b); a) now confirm
it to the use of b) for life with remainder to c) and his heirs male;
with contingent remainders, if c) has no heirs male, to Nicholas, then
Robert, then Thomas, younger brothers of c), and their heirs male;
or in default of heirs male, then to the rightful heirs of Isabel

Witnesses: lord Peter Tilliolf, Lord Robert Pernyng, knights, Alan
of Blannerhasset
Seal: two: one with impression partly erased, the other with
shield impression and legend
NB.   By strict dating this deed would be 1389. The new
regnal year began the same day. The content insists
on a date of 1390.

CW 107 **Final concord:** octave of Michaelmas, 14 Richard II   **1390**

a) Thomas of the Grene and Robert Avenal, plaintiffs
b) Nicholas and Isabel Haveryngton, deforciants

Property: manor of Drumbogh and the third part of the manors
of Bothell, Bemond and Brunskath

It is agreed that a) hold the properties to the uses as in CW 104 above

Witnesses: none
Seal: absent

CW 108 **Gift:**   at Bewmond, Monday after All Saints, 1 November, 16 Richard II   **1392**

a) Nicholas of Haveryngton, knight b) James his son
c) Robert Avenell, chaplain, Henry of Croft, Robert of Crokay, Richard of Knaresdalle

Property: manor of Drumbogh and third part of the manors of Bothell, Beumond and Brunskath with all lands and tenements in Bownes and Cardrunnok

a) grants to b) and c) to hold of the chief Lords of the fee by the usual services, during the term of a)'s life

Witnesses: Peter Tilliolf, Clement of Skeltone, knight, Alan of Blenerhasset, Richard of Skelton, Thomas Pattenson
Seal: shield impression, and legend

CW 109 **Bond in 50 marks:** Sunday after the Purification, 2 February, 21 Richard II   **1398**

a) William of Dacre of Gillesland b) Peter of Legh
c) William of Culwen, heir of William of Horneby

Property: manors of Randolph Ayketon and lands and tenements in Burgh on le Sandys

a) is bound to b) in the matter of the guardianship of c), to be addresses at the next sessions at Lancaster.

Witnesses: none
Seal: none
Conditions of the bond are in Anglo-Norman French

This deed was formerly HMC Box V, 70
CW 110 **Quitclaim:** undated   *c.*1400

a) Thomas of Whiterig b) Robert of Whiterig, father of a)
c) Nicholas of Whiterig, brother of a)

Property: all the lands and tenements which b) gave to a) in co. Cumberland, with the windmill of Whiterig

a) grants to c) to hold for life, with remainder to a) and his heirs

Witnesses: none
Seal: fragment with indistinct impression

CW 111 **Gift:** at Whitrygg 6 May, 4 Hen. V   **1417**

a) Matthew of Wytfeyld, knight   b) Alexander of Wytfeyld, son of a) c) Joan, daughter of Thomas Hunter and wife of b)

Property: moiety of all the lands and tenements of a) in the vill' and territory of Cwitryg in Cumberland

a) grants the property to b) and c) and the heirs male of their bodies; remainders, if there are no such heirs to William, Thomas, Robert, Hugh and John, sons of a) and their heirs male, in sucession, or in default of any such heirs, to the rightful heirs of a)

Witnesses: John Skelton, knight, William Twhates (sic), George Worwye
Seal: simple impression

CW 112 **Gift:** at Carl'e, 8 February, 16 Hen. VI   **1438**

a) John Newby of Newby within Gillisland
b) John Atkynson of Little Thakyngecruk

Property: half of Thakyngecruk, viz. that which lies next to ?Swanipul [text very faint] on one side and the land of Richard of Kirkbrid on the other

a) grants to b) and his heirs to hold of the chief lords of the fee by the usual services

Witnesses: Christopher Culwen the sheriff of Cumberland, [?Robert] Denton, Robert Carlelle, William Cardoille, John Hogeson of Beaumond, William Bowman
Seal: in original wrapper
This deed was found among some strays of the Barony of Burgh series.

CW 113   Gift: at Dronbogh, 14 May 19 Hen. VI   **1441**

a) Nicholas Botiller of Rauclyff, John of Cotone, vicar of the church of Kirkham, Richard Walton, parson of the church of Hymmysworth b) Richard Molynuex, knight, Thomas son of William Haryngton, knights, Richard Baldrestone, Thomas Browyth, John Ellyswyk, parson of the church of Rybchester and Thomas Halsall
c) John Carleton, parson of the church of (blank)
d) Richard Haryngton

Property: manors, messuages, lands and tenements in the vill's of Estone, Fynglaue, Bemonde, Brunschath, Bownes, Cardronnok, Bothill and Dronbogh with the advowson of the church of Bownes, pertaining to the said Manor of Dronboghe

Reciting that a) until recently held the property along with c), by gift of d), a) now grant it to b) and their heirs.

Witnesses: Richard of Daltone, Robert Laurence of Asshetone, Henry Halsall
Seal: three; one reasonable impression, the others poor

CW 114   Gift (mortgage): at Karliole 31 July, 22 Hen. VI   **1444**

a) Thomas of the Sandes, esq. b) William Boweman of Beaumond

Property: one tenement with appurts., in which John Bampton dwells, in Wilmorby next to Burgh by the Sandes

a) grants to b) to hold of the chief lords of the fee by the usual services; to secure a repayment of 40s. of English money.

Witnesses: Thomas Dalamore, sheriff of Cumberland, William Carliole, steward of Burghe, John Hegesone, William Diconsone, Adam Sturdy
Seal: fragment with impression

CW 115   Presentation of a priest: at Karli'e, 10 April   **1445**

a) Alexander Cok, acting Vicar General in the remoter parts [of the Diocese] for our reverend and learned father in Christ, lord Marmaduke [Lumley], Bishop of Carlisle   b) Master William Rouehede, chaplain   c) Robert Somercett   d) lord Robert Haryngton, knight

Property: Rectory of the church of Bowness in Carlisle diocese

On the recommendation of d), true patron of the living, a) presents b) to the rectory which c) lately freely resigned.
Witnesses: none
Seal: fragment of oval seal

CW 116   **Grant (mortgage):** 28 March, 24 Hen. VI   **1446**

a) John Whitfeld, lord of Whitfeld   b) Thomas More of Karli'e, draper

Property: all the lands and tenements of a) in Glassen in the parish of Bowness

a) grants to b) on condition that a) of his heirs regrant the premises absolutely when he repays b) £10

Witnesses: none
Seal: a blob with a vague impression

CW 117   **Declaration:** at Hexham, 6 May, 27 Hen. VI   **1449**

For also mekill as meritore and medfull thyng is to wyttnes the treughe, be it knowyn....
a) William Carnaby and Robert Elleryngtone esqs.   b) Sir Matthew of Whitfeld, grandfather of (*graunfer to*) ... c) Sir Matthew of Whitfeld
d) Alexander, son of b)   e) Jonet, dau. of Thomas Hunter   f) John of Whitfeld, son and heir of b) and brother of d)

Property: half all the lands, tenements, rents and services and appurts. '*in the tone and feld of Whitrigg in the countie of Karleille*'

a) declare that the property was given by b) to d) and e) and their heirs at their marriage; and that d) and e) held it peaceably while f) was alive, and since, in the time of c)

Witnesses: none
Seal: two on one tag, one a fragment with shield impression the other a blob
This document is in dialect English.

61

CW117 A rare example of dialect English in which Alexander and Jonet Whitfield declare their custom of use in premises in the tone and feld of Whitrigg in the countie of Karlielle. The deed was dated at Hexham in Northumberland, 6 May 1449.

CW 118 **copy of court roll:** at the court of Dalstone, Wednesday the vigil of St Thomas, 21 December, 37 Hen. VI   1458

a) Robert Karlelle, steward to the Venerable father in Christ, lord William, [Percy] Bishop of Karliole, lord of the Manor of Dalstone
b) William Beaulieu of Thistilthuayt   c) Humphrey Dacre, esq. son of Thomas Dacre, knight, Lord of Dacre   d) William Normane

Property: one tenement with appurts. called Le Flatt lying within the Barony of Dalstone

Recites that the previous tenant was d); now b) comes to court as attorney of c) and is granted admission of the property by a)

Witnesses: none
Seal: impression

CW 119 **Presentation of a priest:** 31 March   1459

a) Richard of Huthuayte, prior of the cathedral church of the Blessed Mary of Karl'e (Carlisle)
b) Lord William, bishop of Karl'e
c) Thomas Raughtone, priest   d) Richard Haryngton, knight

Property: the church of Bownes in the diocese of Karl'e

a) on behalf of b) presents c) to the living of Bownes at the request of d)
Witnesses: none
Seal: ecclesiastical seal with impression somewhat erased

CW 120 **Bond:**   14 December, 7 Ed. IV   1467

a) Robert Dalstone, John Brakenthropp, John Hutone, esqs.
b) Thomas Ribtone   c) Lancelot [*Lanuslotus*] Threlkeld, William Leyghe, Thomas Lampluygh, knights, Richard Beaulieu

Property: lands and tenements in Dalstone, Drumlynyn, Aykton, Mursthwayt and Partene

a) are bound to b) in 100 marks to abide by the decisions of c) as arbiters of the case concerning possession of the land in question.

Witnesses: none
Seal: three small seals with impressions

CW 121   **Quitclaim:**   feast of St Laurence the martyr, 10 August,   **1474**
14 Ed. IV

a) Thomas Halsall   b) William Haryngton, knight
c) Richard Molyneux, knight, Thomas son of William Haryngton,
knights, Richard Balderston, Thomas Urswik and John Elleswik,
parson of the church of Ribchestre, now decd.   d) Nicholas Botiller
of Rawclif, John Cotom, vicar of Kirkham and Richard Walton,
parson of the church of Hymmesworth

Property: all those manors, lands, rents and services in the vills
of Eston, Fynglane, Bemonde, Brunscath, Bawnes,
Cardrunnok, Bothill and Drumbough and advowson
of the church of Bawnes, which pertains to the manor
of Drumbough

Reciting that he held the premises along with c) according to the
terms of a deed of gift from d) (compare CW 111 above).
a) now releases all rights in the property to b)

Witnesses: none
Seal: impression

CW 122   **Dispute concerning advowson** 22 January   **1478**

a) Thomas, prior of the cathedral church of the Blessed Mary of
Karl'e and Thomas Overdoo his official
b) Edward [Story], bishop of Carl'e   c) Richard Haryngton,
knight
d) William Haryngton, knight, son and heir apparent of c)
e) Giles Redemayn and William Rondhede   f) Giles Elice of
Karli'e
g) Nicholas Coldale, vicar of Stanwig   h) Christopher Curwen
i) Thomas Gayson

Property: advowson of the church of Bownes

On 27 December 1477 b) was requested by h) that i) be presented
to the living of Bownes and he sent a letter dated 7 Jan 1478 to a)
for him to put this into effect. a) then held a meeting in Carlisle
Cathedral where it was affirmed by several rectors, vicars and laity
(named) of local parishes (named) that c) had presented e) as
successive vicars of Bownes and that the right of such presentation
belonged to c) and, after his death, to d); this is disputed by f),
whose case is supported by g)

Witnesses: none
Seal: ecclesiastical seal, part missing
This document does not appear to offer an answer to the dispute.

CW 123   **Gift, ?mortgage:** Trinity Sunday, 22 Ed. IV   **1482**

a) Laurence Whytfyld   b) Clement Skelton of Aynthorn, esq.

Property: all the lands of a) and all their appurts. in Whitrigg
co. Cumbria

a) grants to b) and his heirs ?to secure repayment by a) to b) of £80
(doc. faded and barely legible)

Witnesses: Robert Skeltone, Thomas ?Lathys, James Skeltone, esqs.
Seal: primitive impression, as in CW 111 above

CW 124   **Quitclaim:** morrow of Ss. Peter and Paul, 29 June, 22 Ed.   **1482**

Parties as in CW 123 above

Property: all lands, tenements and appurts. which a) lately held
in the vill' and territory of Quhetrige

a) releases all rights in the land to b)

Witnesses: as in CW 123
Seal: as in CW 123

-oOo-

iii Barony of Burgh, Cumberland
c) deeds 1497-1504

CW 131 **Mortgage agreement:** 3 December, 13 Hen. VII   1497

    a) Thomas, Lord Dacre and of Gylslond
    b) Nicholas Harryngdon, esq. of Adderton co. Lancs.
    c) Dame Isabel Harryngdon, widow of James Harryngdon,
        knight,

Parties a) and b) agree that b) shall pay a) an annual rent of 20
marks out of his properties in Cumbria (no details), that is 17
marks 6s. 8d. being an annual rent formerly granted to b) by c)
which b) now agrees to pay to a) during the life of c); after her
death b) will pay a) the 20 marks out the properties he will inherit
as brother and heir of Isabel's husband James. In return a) now
makes b) a single payment of 520 marks, with proviso that the
annual rent may cease if at any time in the next 20 years b) or d)
repay the 520 marks to a) at his castle of Nawarde

Witnesses: none
Seal: impression, partly erased
This deed, and the next, is in English.

CW 132 **Award:**   1 July, 13 Hen. VII   1498
    a) Thomas Kebeell and John Kingesmyll, serjeants at law

    b) Isabel Haryngtone, wid. of … c) Sir James Haryngton, knight
    d) Nicholas Haryngton, brother and heir male of said James

Recites that a disagreement has arisen between b) and d) regarding
the possession of the manors and lands (no details) which lately
belonged to c). Now, with the agreement of b) and d), a) decree
that the property shall be enjoyed by b) during her lifetime *without
let, interrupcyon or putting oute* by d) or by anyone acting on his
orders. In return b) shall make a deed granting d) an annual rent
of £11 13s. 4d. out of property as in CW 133 below

Witnesses: none
Seal: formerly two, both absent

67

CW 133   **Grant of annual rent:** 27 July, 13 Hen. VII   **1498**

a) Parties b) and d) of CW 132 above

Property: manors, lands and tenements of Bownes, Dunbogh, Penryg, Eston, Brunscarr, and Beamond

In pursuance of the terms of CW 132 above b) grants d) a rent of £11 13s 4. out of the property

Witnesses: Alexander Radcliff, Robert Langley and Christopher Hulton esqs.
Seal: impression

CW 134   **Bond**:   between same parties, 10 August   **1498**

CW 135   **Bond**:   at Carliole, 3 December 14 Hen. VII   **1499**

a) Thomas Lord of Dacre and of Gyllislond
b) Nicholas Haryngton, esq.

a) is bound to b) in £500 to perform the covenants of a deed of the same day's date [which deed appears to be missing from the series].

Witnesses: none
Seal: fragment

CW 136   **Receipt**:   2 May 15 Hen. VII   **1500**

a) Isabel Harryngton   b) Thomas Lord Dacre

a) acknowledges she has receives £13 6s. 8d. from b)

Witnesses: Henry Leylond, Roger Ferrour, Henry Bawer
Seal: a blob

CW 137   **Bond**:   23 July, 16 Hen. VII   **1501**

a) Nicholas Haryngton of Addirton, co. Lancs.
b) Thomas Dacre, lord of Dacre and of Gillisland

a) is bound to b) in £40 to pay b) 20 marks at his castle of Nawart in Cumberland by 2 February next

Witnesses: none
Seal: fragment

CW 138   **Gift:**   14 May, 14 Hen. VII   **1499**

a) William Osmoderlawe, esq.   b) Randolph Dacre, esq.

Property: all that tenement of a) which lies in the vill' and territory of Aynthorne

a) grants to b) and his heirs. See also CW 148 below.

Witnesses: Thomas Beverley, mayor of Carl'e, Thomas Birkbek, Thomas Porter, Richard Kirkbryd
Seal: absent

CW 139   **Gift:**   6 September, 16 Hen. VII   **1500**

a) Randolph Dacre, esq.   b) James Armerar, servant of a)
c) William Osmoderlaw

Property: all the lands, tenements, rents, and services of a) in the vill' and territory of Aynthorn

Reciting that he obtained the property from c), a) now grants it to b) in return for his good service. See also CW 135 above

Witnesses: none
Seal: an indistinct impression

CW 140   **Bond:**   1 December, 17 Hen. VII   **1501**

a) Nicholas Haryngton of Aderton co. Lancs., esq.
b) Humphrey Dacre, Robert Louthre, clerk, John Mier and Adam Mier

Property: a certain acre of land in the vill' of Bolnesse together with the right of advowson [*iurispatronatus*] of the parish church

a) is bound to b) in £200 to perform the covenants of a deed of the same day's date re. the land etc. specified

Witnesses: none
Seal: impression

CW 141   **Bond:**   3 December, 17 Hen. VII   **1501**

a) Parties and property as in CW 140 above

Nicholas Haryngton is bound in £200 to the other parties to guarantee that he has not sold the advowson of Bolnes to any other person

Witnesses: none
Seal: blob

CW 142   **Receipt:** 6 December 17 Hen. VII   **1501**

Nicholas Haryngton acknowledges receipt of 250 marks
from Thomas Lord Dacre

CW 143   **Final concord:** Octave of Trinity Sunday, 17 Hen. VII   **1502**

a) Thomas Dacres, knight, lord of Dacres, Humphrey Dacres, Christopher Dacres and Ralph Dacres plaintiffs
b) Nicholas haryngton, esq., deforciant

Property: 37 messuages, 200 a. land, 40 a. meadow with appurts in Estone, Dunbughe, Fynlanerygg, Cardunnok, Bowenes and Boydon and advowson of the church of Bowenes

Following a plea heard at Westminster on the morrow of Ascension day previously b) recognises that the property rightfully belongs to a), by his own deed of gift, and he therefore quitclaims all his rights in it to them.

Witnesses: none
Seal: none

CW 144   **Sale and bond:** at Carlisle, 17 January, 18 Hen. VII   **1503**

a) Thomas Lord Dacre, Gillesland and Wemme   b) Clement Skelton esq., ?"of Petrelwra"   c) Richard Skelton of Branthuayte, esq.

Property: all the lands of b) in Bownes Town except a tenement held by John Wylde at 4s. a year and a tenement held by Jok Johnson called Jok Jeffreyson at 8s. 6d. a year; and all the lands and tenements of a) in Cardronoke in the Barony of Burghe in Cumberland.

70

Due to the fact that b) has not paid a) the money due on a bond in 500 marks b) now sells the property to a) and his heirs. In return b) is discharged of the said bond and *of the xchetorship for one yere* and *for all the merciments of the xchequier* for a year; a) also discharges b) of "Petrelwra" which b) holds of the King by military service and he appoints c) to take possession of the lands on his behalf; c) is bound to a) in £200 to manage the estate properly on a)'s behalf, delivering up its revenues and profits to a)

Witnesses: Edward Birkbek, mayor of Carlisle, Thomas Birkbek, Thomas Beverley, Sir Thomas Tynding, Sir Robert Louthre
Seal: impression (large bird) and faint legend
This deed is in English.

CW 145 Counterpart of CW 144, identical except that it has three good seals on one tag, each with impression

CW 146 **Further copy** of CW 144 with poor fragments of seals.

CW 147 **Agreement:** at Carlile, 11 April 18 Hen. VII   1503

a) Thomas Lord Dacre   b) Nicholas Haryngton of Addirton, esq.
c) Ralph Smith of Cholbent

Property: lands in Bothill and Beamont in Cumberland

It is agreed between a) and b) that b) will come to London by the 6 May next and will there make over to b) *a jugge of landes and tenementes to the yerely valieu of 20 marks*, i.e. in Bothill to the value of £10 and in Beamont to the value of 66s. 8d. For this a) shall pay b) 100 marks sterling, £29 at the making of this deed, 20 marks at midsummer next and £8 6s. 8d. on 30 November next; with proviso that £4 out of the 20 marks payable at midsummer shall be paid to c)

Witnesses: none
Seal: absent; signature of b)

CW 148   **Receipt:**   9 July 18 Hen. VII   **1503**

Nicholas Haryngton acknowledges receipt of £40 from Thomas, Lord Dacre by the hand of Humphrey Dacre, with agreement for repayment
by Lady Day next.

Witnesses: none
Seal: none

CW 149   **Receipt:**   21 December, 20 Hen. VII   **1504**

a) Parties as in CW 148

Property: lands lying in Drumbughe to the value of 10 marks a year

b) acknowledges that he has received £33 13s. 8d. from Lord Dacre in payment for the property

Witnesses: none
Seal: none; signature of b)

-oOo-

iii Barony of Burgh, Cumberland
d) deeds 1505-1632/3

CW 161   **Agreement to exchange:** at Karliole, 9 October, 21 Hen. VII   **1505**

a) Thomas Dacre, knight, lord of Dacre, Gillesland and Wemme
b) Thomas Curwen, knight

Property: i) one third part of Brunskathe and all the lands and tenements of a) in Stubell [also spelt *Stuble*] ii) various lands and tenements in Grenerig within the demesne of Caldbek; all in Cumberland

The parties agree that a) will give property ii) to b) who in turn will give i) to a) and his heirs in exchange. Morover, when a) delivers to b) other lands in another place between the water of Alne and the water of Derwent, b) will quitclaim to him his rights in property ii)

Witnesses: none
Seal: impression; and signature of b)

CW 162   **Grant in exchange:** date as CW 161   **1505**
a) Parties and property as in CW 161

b) acknowledges that a) has given him property ii) and he therefore gives him i) in exchange

Witnesses: Hugh Louthre, knight, Henry Denton, mayor of the city of Karli'e, Robert Lampleughe, William Brenley, esq.
Seal: impression; and signature of b)

CW 163   **Letters of attorney:** date as CW 161-162 above   **1505**

a) Thomas Culwen, knight   b) John Birket

Property: one third part of Brunskathe with appurts. and all the lands and tenements of a) in Stuble

a) appoints b) to deliver seisin to Thomas Dacre

Witnesses: Hugh Louthre, knight, Hen. Denton, mayor of the city of Karl'e, Robert Lampleughe, William Brenley, esqs.
Seal: impression

CW 164 **Witness to livery of seisin:** 11 October, 21 Hen. VII   1505
Robert Pereson, Robert Whitinge, Robert Gusesalle, John Parke, Rowe Dungalson and Wille Wilson, all of Rowclif, witness livery of seisin as in CW 163 above on behalf of Sir Thomas Curwen of Wirkington, knight
(Paper doc.)

CW 165 **Gift:**   at Karl'e, 23 March, 22 Hen. VII   1507

a) Thomas Elys of Bothill in Cumberland, gent.
b) Thomas Dacre, knight, Lord of Dacre, Gillesland and Wemme

Property: one third part of Brunskathe

a) grants to b) and his heirs

Witnesses: Robert Louthre, rector of Aiketon, John Rigge, William Skelton, Rouland Ratclif
Seal: impression

CW 166 **Gift (mortgage):** 14 October, 9 Hen. VIII   1517

a) John Cwhitfeild of Qwhitfeild Hall in Northumberland, esq.
b) Thomas Barkar of the city of Karl'e, tanner

Property: the two tenements of a) which lie in the vill' and territory of Qwhitrygge within the Barony of Burghe by [per] Sands, one in the occ. of Edward Haryngtone at ann. rent of 18s., the other in the occ. of Robert Farlaham at annual rent of 8s.

a) grants to b) to secure repayment of £20 by, and within, the week following 2 February next.

Witnesses: Thomas Blanerhasset, gentleman in the city of Karl'e, Cuthbert brother of a), John Chalaner in the city of Karl'e, John Graham

Seal: fragment, with impression

CW 167   Counterpart of CW 166 above

> **Witnesses:**   as in CW 166
> **Seal:**   impression

CW 168   **Bond:** date and parties as CW 166-167

> a) is bound to b) in £40 for performance of covenants of CW 166-7

> **Witnesses:**   none
> **Seal:**   tiny impression

CW 169   **Gift:**   20 Nov. 9 Hen. VIII   **1517**

> a) Robert Ogle, Lord Ogle   b) Christopher Dacre, knight, and William Husbande, master of the College of Graystok   c) William Geffreyson, John Peell, William Smethes, Henry the vicar of Thurisby and the wife of John Geffreyson of the Park   d) John Geffreyson and Robert Moyses

> **Property:**   all lands, tenements, rents and services, and appurts. in Thurisby, in the occ. of c), with all woods and underwoods growing in the same

> a) grants to b) and their heirs and appoints d) as his attornies to deliver seisin.

> **Witnesses:**   none
> **Seal:**   absent; signature of a)

CW 170   **Grant of annuity:** at Morpeth, 4 December, 9 Hen. VIII   **1517**

> a) Thomas Lord Dacre
> b) Christopher Dacre and William Husbands (parties (b) of CW 169 above)   c) Robert Ogle, Lord Ogle

> **Property:**   property as in CW 169 above

> Reciting 169 above a) directs b) to allow c) the clear yearly value of the property, viz. £5 a year for the next 3 years

> **Witnesses:**   none
> **Seal:**   absent; signature of c)

CW 171 **Gift:** 19 December, 9 Hen. VIII   **1517**

Parties a) b) and d) as in CW 169 above
c) George Geffreyson, Robert Arloshe, Robert Robynson, William Bawne and William Jakson, chaplain

Property: all the lands, tenements, rents and services of a) in Thurisby in the occs. of c)

a) grant to b) and appoints d) to deliver seisin

Witnesses: none absent; signature of a)
Seal: absent; signature of a)

CW 172 **Letter:** at Kirkoswald 19 January, 11 Hen. VIII   **1520**

a) Thomas ?Hugel
b) William Skelton, "son to Robert Skelton of Karlell"

A royal writ dated at Grenewich on the 17 November last was delivered to a) by b)'s wife. In pursuance of its terms, a) now asks b) to meet his son in Glassen on the morning of the 26th January next in order to see to the business (unspecified). Alternative dates are suggested.
A paper doc., fragile and torn.

CW 173 **Conveyance:** 13 May, 12 Hen. VIII   **1520**

a) Alexander Ratclyff, knight, Adam Hulton, esq., Robert Langley, esq., Thomas Ratclyff, clerk   b) James Harryngton, son and heir of Nicholas Harryngton, esq. who was kinsman and heir male of James Harryngton, knight   c) Thomas Blanerhasset and Edward Blanerhasset

Property: manors of Bothell, Beamond, Bolnes with advowson of the church of Bolnes; manors of Drumbughe, Eston, Fynglond, Fynglaryg, Stubhill, Brunskathe and Cardrunnok with appurts. in Cumberland; and with all lands, tenements, meadows, feedings, pastures, moors, marshes, rents and services in the same places.

a) grants to b) and his heirs and appoint c) to deliver him the seisin

Witnesses: none
Seal: of the four persons of party a), each with impressions; and their four signatures

CW 174   **Bond**:   date as CW 173

a) James Harryngton, esq.   b) Thomas Dacre, knight
c) Richard Elyott and Lewes Pollard, knights, King's justices

Property: as in CW 173

a) is bound to b) in £500 sterling to abide by the award of c) as to
the right of possession of the properties and upon all other matters
of variance already brought up between a) and b)

Witnesses: none
Seal: small impression, broken; mark of a)

CW 175   **Receipt and discharge:** 2 August, 13 Hen. VIII   **1521**

a) Parties as in CW 174; J. Harryngton is described as *'heir... of
Sir James Harryngton of Brixwell'* [co. Northants.]

Property: manors of Drumbighe, Eston, Synglond and
Synglamryge [sic, should be Fynglond, Finglanryge]
with ⅓ part of the manors of Bothell, Beamonde,
and Brunscathe, ½ the manor of Bowness with the
advowson of the church of Bownes; and $\frac{1}{8}$ part of
the other half; and all the lands of a) in Cardronnoke
and Stubyll in Cumberland

Referring back to the award mentioned in CW 174, a) now acknowledges receipt from b) of 50 marks sterling, parcel of the sum of
250 marks which b) has to pay a) by virtue of the same award.

Witnesses: William Holgill (signature)
Seal: impression

CW 176   **Agreement and bond:** 24 August, 13 Hen. VIII   **1521**

a) The Hon. Lord Thomas, lord Dacre   b) Cicely Glaysters, formerly
the wife of Richard Glaysters, sister of Clement Skelton decd.

Property: lands late of Clement Skelton, decd. (no details)

b) agrees and is bound to a) in £40 that, when she inherits the
property late her brother Clement's, she will convey it to b); who
in turn agrees that he will then convey her some other land to the
clear yearly value of 20s.

Witnesses: none
Seal: absent

CW 177   Agreement and bond: date as CW 176

a) The Hon. Thomas, Lord Dacre   b) Robert Lathys, son and heir of Janett Lathys who was sister and heir of Clement Skelton

Property: lands late of Clement Skelton deceased (no details)

b) agrees and is bound to a) in £40 that he will convey to a) the land he will inherit as heir of Clement Skelton.

Witnesses: none
Seal: absent

CW 178   **Quitclaim:**   30 August, 13 Hen. VIII   **1521**

a) Katherine Bryscoe (?Brystoe)   b) Rt. Hon. Lord, lord Thomas Dacre c) Clement Skelton

Property: lands, tenements, messuages, meadows, feedings and pastures in the vills' of Bowness and Cardronnok lately held by c)

Recites that the property was purchased by b) from c); now a) releases to b) any right she may have had in it as heir of c)

Witnesses: John Briscoe, son of the said Katherine, John Dalston, Richard Barion
Seal: erased and damaged impression

CW 179   **Quitclaim:**   date as CW 178.
John Briscoe, son of Katherine, makes an identical release.
No witnesses or seal; doc. bound into CW 178.

CW 180   **Receipt and discharge:** 1 August, 14 Hen. VIII   **1522**

Parties and property as in CW 175 above

b) acknowledges receipt of 50 marks in full and final payment of the 250 marks owing to him by Thomas Dacre and he discharges him of any liability to make any further payments.

Witnesses: none
Seal: absent; signature of b)
CW 181 **Quitclaim:**   17 February,   1632/3

a) George Graime alias Grame of The Fawld, son of William Graime decd. who was son of Robert Graime late of The Fawld, decd.
b) The Right Hon. Thomas Earl of Arundel and Surrey, Earl Marshall of England and Knight of the Most Noble Order of the Garter
d) Anne, late countess of Arundel, decd., mother of b)

Property: messuages, lands, tenements, rents etc. in the manors, towns, fields, hamlets and territories of Bownes, Cardronnock in the Barony of Brough by Sands

Reciting that the premises were lately in the possession of himself or his father or his grandfather, and also lately in the possession of d), a) now quitclaims any rights he may have in them to b)

Witnesses: signatures endorsed of: Francis Howard, William Radclliffe, John Hatton. ?Roger Brograve
Seal: absent

-oOo-

THE DUKE OF NORFOLK'S DEEDS
AT ARUNDEL CASTLE

CATALOGUE 1   PART I

Dacre Estates in Northern Counties

iv

Carlisle and area, co. Cumberland

iv Premises in Carlisle and area c.1280-1438

INTRODUCTION

The deeds in this group do not adhere to the title of any particular property. As with other sub-sets in the medieval deeds series at Arundel, they are united by the broad area to which they relate rather than by the legal transactions they represent. Although not explicit in these deeds, it may be assumed that the Dacre family acquired several properties in Carlisle by purchase or by inheritance. Some of the tenements in this section may pertain to the Barony of Burgh or to the Dacre lordship itself. It was common in the early medieval period for outlying manors to enjoy burgage rights and land inside the chief town of the area, for the protection of vassals and the enhancement of trade within a feudal framework. Indeed, the Barony of Burgh was itself established as part of Carlisle's defence system after the Norman Conquest.[*]

Ranulph, Lord Dacre is mentioned as a neighbouring owner to the tenement(s) conveyed in 1373 and 1374 in CW 273 and 274 below, but not as owner himself of any of the deeds in this group. Premises in Fisher Street are mentioned in 1306 (CW 196) and in 1421 (CW 207). At the splitting of the Dacre inheritance in 1569 a messuage in Fisher Street was among the possessions that fell to Elizabeth Dacre. However, Anne Dacre, of whose inheritance these deeds are part, did not inherit any Carlisle premises. It is possible, therefore, that a very early antiquarian hand may have selected these particular medieval deeds for preservation - perhaps that of Anne Dacre herself. For, clearly, the several properties represented here did not descend with the Howard family beyond her lifetime.

Among the parties and witnesses to these deeds are a few persons of note. Sir William Dacre (b. 1265, d. 1318), the purchaser of premises in Bochardeby outside the City around 1300 (ref.CW 213), was one of the early members in the Dacre lineage, living at Dacre Castle north of Ullswater. His father and grandfather before him had been sheriffs of Cumberland. Lord Anthony of Lucy is the first named witness to this deed. His family, from the Egremont region, was already connected by marriage with the Dacres. His daughter, Lucy, later married into the de Greystoke family. So, the Dacres and the Greystokes, later to be united themselves, were already connected through the Lucys.

Lord Anthony Lucy and Ranulph, the first lord Dacre (b. c.1290, d.1339, son of William above), were both prominent figures in engagements against the Scots in the early 14th century, gaining lands and plunder for their pains. In CW 192, circa 1280,

---

[*] This introduction is based upon the sources cited on page 3 above and, additionally, Henry Summerson, *Medieval Carlisle* (Cumb. Antiq. Soc. 1993)

Thomas of Multon, described as lord of Burge, was Ranulph's future father in law. As well as Burgh, he also possessed the lordship of Gilsland, north east of Carlisle in the Cheviots, a combination which no doubt caused his only daughter Margaret to be seen as a good catch. Ranulph eloped with her around 1314-1315, spiriting her from under the noses of her wardens in Warwick Castle, and married her, thus bringing the Gilsland and Burgh baronies to the Dacres.

For the place name, Carlisle, this catalogue transcribes the style found in the deeds, which is usually an abbreviated form of the name. The convention was for "*Karl*", or "*Karli*", to be followed by an abbreviation symbol and the Latin case-ending appropriate to the syntax. I have reproduced the abbreviated style wherever it occurs but substituted an Anglicised final 'e' for the various Latin endings. The penultimate deed of the group, CW214, contains, in the date and in the names of witnesses, a variant form for Carlisle, that is, *Kaerd* for *Kaerl*, ie Caerdeole instead of Caerleole (perhaps substituting Latin de for French le as the second element of the name). This duality is echoed in witnesses surnames Carlelle and Cardoille found, for example, in CW 212.

The particular value of these deeds is in the medieval topography of the City that they reveal and in the wealth of personal names that come to light. For a gazetteer of localities mentioned, see below.

iv Premises in Carlisle and area

Gazetteer

Because so few runs of deeds in this group relate to any specific property, they are presented in chronological order. The following 'Place Index' gives the deed reference for the localities and locational clues that are mentioned in the property clauses.

CW	
195	bakers' street
200	Blakhale
213	Bochardeby
200, 205	Bochardegate
204	Caldew Gate
204, 198	Castle, castle ditch
192	city wall
197	Eden, water of
196, 207	fishers' street
205	Hobryghtby
214	Lustelbont
201-202	Holme Cultran, tenement of the Abbot of
195	market place
194, 197	Richards Gate, Richard Street
207	St Alban's Chapel
191, 197	suburbs
215	Stanwix

CW 200 is dated at Wrestlingworth, Beds.

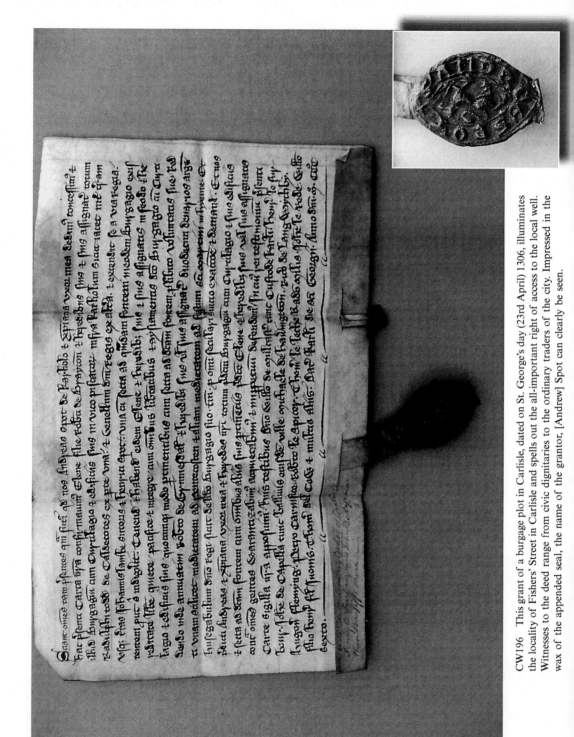

CW196 This grant of a burgage plot in Carlisle, dated on St. George's day (23rd April) 1306, illuminates the locality of Fishers' Street in Carlisle and spells out the all-important right of access to the local well. Witnesses to the deed range from civic dignitaries to the ordinary traders of the city. Impressed in the wax of the appended seal, the name of the grantor, [Andrew] Spot can clearly be seen.

iv Premises in Carlisle and area

CW 191 Quitclaim: undated   **circa 1280**

a) Alain le Wayte of Karli'e
b) William son of Henry the tailor of Karli'e

Property: all that land with the buildings and all appurts. in the
suburb of Karli' lying between the way which leads
towards the field of the castle of Karl'e on one side
and the wall of the city of of Karlisle on the other,
extending in length from the said way at one end as
far as the land of b) at the other

a) releases all rights in the land to b) and his heirs

Witnesses: lord Gilbert of Culwene then sheriff of Cumberland,
lord Geoffrey of Tylolf, lord John of Teryby, knights,
Alex of Boltona then Mayor of Karli', Gilbert of
Grinesdale, Thomas of Tybay, Alan of Peningtona
then bailiff of Karli', John the skinner [*pelliparius*],
Peter the apothecary [*appotecar'*], Peter of Penred,
John the bursar [*dispensator*], ?Win of Tybay, Henry le
Furbur, Robert son of Jelian, William Mus, Laurence
le Furbur then reeve, Richard of Appelby, clerk
Seal: oval seal with impression and legend

CW 192 Gift: undated   **circa 1280**

a) Robert son of Amyas [*filius Amisii*]
b) Thomas the younger of Multone, lord of Burge [Burgh]
c) Adam White [*Albi*] and Margaret, daughter of a)

Property: all that land which a)'s father held in the city of Karleol
lying between land which was once of Walter the clerk
and land which a) gave to c)

a) grants to b) but reserves to himself a strip 38 feet from the

highway as far as the Wall, in breadth all along the highway; for
b) and his heirs to hold free of all taxes and demands.

Witnesses: lord William of the Vales (or Devaux, *de vallibus*), lord
Adam of Neutone, lord Ralph of Feritate, Robert of
Tibey, Alexander son of Ralph, Adam son of Roger,
Henry his brother, William of Timp', Robert of Ireland
[*de Hibernia*], Robert of Kirkebi
Seal: absent

CW 193   Sale: undated   **circa 1280**

a) Agnes daughter of Helen of Karleole
b) Thomas of Karleole, rector of the church of St Mary in
Bedeford,
uncle of a)   c) William son of Juetta [? 'the Jewish woman']

Property: one third part of a certain piece of land in Karleole
with appurts.

Recites that the land used to belong to c) and that a) holds it by
right of dower. She now grants it to b) and his assigns reserving
service to the lords of the fee, if demanded.

Witnesses: Henry the sacrist of Lincoln, Richard and Walter the
chaplains to the lord Dean of Lincoln, Master Henry
the rector of the church of Swalwe, master Richard
of Burge, Jordan, Thomas of Hylle, Robert the cook,
servants of the lord Dean of Lincoln, Richard of
Strettone, clerk.
Seal: oval with impression and legend

CW 194   Gift: undated   **circa 1300**

a) John le Barker of ?Richard Street [*vico Ric'i*]
b) Adam of Warthewick

Property: all that land with its buildings in Richard Street outside
the gates of Karl'e, lying between the land of John le Wadder on
one side and land of Adam the tailor [or ?shoemaker, *sutor*] on
the other, in length from the highway as far as the land of Lord
Robert of Tillhol

a) grants to b) to hold in fee by hereditary right, paying an annual
rent of 4s. silver to the Master of the Hospital of St Nicholas
outside Karl'e

Witnesses: lord John of the Castle [*de Castre*] then sheriff, Adam
the Shire man [*le Sherman*], Ralph of Longmaban,
Michael le Wadder, Thomas of Dumfres

Seal: absent

CW 195 **Gift:** undated **circa 1300**

a) John of Glych of Karl'e b) Ralph the Parker

Property: a messuage with appurts. in Karl'e, lying between the
messuage of William of ?the Brothers (*de fr'ibus*) on
one side and the messuage of Walter the spicer on the
other, one head abutting on the bakers' street (*vicus
pistor'*) and the other on the market place (*forum*) of
Karl'e

a) grants to b) and his heirs to hold of the chief lords of the fee
by the usual services

Witnesses: William son of Henry son of Ivo, then Mayor of the
city of Karl'e, John of the Chapel and Thomas Colstane
then bailiffs, John of Crofton, Robert of Grinnesdale,
? Bernard le Pulter, Nicholas le Spenser, Robert of
Gonertone, John Fleminge, Norman of Redmanne,
John Keke, Alan the clerk

Seal: absent

CW 196 **Gift:** at Karl'e, St George's day, 23 April **1306**

a) Andrew Spot of Karliole and Christine his wife
b) Helen, daughter of Robert of Braytone

Property: all that burgage with its curtilage and building in
the fishers' street [*in vico piscatorum*] within Karliole,
lying between the land of Ralph Todd of Caldecotes
on one side and a public lane [*venella domini Regis*]
on the other, in length from the highway as far as
the lands of John Lambe the tailor [*sutor*] and Henry
Spot; with access to a certain well [*fons*] in the same
burgage whenever necessary and with all liberties and
easements belonging to the burgage

a) grant to b) and her heirs to hold in fee, paying a) an annual
rent of 12d. of silver

Witnesses: lord William of Mulcaster then Warden (*custos*) of
Karl'e, Henry le Furbour and John of the Chapel, then

bailiffs of the same vill', Michael of Haveringetone, Richard of Langwaythby, Hugh Flemyng, Peter the butcher [*carnifex*], Robert le Spicer, Thomas le Leche, Ralph Milis, John le Rede, William son of Henry son of Ivo, Thomas of the Cow

Seal: one (formerly two); impression and legend

CW 197 Quitclaim: at Karl'le, 20 November **1339**

a) John Hardyng of Salkeld

b) Euphemia [*Eufemia*] and Agnes, daughters and heirs of Adam Sherman of Karli'e c) John Wadder, kinsman of a) d) Cecily of Ulnesby

Property: i) One messuage with a garden in the suburb of Karli' outside Richard's gate; ii) a garden next to the water of Eden, one head of which extends from the highway as far as the garden of Michael the dyer and the north side from the way leading towards the meadow of Swift as far as the garden of Adam Sherman iii) a certain house within the city of Karl'e; iv) an annual rent of 3s. from the house of Robert Fourbour

Recites that property i) was formerly held by c) and that property iii) is currently held by d) as b)'s inheritance. a) now releases all rights he has in the properties to b) and their heirs

Witnesses: Lord Antony of Lucy, sheriff of Cumberland, John Flemyng, mayor of the city of Karli', Robert Fourbour, Robert son of Avice, Adam Louson, Robert Grout, William son of Gilbert

Seal: absent

CW 198 Quitclaim: at Karli'e Monday before Christmas 30 Ed. III **1356**

a) William of Parcane b) Stephen of Karl'e, clerk
c) Gilbert of Kirkandrew, kinsman of a)

Property: all that tenement in Karli'e which once belonged to c), lying opposite the castle ditch between the tenement of William Walays on one side and the tenement of William of Brumfelde on the other

a) releases all his rights in the property to b) and his heirs.

Witnesses: Robert of Tebay, then mayor of the city of Karl'e, Alan of Blenerhayset and Robert of Burghe then bailiffs of the same city, William of Arcurheth, Robert Grout, John of Musgrave, William of Whitteby

Seal: impression and legend

CW 199   Gift: at Karl'e, Ss. Philip and James, 1 May, 36 Ed. III   **1362**

a) William Parekere b) John of Wittone and Joan his wife

Property: one messuage with appurts. in the city of Karl'e except one room in the same messuage 14 feet in width by 30 feet in length; the messuage lying between the messuage of b) on one side and the messuage of master William Fentone on the other; with all liberties and easements pertaining.

a) grants to b) and their heirs to hold of the chief lords of the fee, paying to b) and his heirs 14s. sterling annual rent; with power reserved for a) to distrain for non-payment

Witnesses: Thomas of Alaynby then Mayor of the city of Karl'e, Alan of Blenerhaicet and William of Birkenside, then bailiffs of the same city, William of Arcurrethe, Robert of Tibay, Norman of Redemane, William of Londyn, John of Dundraue, John Marschalle

Seal: two, with impressions and legends

CW 200   Receipt: at Wrestlingworth, Monday after the circumcision of Our Lord, 1 January   **1363**

a) Thomas son of John of Raghtone of Carlhulle
b) John of Raghtone, King's esquire

Property: one tenement in the vill' of Carliole, one messuage outside Botchardyate; 40 acres of land in the fields of Carliole, Hubbridby and Blakhale and 5 acres of meadow in the same fields

a) acknowledges receipt of £20 sterling from b) as a purchase price for the property

Witnesses: none
Seal: absent

CW 201   **Gift:**   at Karl'e, Sunday before St Thomas the Apostle, 21 December   **1370**

a) John of Mideltone and John of Cane (?Cave), chaplain
b) Robert of Tybay and   c) Beatrix his wife

Property: all that tenement in the city of Karl'e lying between the tenement of the Abbot of Holmecoltran on one side and the tenement of Thomas of Sandford on the other

Reciting that they received the property from b), a) grant it to b) and c) and the heirs of their bodies to hold of the chief lords of the fee; in default of joint heirs of b) and c) the property shall remain to the heirs of b)

Witnesses: Alan of Blenerhayset then Mayor of the city of Karl'e, Richard of Lundyn and William of Carleton the younger, then bailiffs of the same city, William of Lundyn, William of Birkensyde, John Marschale, John of Dundrawe, Robert the goldsmith (*aurifaber*), Adam the tailor [*sissor*], Thomas Colt

Seal: one of two remains, with impression and legend

CW 202   **Gift:**   at Karl'e, Wednesday St Mary Magdalene, 22 July 47 Ed. III   **1373**

a) Robert of Tybay   b) Robert Taillour, chaplain

Property: one annual rent of 40s. arising out of the tenement that Robert Wourschipp holds in the city of Karl'e between the tenement of the Abbot of Holmecoltran on one side and the tenement of Lord Ranulph of Dacre on the other

a) grants the rent to b) with power to distrain for arrears

Witnesses: Alan of Blenerhayset, mayor of the city of Karl'e, Richard of Lundyn and William of Carleton the younger, bailiffs of the same city, Richard ?Syfener, John of Kardoille, Robert Goldsmythe, Patrick Bakester, Adam Taillour

Seal: impression erased

CW 203 **Quitclaim:** at Karl'e, in the feast of the Conception,
8 December 48 Ed. III   **1374**

a) Richard of the Sandes   b) John Clerk of Anaud (or variants)
c) Norman of Redmane

Property: tenement in the city of Karl'e lying between the tenement
of William of Lon-[?dyn] on one side and the tenement
of Lord Ranulph of Dacre on the other, one head of
which abuts on the highway and the other on the wall
of the said city

Reciting that a) has rights in the property pursuant to a warranty
clause in a deed made by c), a) now releases these rights to b)

Witnesses: William of London then mayor of the city of Karl'e,
Robert Goldsmyth and William of Carletone, then
bailiffs of the same city, John of Dentone, John
Dalmore
Seal: impression all but erased

CW 204 **Quitclaim:** at Karl'e, 6 April 19 Richard II   **1396**

a) Robert of Grynnysdale, son and heir of Gilbert Pepir and
Margaret his wife   b) Stephen of Karli'e

Property: tenement with its appurts. in which b) lives, in the city
of Karl'e between the tenement of Walter of Bamtone
on one side and the tenement once of William of
Bromfeld on the other; in length, one head upon the
tenement of Roger Wily and the other on the way
which leads from the gate of Caldewe to the castle

a) releases all rights that he has in the property to b) and his
heirs

Witnesses: John of Blencansopp then Mayor of the same city,
William Napet then bailiff, Alan of Blenerhayset,
Robert of Karlele, Robert Sperri, Roger Wily,
Seal: broken: remains of impression

CW 205 **Gift:**   at Karliole, Saturday after Easter, 21 Richard II   **1398**

a) Oliver of Raghtone
b) Thomas the vicar of Edenhale, son of John Scayfe

Property: all lands, tenements, rents and services in Bochardegate within the vill' of Karliole and within the vill' of Hobryghtby

a) grants to b) to hold of the chief lords by the usual services

Witnesses: none
Seal: vague impression, deeply recessed

CW 206 **Gift:**   at Karliole, St James the Apostle, 25 July, 1 Henry V   **1413**

a) John of the More [*del More*], clerk and Joan his wife
b) William of Legh, esq. and Agnes his wife

Property: one messuage with appurts. in the city of Karl'e, sited between the tenement of Walter of Bamptone on one side and the tenement of b) on the other

a) grant to b) and their heirs to hold of the chief lords of the fee by the usual services

Witnesses: William of Dentone, mayor of the city, William Cardoille and Robert of Blenerhaiset bailiffs of the same city, Robert of Karlelle, John Cardoille, John of Hirneby, John of Ireby, Walter of Bamptone, Henry Porter
Seal: impression

CW 207 **Quitclaim:** 8 May 9 Henry V   **1421**

a) John of Stapilton of Salkeld
b) Thomas Delamore c) John Delamore

Property: one annual rent of 2s. silver from one tenement in the city of Karl'e next to the chapel of St Alban in the fishers' street

Reciting that the property formerly belonged to c), a) now releases his entitlement to the rent to b) and his heirs

Witnesses: William of Stapilton then sheriff of Cumberland, William of Stapilton the younger, John of Hirneby of Karli'e, Robert of Karlelle, John of Cardoile, John of the More,
Seal: impression

CW 208 **Gift:** at Karliole Monday before the Purification,
2 February 6 Henry VI   **1428**

a) John Atkynson of Karliole, merchant
b) Lord John Bradewath, chaplain and Master John Atkynson,
clerk

Property: all lands and tenements of a) with appurts. within the
city of Karl'e or elsewhere in co. Cumberland

a) grants to b) and their heirs to hold of the chief lords of the fee
by the usual services.

Witnesses: Robert Carlelle then mayor of the city of Karleole,
William Cardoyle and Richard Morisson then bailiffs
of the same, John Hyenby, Thomas Fraunkys, John
Mydlame, John Fraunkys,
Seal: with parchment trim and faint impression

CW 209 **Gift:** at Karl'e, 9 Sept. 9 Henry VI   **1430**

a) John Cletherowe and Agnes his wife of Karl'e
b) Thomas Dooge

Property: all lands and tenements of a) within the city of Karl'e
and in elsewhere co. Cumberland

a) grant to b) and his heirs to hold of the chief lords by the usual
services

Witnesses: John Blanerhasset then Mayor of the city of Karl'e,
Thomas More and Henry Strikland then bailiffs of the
same, William Laton and Thomas Beiauchamp esqs.,
John Herneby, John Atkynson, Thomas Frankisch,
Richard Moressone, William Cardoile
Seal: impression, broken

CW 210 **Gift:** 24 February 9 Henry VI   **1431**

a) Agnes Cletherowe, *lately wife of John*, widow b) Thomas
Dooge

Property: as in CW 209

a) confirms the property to b) and his heirs

Witnesses: John Blanerhasset then Mayor of the city of Karl'e, John Graveson and John Midelham then bailiffs of the same, William Latone, John Herneby, Thomas Beauchamp, William Sharpe, Richard Moresson, David Devias

Seal: impression

CW 211 **Quitclaim:** 28 April 9 Henry VI   **1431**

Parties and property as in CW 209-210 above

a), *in her pure widowhood,* releases all rights in the property to b) and his heirs

Witnesses: none
Seal: impression
Endorsed in a 16thc. hand, *Camyzland and Carlyll*

CW 212 **Quitclaim:** at Carliole, 5 June 16 Henry VI   **1438**

a) John Atkynson, clerk   b) Lord John Bradeworthe, chaplain
c) John Atkynson, father of a)

Property: a certain tenement lying within the city of Carl'e

Reciting that a) and b) hold the property by gift from c), a) now releases all his rights in it to b) and his heirs

Witnesses: Robert Carlelle then Mayor of the city of Carliole, William Cardoille and Henry Striklande then bailiffs of the same, Thomas Frankysshe and John Frankysshe, William Loffe

Seal: vague impression

The three final deeds in the Carlisle collection relate to places assumed to be outside the City. The first, Bochardeby is presumably related to Bochardegate, mentioned in 200 and 205 above. For the second, 'Lustelbont', a modern location has not been found, though several alternative spellings were searched for, including 'Luftel-', Buftel- [first letter *could* just be a B]. The third, Stanwix, is just north of the City.

"BOCHARDEBY"

CW 213 **Gift:**   undated   **circa 1300**

a) Peter the butcher of Carliole   b) William of Daker, knight

Property: one messuage with its curtilage and all the land of
a) in the vill' and territory of Bochardeby and all
appurts.

a) grants to b) and his heirs to hold of the chief lords of the fee
by the usual services.

Witnesses: Lord Anthony of Lucy, Lord William of Mulcastre,
Lord John of the Castle [*de Castr'*], then the sheriff
of Karl', Lord Robert of Kirkebride, knights; John of
Warwyke, Michael of Haveringtone of Caldecotes, John
of Grinnesdale then mayor, John of Cap-[missing]

Seal: absent

"LUSTELBONT"

CW 214   Gift: at Kaerd', Wednesday after St Lucia, 13 Dec., 2 Ed. III   1329

a) William Moryn   b) Roger le Longe

Property: 3 acres 1½ roods of land lying in Lustelbont: of which
1½ acres 1½ roods lie in length between the Highway
on the W. and the land of John Gilbert on the E. and
in width between land of John Odyn on the S. and
land of John Moryn, brother of a), on the N; 1½
acres lie in

length between land of John Odyn on the W. and the common
pasture of the Heeth on the E. and in width between land of said
John Moryn on the N. and land of Jeva [or ?Jena, or ?Ieva for
'Ivan'] Gogh on the south

a) grants to b) and his heirs to hold of the chief lords of the fee
by the usual services and by hereditary right

Witnesses: Roger the skinner [*peliter'*], Andrew the goldsmith then
Reeve of the Borough of Kaerd', Walter of Barry
then bailiff of Kaerd', John Odyn, Richard Elys, John
Gilbert, Jeva [or ?Jena, etc. as above] Goch

Seal: impression, broken in two

STANWIX

CW 215   Gift: At Staynwigs, St Katherine the virgin,
25 November, 44 Ed. III   1370

a) Robert of Bolton, parson of the church of ?Bochastre, John
Scyrtour and John Hog, chaplain

b) Gilbert son of William of ?Quelpedalle   c) Hugh Lowe

Property: lands and tenements in the vill' of Stayniwigis

Reciting that they received the property from c), a) now grant to
b) and his heirs to hold of the chief lords of the fee by the usual
services.

Witnesses: Adam Parnynge then sheriff of Cumberland, John of
Warwic, knights, Alan of Blenerhaiset then mayor of
the city of Karl'e, William of Karlton and Richard
of Londen then bailiffs of the same, John Ferrour,
Thomas Hog

Seal: three with impressions (two poor)

-oOo-

THE DUKE OF NORFOLK'S DEEDS
AT ARUNDEL CASTLE

CATALOGUE 1 PART I

Dacre Estates in Northern Counties

v

Kirkoswald, Penrith and area, co. Cumberland

v *Kirkoswald, Penrith and area*

An estate based at Kirkoswald in the Eden valley, north-east of Penrith, formed part of the inheritance of Joan Multon who married Randolf Dacre in 1286. She obtained it, together with the Barony of Burgh (above), from her mother Aude, wife of Richard Lucy of Egremont. The 15th-century deeds in this group contain evidence of Dacre family ownership but, as for other series of deeds in the Duke of Norfolk's archives, the early titles do not follow through. They hang in mid air with no obvious thread to anchor them to the Dacre family. In being saved for their historic interest they were, unfortunately, 'lost' to their context.

The Kirkoswald estate did not pass to the Dukes of Norfolk through Anne Dacre's portion at the division in 1590. According to the family historian, Henry Howard of Corby, it seems to have fallen to the share of the Dacres of the South.[*]

A substantial part of this series relates to Carleton. There are four places called Carlton/Carleton in Cumberland, of which this seems to be the one near Penrith. CW 225 and CW 230 in this bundle were found among the Appleby deeds (see below). Among the Cumberland Carltons were also found two deeds relating to a Carlton, which, from the witnesses names, I have taken to be the Nottinghamshire Carlton. Further deeds bundled in the same group would appear, again from the witnesses names, to relate to Meynell family properties in Carlton in Cleveland. These have all been relocated with their proper counties and catalogued as NT/- and YK/- respectively. For the Carlton in Cleveland, see *Section x* of this catalogue (Dacre inheritance in North and East Yorkshire). Of the undated Carlton deeds CW 221-227 in this section, CW 223 perhaps appears to be in an earlier hand than the rest; but personal names throughout suggest an overlap and I have therefore guestimated them all at *circa 1300*.

Some unspecified properties in Penrith and Carleton were part of the attainted Lancaster family estates purchased by William, lord Dacre in 1544 (see CW 316 below) The deeds listed here do not demonstrate any obvious link with the Lancaster family but the possibility of a connection should not be ruled out.

---

[*] H. Howard, *Memorials of the Howard Family*, xi appendix H (Corby Castle, 1834)

Contents

CW224   Relating to the arable fields and meadows of Carleton near Penrith, circa 1300, this deed is typical of many in the collections at Arundel - robbed of its seal and without much visual charm; but nevertheless containing riches in its text. The names of neighbouring land holders are named. Many minor locations are named. Some people have developed surnames in the modern sense: others are still distinguished in an old-fashioned way, by reference to their father or grandfather. The witnesses include the sheriff of Cumberland.

v *Kirkoswald, Penrith and area*

CW 221 **Gift:** undated **circa 1300**

a) William of Wilton and Joan his wife
b) John son of Adam del Wra

Property: one messuage and 20a. land in the vill' of Blenkarne in Cumberland lying between the land of John the miller [*molendinarius*] on one side and land called Canittlande on the other

a) grants to b) to hold of the chief lords of the fee by the usual services

Witnesses: Roger of Salkelde, William of Hotone of Salkelde, Clement of Croftone, John Hunter, John of Layfingby
Seal: two, small, with impressions

CW 222 **Gift:** undated **circa 1275**

a) William son of Henry of Dolfineby b) Peter son of Hugh the butcher [*carnifex*] of Karl'e

Property: one messuage, one sheepfold [*bercaria*] and four acres of land and one acre of meadow, ½ acre of which lies (extends) from the way which leads to the church as far as the mill way to the E., with appurts in Dolfynby in Edinhale; one rood of land on which the mill of Dolfineby was once [sic, *quondam**] erected, with all liberties and easements whatsoever [*The rood is later summarised as *terra molendini*, which perhaps implies that the mill was still there]

a) grants to b) to hold by hereditary right from the chief lords of the fee by the usual services.

Witnesses: lord William of Mulcastre then sheriff of Cumberland, Walter of Bamptone, John of Staffol, Adam of Hotone, Thomas of Hotone, Adam Turpe of Edenhale, Adam of Carletone, Robert of Loncastre, William le Mareschale

Seal: absent

CW 223   **Gift:**   undated   **circa 1300**

a) John son of Gilbert le Quite of Carletona
b) William son of John of Brau'wra

Property: one messuage with curtilage in the vill' of Carletona lying between the tenement of John son of Bruce (or ?Brice) on one side and the tenement of John Sappekunt on the other; and 13 acres 3 roods of land in the territory of the said vill' with a certain meadow in Le Halle Enghis; 3 acres of which lie pertaining to and in the croft of the said messuage between the land of the said John son of Bruce on one side and the land of one Thomas son of Paul of Edenhale on the other; three acres lie under Le Stanygatbanck between land of John Bone on one side and land of John son of Peter on the other; 1½ acres lie upon Rokelund between the land of John Bruce on one side and land of Thomas son of William on the other; ½ acre lies in Le Mire [*in le miro*] between land of said John Bone on one side and land of said John son of Brice on the other; ½ acre lies upon Le Koldebanck between land of said John Bone on one side and land of William son of Peter on the other; and one [illeg.] lies on Balledbuske between the land of John Bone and William son of Peter; 3 roods lie in Le Wattehale between the lands of said John Bone and William son of Peter on both sides; ½ acre lies beyond Le Buretrebuske between lands of said John Bone and William son of Peter on both sides; 3 roods lie this side of Le Buretrebuske between lands of the same John and William; 1 acre lies upon Loc Twayt between land of said William on one side and land of Thomas son of Gerard on the other; with all liberties and easements

a) grants to b) and his heirs to hold of the chief Lords of the fee by the usual services

Witnesses: Robert of Bartone then bailiff of Penreth, Alexander of the Chapel [*de capella*], William of Dolfanby, Adam of Carleton, John Bone, Adam ?Dunnyng, John son of Bruce then the reeve [*prepositus*].

Seal: absent

CW 224 Gift: undated circa **1300**

a) John son of Gilbert le Quite of Carletona b) William son of John of Brau'wra c) Joan, mother of a) d) Gilbert, grandfather of a) e) Mariota, wife of John of Bran'wra

Property: four acres and one rood in the territory of Carleton and that meadow which a) holds, in four different places in the territory of the said vill'; of which 1½ acres lie upon Le Staynnigatbanck between land which c) holds as her dower on one side, being the former land of d), and land which e) holds as her dower, also the former land of d), on the other; 1 acre lies upon Rokeland between land which c) holds as dower on one side and land which e) holds as dower on the other, both former land of d); ½ acre called Le Keldland, between land of John Bone and land of William son of Peter; ½ acre land lies at Le Balledbuske between land of said John and said William; 1½ roods lies at Le Halleenghis between land of same persons; 1½ roods lie upon Le Buttis between land of John son of Brice and land of said William son of Peter; and two portions [*partes*] of meadow in Le Pottis; and that dole [*illud dale* {accusative tense}] of meadow in Le Halleenghis which lies between the meadow of John Bone and the meadow of John of the Banck; and that dole of meadow in Le Halleenghis which lies between the meadow of said John Bone and the meadow of Adam son of John son of Gerard

a) grants to b) and his heirs to hold of the chief Lords of the fee by the usual services

Witnesses: lord John of the Castle [*de castre*], knight, then sheriff of Cumberland, William of Quitholm, Adam of Carletona, William of Dolfanby, William son of Peter of Carletona

Seal: absent

CW 225 Grant: undated   **circa 1300**

a) John son of Gilbert le Quite of Carletona   b) William son of
John of Braumwra of Penrethe

Property: one plot of land with its curtilage in the vill of Carletone
lying between the tenement of (a) on one side and that
of John of Sappekunt on the other; 1a. 1r. of land in
the vill of which the acre lies upon Loccwayt between
land of William son of [missing] and land of Thomas
son of Gerard, and the rood lies in Le More [or could
be *myre* - hole in doc.] next to the land of John son
of Bruce to the north

a) grants to b) together with the reversion of a further 5a. land
which Mariota, relict of Gilbert le Quite holds for life.

Witnesses: Robert of Burton, then bailiff of Penreth, Alexander
of the chapel, ?Adam of Carleton, John Bone, William
son of Peter of Carleton, William of Dolfanby.
Seal: none
This document is 'moth-eaten'

CW 226 Grant and lease to fee farm*: undated   **circa 1300**

a) Alexander of the Chapel   b) Thomas son of William of Carletone
c) William son of Gilbert

Property: the toft and croft with all its land and meadow in the
territory of Carletone which once belonged to c) and
lies between the croft of Thomas of the Bank on the
east and the croft of b) on the west; with all liberties
and easements within the vill' and without

The land formerly belonged to c). Now a) grants to b) and his
heirs to hold of the chief lords by the usual services and to hold
of a) and his heirs by a 12s. annual rent and by plough service
of an acre of land, assuming he has an ox in the plough team [*si
pred' Tho' aliquem bovem in caruca possideat*].

Witnesses: Thomas of Bank, John of Bramwra, William son of
Peter, John of Bank, William son of Nicholas, Adam
son of Beatrice, Peter Dicheman
Seal: absent
* full phrase is: *concessi, dedi et ad firmam feodi dimisi*

CW 227   **Grant of reversion:** undated   **circa 1300**

a) John son of Thomas son of William of Carleton
b) Adam son of John son of Gerard of Carleton
c) Alice, mother of a)

Property: one rood of land upon Le Lathestedis in the territory of Carleton, lying between land which b) holds by gift from a) on one side and land of John Bone on the other

Reciting that c) holds the land for life, a) grants the reversion expectant upon her death to b) and his heirs to hold of the chief lords by the usual services.

Witnesses: lord John of the Castle, knight, then sheriff of Cumberland, William of ?Wycclan [text very faint], Adam of Carletone, William of Dolfanby, William son of Peter of Carletone.
Seal: fragment

CW 228   **Quitclaim:**   at Carleton, on the Exaltation of the Holy Cross, 14 September, 11 Ed. III   **1337**

a) John son of William of Carleton   b) William of Bramwra

Property: all the lands and tenements which b) received from a) when b) was a minor

a) now releases to b) all his rights in the property

Witnesses: John Bone, Geoffrey Taillour, William of Dolfanbi, John of Boltone, Thomas son of William son of Peter, William of the Bank, Adam Gerard
Seal: impression mostly erased

CW 229   **Lease for lives:** at Carletone, 12 August 7 Ed. IV   **1467**

a) William Blyrthorne of Bernardscastell and Elena his wife
b) Thomas Patonson and John Newton of Carlton

Property: two tenements in the vill' and territory of Carlton next Penreth

a) grant to b) to hold of themselves during their lives at annual rent of 19s. of English money, payable half-annually, with power for distraint if the rent is more than 40 days overdue. **Additional clause in English**: that after the decease of *Wilyam and Elyn*, b) shall leave the premises in a good state of repair with *thak and wagh* (thatch and ?wattles)

Witnesses:	Thomas Carlton, John Bost (or Bosc), William Henreson, John Browne, William Bolton
Seal:	two fragments

CW 230 **Counterpart** of CW 229 with slightly better seals

CW 231 **Gift:**   undated   **circa 1300**

a) Hudd the smith [*Eudo faber*], son of Robert Collan of Penrethe

b) Adam son of John son of Gerard of Carletone

Property:	three roods of land in the teritory of Penrethe; of which ½ acre lies upon Partegil between the land of Thomas of Hotona on one side and land of Adam son of Robert on the other; one rood lies at Le Potterwat between land of said Thomas on one side and the meadow of said Adam on the other.

a) grants to b) to hold of the chief lords of the fee by the usual services.

Witnesses:	Robert of Bartone then bailiff of Penrethe, Alexander of the Chapel, Adam of Carletone, John Bone, Thomas of Appilby, Adam son of Robert then the reeve.
Seal:	absent

CW 232 **Gift:**   undated   **circa 1300**

a) William son of Geoffrey Helfe of Penrethe

b) Adam son of John son of Gerard of Carletona

Property:	all the land of a) in the territory of Penrethe which lies between the ?way out of [*exitus de*] Carletone on one side and land called Carleton Lofttwaye on the other; with all liberties and easements pertaining

a) grants to b) and his heirs to hold of the chief lords of the fee by the usual services.

Witnesses: Robert of Bartone then bailiff of Penrethe, Alexander of Chapel, Adam of Carletona, John Bone, John son of Bruce, Thomas of Appilby, Adam son of Robert then reeve.

Seal: impression

CW 233 **Request for an investigation:** at Devyses, 6 August 8 Hen. VI   **1430**

a) The Hon. Lord Dakre
b) Thomas Coventre, mayor of Devyses, William Coventre, John Coventre, William B-[illegible]-grove, Robert Chaundeler, William Smythe, John Saunders, John Fawkener, John Gray, John Baker, chapman, Roger Barbour, John Smythe, William Hendelous, burgesses of the same town
c) William Burton, son of Adam Burton of Staffelle
d) William Burton, uncle of c)

Property: lands and tenements of c) in Staffelle (no details)

Recites that b) examined c) on 1 Aug. last who claimed that he was entitled to the property in Staffield and that d) was not. Now b) require a) to investigate the truth of the matter.

Witnesses: none
Seal: ten small seals and fragments, some with impressions; and one great seal of the borough, legend fragmented but impression good

CW 234 **Gift:** at Staffulle, Wednesday after Michaelmas
13 Hen. VI   **1434**

a) Ralph of Kyrkeby, son of John of Kyrkeby
b) Lord Thomas Dacre, lord of Dacre and of Gillesland

Property: moiety of the manor of Staffulle in Cumberland, with all rents, services of the free tenants and all appurts.

a) grants to b) and his heirs to hold of the chief lords of the fee by the usual services

Witnesses: none
Seal: impression

CW 235 **Gift:** at Keverhughe, Wednesday before Michaelmas
37 Hen. VI **1455**

a) John Helton, son and heir of Thomas Helton of Gamellesby
and Christine his wife, dau. of ... b) Joan, former wife of William
Patrikson c) Humphrey Dacre son of Thomas, lord Dacre late
of Gillesland, knight

Property: one messuage, built upon, at Keverhugh within the
territory of Kirkoswald and all lands and meadows
adjoining, with all appurts.

Reciting that he received the property from b) in her widowhood
a) now grant it to c) and his heirs to hold of the chief lords of
the fee by the usual services

Witnesses: William Marshall, rector of the church of Kirkoswald,
John Wherton of Kirkbythore, John Vyell, John Couper,
William Vyell.
Seal: fragment

-oOo-

THE DUKE OF NORFOLK'S DEEDS
AT ARUNDEL CASTLE

CATALOGUE 1 PART I

Dacre Estates in Northern Counties

vi

Appleby and area, co. Westmorland

vi. *Appleby and area, Westmorland*

The following deeds are centred on the market town of Appleby in Westmorland, relating to the town itself and to various parishes in the vicinity as listed in the *Contents* below.

A 'Barony of Dufton' was mentioned by the Howard family historian, Henry Howard of Corby, as part of Anne Dacre's inheritance in 1571 (ie. the half of the Greystoke holdings that descended to the Dukes of Norfolk).[*] The pedigree of this 'Barony' is unclear, and it may simply have been a Dacre family expression for their possessions in the Appleby area. Dufton itself, a parish lying north east of Appleby, backing onto the fells, is mentioned only incidentally in this series. However, it was an early Greystoke family possession (see *i. Greystoke family etates, Introduction*, above). In 1344 the manor of Dufton was mentioned as a Greystoke family possession (CW 11). This manor, with its outliers, would have covered a much larger territory than the parish itself. In 1472, a rental of the Greystoke estates includes around 22 holdings and a tenement in Appleby under the heading 'Dufton'.[†] In 1565 the Dufton territory amounted to upwards of 9,000 acres.[‡]

Dufton had come into the Greystoke family by the 13th century. In early medieval Westmorland there were only two baronies, 'Kendal' and 'Westmorland'. The former covered the central Lakeland, the Kendal area and south to Kirkby Lonsdale and the Lune valley. The latter covered eastern Lakeland from Ullswater, straddling south and east across the Eden valley to Appleby and its surrounds. This barony was held by John de Veteripont who, in 1202-3, held the custody of Appleby and the shrievalty of Westmorland. He died in 1228-9 and, while his male line subsequently descended by marriage into the Clifford family (the chief lords of Appleby), a female descendant, Christian (or Christine), married into the Fitzwilliams of Greystoke around 1227. By this route the Greystoke barons may have gained an early stake in Westmorland. In 1315-16 Ralph, son of William of Greystoke (who died in 1289) was found by inquest to hold the vills of Dufton, Brampton, Bolton and Yanewith from the Cliffords.[§]

The Dacre family, as well as the Greystokes, had an interest in the Appleby area in their own right. For Margaret Multon, the Gilsland heiress, had married Ranulph Dacre in 1315, bringing not only the Gilsland inheritance to the Dacres but also the manor of Hoff and Drybeck near Appleby. A relative of hers, Sir Hugh of Multon, was a juror at Appleby in 1291-2, a factor which points to his being a local landowner.

---

[*] H. Howard, Memorials of the Howard Family (Corby Castle, 1834), XI, appendix.
[†] Carlisle Record Office D/HG/16
[‡] See D7113 on page 255 below.
[§] J.Nicholson and R. Burn, *The History and Antiquities of the Counties of Westmorland and Cumberland* (1777; republished in 1976 with introduction by B.C.Jones), vol I, pp 271, 356

Indeed, in CW 283 below a deed of gift specifies the rent should be paid to him at Hoff - which was presumably his seat.

The manor of Hoff subsequently passed to Thomas of Multon and the entitlement of his heir (Margaret) was affirmed at inquests in 1308-9 and in 1315-16. Under age at the first inquest, she had married Sir Randolf Dacre by the second.* She is party to one of the deeds in this series (CW 257), in 1341, described as 'the Lady of Gilleslande'.

Both Dufton and Orton, a village which the historian Henry Howard of Corby associates with the Barony of Dufton, also occur later in the catalogue (section *vii*, CW 281-314) as properties in the hands of the Lancaster family; while Kirkby Thore occurs here, in a Dacre connection, and in section *vii* under the Lancaster family.

As the *Contents*, below, shows, most deeds in this group demonstrate some connection both with the Greystokes or the Dacres. As well as CW 257, cited above, another deed, CW 253 below, mentions premises held in remainder by Ralph, lord Greystoke in 1406. It was the grand-daughter of this Ralph whose marriage to Thomas, 2nd lord Dacre and Gilsland, *c.*1488, brought the Greystoke lordship and possessions into Dacre hands. Other deeds, relating to small purchases of land, must reflect piecemeal consolidation by the Dacres of the ancestral hold they already enjoyed in the Appleby area of Westmorland.

For further premises in Dufton, see CW 287-289 below. For an inquisition at Appleby in 1593, see CW 351 in section *ix*, *Casterton,* below.

---

* Nicholson and Burn (cited above), Vol I, pp 337-8

Contents

vi. *Appleby and area,*[*] *Westmorland*

CW 241 **Grant:** undated circa 1350[*]

a) Robert Overdo of Appelby
b) John of Hurworth, the forester of Flakebrig.

Property: burgage in Appleby, which lies in the street called Peresgate between the tenement of John of Colby on one side and the tenement of the chantry of the Blessed Virgin Mary on the other.

a) grants to b) and his heirs.

Witnesses: John of Threwele of Appelby, Robert Ackynsone, William of Coldale, Robert Smythe, William Praysone.
Seal: impression.
* This deed could perhaps be later: compare CW 245 below.

CW 242 **Grant:** undated circa 1350

a) John son of John of Goldington of Colleby
b) William of Bolton, clerk

Property: one toft in Appilby in the barony of Persgate between a toft once of lord Guy [Wydonis] the chaplain on one side and the end of the bridge of St. Lawrence on the other

a) grants to b) to hold of him at annual rent of 8d. of silver.

Witnesses: William Lengleys, Thomas son of Walter the clerk, Robert of Sandford, John Wynde, Adam the taylor [cissore], William of Caterlene.
Seal: rough.

---

* For Hoff, near Appleby, as the seat at which a deed originated, see pp.47, 146.

CW 243 Gift: at Appleby, Monday after St. Thomas the Martyr, (29 Dec) 26 Ed. III   **1352**

a) William son of Thomas Nelson of Appleby, chaplain
b) John Puddyng, skinner, and Christine his wife
c) William Wrangwys

Property: all lands and tenements of a) in the vill' of Appelby in a street called Persgate, lying between the tenement once of John of Colleby and the tenement of Walter Lifte.

a) grants to b), having obtained the property by gift of c), to hold in chief, rendering customary service to the borough of Appleby.

Witnesses: John of Colleby, then mayor of Appelby, Thomas of Walles, William del Vickers, then bailiff of the same town, Thomas of Goldyngton, John del Oncyles, Thomas Makatdo, John of Burgh, clerk.
Seal:
         none

CW 244 Gift: at Appleby, Monday before St. Martin in Hieme (11 Nov) 39 Ed. III   **1365**

a) John of Langley, walker
b) Robert of Ordo [or ? Eyde] of Appelby.

Property: a burgage which lies next to the street called Persgate between the tenement of St. Nicholas on one side and the tenement of the Chantry of St. Mary on the other, in the vill' of Appelby.

a) grants to b) and his heirs.

Witnesses: John of Trelkeld of Appelby, Thomas Makeatdo of the same, William Praysone of the same, John of Burgh.
Seal: impression.

CW 245 Gift: at Appleby, Monday after Christmas, 45 Ed. III   **1371**

a) Robert Overdos   b) John of Hurworthe, forester of Flakebrig

Property: messuage in the borough of Appelby in Persgat between the tenement of b) and the tenement of a)
a) grants to b) and his heirs.

Witnesses:	none	
Seal:	good impression	

CW 246   **Quitclaim:**   at Appelby, Tuesday before Simon the Apostle, 28 October, 9 Ric. II   **1385**

a) Adam of Bolton   b) John of Hortheworthe

Property: one tenement, once of Adam Walkar's in the town of Appylby next to the end of the town bridge.

a) quitclaims all his former rights in the property to b).

Witnesses:	Robert of Goldyntone, William of Coldale, Robert Overdu, Joan Overdu.
Seal:	damaged but good impression

CW 247   **Gift:**   at Appelby, Monday before Simon the Apostle, 28 October, 9 Ric. II   **1385**

a) Thomas Forster of Hexham   b) John of Hurtheworthe

Property: one tenement in the town of Appylby, lying between the end of the bridge on one side and the tenement of the Lord of Clifford on the other.

a) grants to b) and his heirs.

Witnesses:	as in CW 246 above.
Seal:	damaged, with impression.

CW 248   **Gift:**   at Exham (Hexham), St. James the Apostle, 25 July, 10 Ric. II   **1386**

a) William Horde and Margaret his wife
b) John of Horeworthe of Appelby

Property: one burgage in Porsgat in the town of Appelby, lying between the grange of Master John Wateresson on one side and the burgage of Adam Walker on the other.

a) grants to b) and his heirs.

Witnesses:	Robert Owerdos, then mayor, William of Coldalle, John Overdos, John ?Tawer, John Wynde.
Seal:	impression.

CW 249 **Quitclaim:** at Appleby, date as in CW 248 above   **1386**

a) Adam of Bolton   b) John of Horeworth

Property: one messuage and appurts. in Persgat in Appelby. Abuttals as in CW 248 above.

a) quitclaims to b) his rights in the property.

Witnesses: Robert Ordu, then maior, John Wattesson, John Ordu, Daw Peny.
Seal: impression

CW 250 **Gift:**   at Appleby, Thursday in Easter week, 3 Hen. IV   **1402**

a) John of Hurworth of Appelby   b) Henry, parson of the church of Mertone   c) William, parson of the church of Dunstane   d) John of Lancaster of Bramptone   e) John of Heltone

Property: all the lands and tenements of a) in the town and territory of Appelby.

a) grants to b), c), d), and e).

Witnesses: none
Seal: small, simple impression.

CW 251 **Gift:**   at Appleby, Monday before St. Lawrence, 10 August,   **1402**

a) John Hurworthe of Appelby
b) parties b), c), and e) of CW 250 above   c) William Watson

Property: all lands, tenements and rents of a) both within and without the borough of Appelby.

a) grants to b) and c).

Witnesses: none, as in CW 250 above.
Seal: impression

CW 252 **Gift:** at Appelby, Vigil of Ss. Simon and Jude, 28 October, 7 Hen. IV **1405**

a) John of Hurthworth of Appelby b) William of Wenceslaw, parson of the church of Duffeton c) Robert Goldale, chaplain.

Property: i) tenement at the end of the bridge of Appleby
ii) two burgages in the same town.

a) grants the two properties to b) and c) to hold of the chief lords of the fee by the respective sevices that pertain to them

Witnesses: John Mawchele*, John of Heltone, John Saghier, John Overdo
Seal: as in CW 250-251 above.
*Though this could equally be read as 'Mawthele', compare CW295-296 below where an earlier family member is 'Maukael.

CW 253 **Gift:** at Appelby, 12 October 8 Hen. IV **1406**

a) William of Wenceslaw, rector of the church of Duffetone
b) Robert of Goldale, chaplain
c) John of Hurthworth of Appelby
d) Ralph [Dacre], Baron of Greystok.

Property: as in CW 252 above.

a) and b) grant to c) with remainder to d) and his heirs.

Witnesses: none
Seal: two on one tag, each with simple impression

CW 254 **Grant:** 12 October, 8 Hen. IV **1406**

Parties and transaction as in CW 253 above

Property: as in CW 253 above

Witnesses: none
Seal: impression 'w', presumably of party a)
253 and 254 are a matching pair of indentures

CW 255   **Declaration:** at Hexham, 31 August 8 Hen. VI   **1430**

[to all men]...*hele in owr Lord Aylastyng Syne medefull thyng is to bere wytnes to trewthe.....*

a) Paton ?Laveroke, John Forbes, Richard Peresone, Robert Monke, Thomas Baxter, John Monke, William Werthingtone, William Dode, Robert Dixon, Thomas Sparkes, Robert Baxter, Stephen Hunter, all burgesses of the town of Hexham
b) Thomas Forster of Hexham, son and heir of Jonet Forster who was daughter and heir of...
c) Thomas of Boltone, son and heir of William of Boltone

Property: a place [ie, *plot of land*] in Appilby in Westmorland which joins upon the br[idge] of St. Lawrance.

a) declare and witness that the property was bought by c) and that
b) is his rightful heir.
NB This document is in dialect English, not Latin.

Witnesses: none
Seal: none

CW 256   **Quitclaim:**   at [illegible -oth], 14 August, 27 Hen. VI   **1449**

a) Thomas Foster of Hexham, son and heir of Isabelle Foster, deceased
b) Ralph [Dacre], baron of Graistok and Wemme

Property: one toft and appurts. in Appilby

a) quitclaims his rights in the property to b)

Witnesses: none
Seal: impression

-oOo-

vi cont. *Appleby and Drybeck*

CW 257 Confirmation: at the manor of Hoffe, Tuesday after
the Octave of Michaelmas, 15 Ed. III   **1341**

a) Thomas of Berwys, knight
b) Lady Margaret of Dacre, lady of Gilleslande

Property: one acre of meadow in the vill' of Dribek called
Cokemancrokes

a) confirms to b) to hold of the chief lords by the services
pertaining

Witnesses: lord Hugh of Louthre, John of Derwentwatre, John
of Stirkeland, John of Lancastre, knights, Thomas
of Musgrave then vicar of Westmorland, Thomas
Maunchel, Robert of Crakanthorppe, Hugh of
Ormesheued, John of Helletone, Thomas son of
Julian.

Seal: good impression of shield and crest; with legend

CW 258 Gift: at Appelby, Monday in the Vigil of St. James,
25 July, 37 Ed. III   **1362**

a) John of Threlkeld   b) John of Threlkeld, father of a)
c) Thomas Johnson of Drybek

Property: two acres of meadow in Appelby, Skyeterygate

a) gives the premises, which he received from b), to c); to hold of
the chief lords of the fee by the usual services

Witnesses: Thomas of Blenkansoppe, Thomas of Warthetoppe
[or ?-coppe], William of Warthetoppe, William of
Crakanthorppe, John of Burgh, clerk.

Seal: border and good impression of ?an angel

CW 259 **Re-grant:** at Drybek, 5 November 28 Hen. VI   **1449**

a) Robert Salkeld, John Syward, vicar of the church of Penrethe and Thomas Burgham the elder b) Hugh Forstere of Penreth and Mariota his wife c) Gilbert Bukthorpe

Property: i) all lands and tenements of a) and c) in Drybek
ii) two acres of meadow in Skytersgate in the vill' of Appilby

Recites that a) and c) held the property by gift from b). They now give it back to him, to hold of the chief lords of the fee

Witnesses: none
Seal: formerly three, of which two remain, with reasonable impressions

CW 260 **Quitclaim:** 20 September, 30 Hen. VI   **1451**

a) Thomas Burghham the elder   b) Robert Salkeld
c) John Syward, vicar of the parish church of Penrethe
d) Thomas Colt

Property: all lands and tenements in Cumberland and Westmorland which a) held together with Gilbert Buckthorpe, now deceased, by gift of Hugh Forster of Penrith

a), b) and c) quitclaim to d)

Witnesses: none
Seal:

formerly three, of which two remain, with impressions

-oOo-

CW263 The larger landowners were able to appoint representatives to do their business. This deed of 2 April 1500 was drawn up at Kirkoswald, and the seal shows Lady Mabel Dacre's crest of a stag in full antler. She had just bought some meadowland at Ellercar in Crackenthorpe. Now John Tibbey of Kirkbythore is given the job of going over there to finalise the transaction by entering upon the premises.

vi cont. Crackenthorpe, co. Westmorland 1483-1500

CW 261 **Grant and letters of attorney:** 13 January 22 Ed. IV   **1483**

> a) John Robertson, son and heir of Robert Robertson alias Hobkyn Robertson of Crosby Garrard   b) Christopher Messanger and Katherine his wife, one of the daughters and heirs of Robert Smyth late of Kirkebystephan and Alice his wife   c) John Johnson of Kirkebystephan, son and one of the heirs of Margaret late wife of Robert Johnson of Kirkbystephan, who was sister of said Katherine and her co-heir   d) William Thomlynson of Kirkebystephan and Isabel his wife, sister and co-heir with Margaret and Katherine above
> e) Henry Cady of Bolton
> f) John Cady the elder and William Hogeson
>
> **Property:**   one acre of meadow in Ellercar in Crakanthorpe
>
> a) - d) grant to e) and appoint f) to be their attornies for livery of seisin.
>
> **Witnesses:**   John Wherton of Kirkbythore, John Wherton of Appelby, Christopher Ratcliff, Edward Ratclif, Alan Walton
> **Seal:**   formerly six, of which five remain; small, with faint impressions
> Part of the text of this deed is spoiled by insect damage

CW 262 **Grant:**   at Ellercar, 2 April 15 Hen. VII   **1500**

> a) Henry Cady of Bolton   b) Mabel, late wife of Lord Humphrey Dacre, late lord of Dacre and Gillesland
>
> **Property:**   as in CW 261
>
> Reciting title as in CW 261 above a) now grants to b) and her heirs

Witnesses: Philip Dacre esq., John Rigge, Roland Thomson of
Kirkbythore, John Wolfe the elder of the same.

Seal:
impression of a bird

CW 263   **Letters of attorney:** at Kirkoswald, 2 April, 15 Hen. VII   **1500**

a) Mabil Dacre as in CW 262 above   b) John Tibbey of
Kirkebythore

a) appoints b) to receive seisin of property as in CW 261 above
from Henry Cady

Witnesses: none
Seal: impression of a stag

-oOo-

vi cont. Firbank, co. Westmorland

CW 264 **Grant:** at Netherburghe, Tuesday after Michaelmas 4 Ed. III **1330**

a) John of Frethebank   b) Richard of Preston

Property: lands and tenements in the hamlet of Frethebank, co. Westmorland

a) grants to b) with all rents, services and appurts., to hold of the chief lords by the usual services

Witnesses: William of Medyltone, Adam of Berburne, Ketil of Myrewra, John of Donebegyng, Hugh of Thorneton
Seal: absent

CW 265 **Quitclaim:** at Kirkby in Kendale in the Vigil of (Easter), 36 Ed. III **1362**

a) Richard of Preston   b) Thomas, son of William of Freyebank

Property: tenements, meadows, houses and gardens within the hamlet [*hameletta*] of Freyebank

a) releases to b), with an annual rent of 4 shillings out of the premises

Witnesses: Thomas of Stirkeland, lord James Pickering, knights, Matthew of Redeman, Thomas of Redemane, John of Pikering
Seal: good impression of arms; and legend
Much of this deed is faded and illegible through insect damage.

CW 266 **Grant:** at Frethebank in the vigil of Palm Sunday, 1 Hen. VI **1423**

a) Thomas Frethbank   b) Robert Frethbank, son of a)

Property: all his lands, tenements, meadows and wastes with common of pasture and all liberties, in Frethbank

a) grants to b) and his heirs male; reversion to a) and his heirs in default of heirs male of b)

Witnesses: John Mylnthorpe then sub-vicar of Westmorland, Robert Docwra, John Layburn, John Cayrons of Kyrkeby in Kendall, Richard Ward.

Seal: impression

CW 267   **Declaration:** in the church at Kirkebykendall, St. Wilfrid's day, 12 October, 12 Hen. VI   **1433**

a) Richard Garesdall, vicar of the church [*kirke*] of Kirkebykendall, Robert Laybrun, knight, Richard Duket, '*swhier*' (? esquire), William of Levenes, Robert Dokwray, Thomas of Dokwray, John of Chaumbre, Robert Colynson, John (?of) Brigges
b) John Nelson   c) Jhankyn of Stanegreff, clerk
d) Thomas of Frethbank   e) John of Frethbank, his son

Property: lands formerly belonging to d) in co. Westmorland

At an inquest held before the parties of a) in the church of Kirby Kendall on the date of this deed, a), at the request of b) require c) to speak the truth *as he would at the day of dome*'; whereupon c) claims he executed a deed at the bidding of e) whereby the lands came to e) after the death of d); but he denies any knowledge as to whether this accorded with the last wishes of d)

Witnesses: none
Seal: 7 small seals, some with impressions
This document in dialect English

CW 268   **Verification of deed:** at Appelby, 5 March 12 Hen. VI   **1434**

a) John of Milthorppe   b) Robert of Frethebank, son of Thomas of Frethebank   c) John of Frethebank and John his son.

Property: as in CW 267

a) verifies the deed CW 266 above which was made in the presence of Adam Warde of Frethebank, Richard his son, William Thomlynson of Frethebank, William Gilpyne, Richard son of John of Redeman; the deed was made as the result of an argument between b) and c)

Witnesses: none
Seal: impression

CW 269 A 16th-century copy of CW 267 above.

-oOo-

vi cont. premises in Kirkby Thore

(see also vii., Westmorland deeds, **below)**

CW 270 **Grant:**   at Kirkebythore, 13 November 5 Hen. VII   **1489**

a) John Kirkeby of Hawthorne in the Bishopric of Durham, esq.
b) Mabel, Lady of Dacre and of Gillesland

Property: two tenements in Kirkebythore, one in the occ. of
John Tybey of the Grene, the other in the occ. of John
Grayson, with all lands and meadows adjoining, and all
appurts; one parcel of meadow there which lies between
the water of Troutebek and the watercourse of the corn
mill there [*molendinum ad blad'*], late belonging to a),
called Kirkebymylneholme, in the occ. of Alan Walton
and Robert Thomson the elder; all the tenants being
tenants at will.

a) grants to b) and her assigns to hold of the chief lords of the fee
by the usual services.

Witnesses: Christopher Cannesfeld, rector of the church of Aykton,
Robert Chapman, rector of the church of Beamount,
Roland Ratclif, Robert Skelton, Alan Walton.
Seal: a blob

CW 271 **Quitclaim:** date, parties and property as in CW 270.
Witnesses: Christopher Cannesfield, rector of Ayketon, Robert
Chapman, rector of the church of Be[amont], [missing-]-
?myre Thomas Beverley, Alan Walton
Seal: a blob

CW 272 **Letters of attorney:** 19 February, 5 Hen. VII   **1489**

a) Mabel, Lady Dacre of Dacre and Gillesland
b) Edward Parro and William Newton

a) appoints b) as her attornies to receive seisin from John Kirkeby
of property as in CW 271
Witnesses: none
Seal: fragment

vi cont. Milburn, Westmorland

CW 273   **Grant and confirmation:** undated   **?circa 1250**

a) Adam son of Alan Bouscier of Milneborn
b) William Surays and Beatrice his wife
c) Hudd of Milneborn   d) Bertine [*Bertinus*] of Jonesby

> **Property:**   all the land with all its appurts. in the vill' of Milneborn
> which c) gave to b), together with ⅓ part of the mill
> of Milneborn and ⅓ part of the multure [*multura*,
> 'payment for grinding'] of those using the mill; and
> with common of pasture and all liberties within the
> vill' of Milneborn and without

a) confirms to b) and their heirs all the rights in the property that
c) gave them by his charter; so that b) will hold the premises of a)
and his heirs at 20d. silver per ann. in lieu of all secular demands;
and paying a further sum of one mark of silver to d) each year
on behalf of a) ("nomine meo"); with liability to foreign service
proportionate to that amount of land; and liability to a fine of 6d
in case of forfeiture without bloodshed or 12d. if bloodshed occurs
(to persons other than a) or his heirs.)

> **Witnesses:**   Roger of Stokes, Nicholas of Corby then bailiff of
> Westmorland [*Westmeria*], lord Richard of Scirburn,
> Thomas of Musegraf, Henry of Stanelay, John of the
> Chapel, Walter of Meburn, Robert of Yun [initial Y is
> accentuated, ?making it a two-syllable name], Simon
> of Bra'tu' [?Brampton], John of Helt'

Seal: absent
This deed has been repaired

CW 274   **Quitclaim:**   undated   **?circa 1260**

a) Timocke, once wife of Adam Bousquiere of Middiltone
b) William le Surays of Appilby and Beatrice his wife

Property: all the lands and tenements that a)'s former husband held within the vill' of Milneberne and without

a), in her chaste widowhood, releases all her rights in the property to b and their heirs

Witnesses: Richard of Crippinges then sheriff of Westmorland, Walter of Raffnessby, William lord of Barton, Simon son of William the clerk of Barton, Robert the stranger [*extraneus*], John of Broy, Adam son of Gilbert, lord of Kirkebyth', Richard of Appilby, clerk

Seal: absent

This deed has been repaired

-oOo-

THE DUKE OF NORFOLK'S DEEDS AT ARUNDEL CASTLE

CATALOGUE 1   PART I

Dacre Estates in Northern Counties

vii

Westmorland deeds including Barton Barony

vii. *Westmorland deeds: Lancaster family and Barton barony*

Two strands link this group of deeds: firstly, the Barony of Barton and secondly, the Lancaster family. The Barony of Barton was reputedly one of the possessions of the Dacre family in the 16th century (H.Howard *op. cit.*). The barony was named from what is now a tiny village south west of Penrith and its territory spread out from the south side of Lake Ullswater, to include Glenridding and Glencoyne at the head of the Lake.

John of Lancaster, later Sir John (d.1334), was the earliest member of the Lancaster family to be mentioned in these deeds, receiving a grant of Glenridding in the territory of Barton from Hugh of Multon and Joan his wife in 1292 (CW 272). In 1300 he was described as 'lord of Grisedale in Barton' and, following the settling of his estates in 1319, Ranulph lord Dacre became entitled to a reversion of the manor of Barton (*Complete Peerage*, VII, pp.274-5). This entitlement probably emanated from the latter's marriage in 1315 to the Gilsland heiress, Margaret Multon, who clearly inherited some of Hugh's properties (see vi, *Appleby and area: introduction*, above).

As with previous groups, this is a patchy collection culled, one suspects, from a fuller series that has not survived. Some runs can be traced through to the Lancaster family; others, generally the earlier deeds, cannot. Those for Melkinthorpe (CW 281-290) leap from the Brampton family in the 14th century to the Lancaster family in the 16th century, with no clear link from the one to the other. Other Brampton family deeds, CW 287-289, have been catalogued here even though they mention Dufton and Appleby (see *vi. Appleby and area*, above), on the grounds of a presumed link between their properties and those of the Lancasters. It is possible that CW 273-274 above should properly belong to this section.

The final section in this group demonstrates that in 1544 William, lord Dacre of Greystoke, obtained substantial Lancaster family holdings not only in Westmorland but also in Cumberland and Lancashire following the attainder of William Lancaster, gentleman. As with earlier groups, we may perhaps assume that the Dacres were buying up properties to consolidate their ancestral holdings, in this case, within and around the Barony of Barton.

Because William Lancaster's holdings included, in 1544, premises in Carleton and Penrith, it is possible that the deeds CW 221-235, catalogued in section v above, *Kirkoswald, Penrith and area*, should be considered as part of this collection.

141

Contents

---

* Other places mentioned: Asby, Colby, Bolton, Dufton, Knock (in Long Marton), Maulds Meaburn, Melkinthorpe, 'Merton' (?Long Marton) and Sandford, all near Appleby in Westmorland.

† Other places mentioned: Langdale and Kelleth

‡ Other places mentioned: Smardale and Patricksdale (Patterdale)

§ Places mentioned: Carlton, Deepdale, Farleton, Newby, Patterdale, Penrith and Sandwick in Martindale and Thackthwaite in Cumberland

vii. i Westmorland deeds: Barton and elsewhere

CW 281 **Gift:** undated **circa 1250**

a) John of Sandwik b) John the baker [*pistor*] of Pulhou

Property: one acre of land in a)'s demesne of Bartone, that is, in the place called Mousehennan, upon which lies the great stone called Grayostan; with all commons, liberties and easements and other appurts. nearby within the limits of the vill' of Bartone, and without, and in all places named and unnamed.

a) grants to b) and his heirs, in return for his free service, to hold of a) and his heirs at 1d. ann. rent payable at Christmas in lieu of all other demands.

Witnesses: lord Robert of Quenewyt, lord Thomas of Hollebet', Roger son of Gilbert of Loncastre, Robert of ?Morville, Richard son of Henry of ?Tyrreh'r [?modern Tirrill], Ralph son of Ely of Wyndr', Richard of Burbank, Roger son of ?Erme [*Ormi*], Simon of Lourdal

Seal: oval with partial legend

CW 282 **Gift:** undated **circa 1250**

a) John of Sandwik b) Eli of Windr's
c) Henry of Sandwik, brother of a)

Property: two parcels of land in the field [*campus*] of Sandwik which lie together in le Gayrbo'r, from the land of Roger of Sandwik, as far as the hedge, as the deed of of c) describes [these details are not cited]

a), mentions that he got the land from c) and that he has his deed [*carta*] in his possession. He grants the premises to b) in return for hhis free service, to hold it freely, honourably and peacably together with all the liberties and common easements that pertain to the land of Sandwik [*cum omnibus libertatibus et communis assiamentis tante terre de Sandwik adiacentibus*]; paying 1d. in rent to c) within the Christmas period for everything that his original deed specified in making a length of hedge in the vill' of Sandwik proportionate to the land conveyed [*....pro omnibus sicut carta originale testatur faciend' unum sepem quantum pertinet ad tantam terram...*];

Witnesses:	lord Robert of Quenewit, Henry of [illegible, *?Tyrr'*], Richard of Windr', Gilbert of Tyrr', Ralph son of Elye, Gilbert son of Robert, Robert of Holenewayr, Roger of Lourdal, William son of Adam
Seal:	oval with impression

CW 283 **Gift:** at Hoff, Saturday before All Saints, 1 November, 20 Edward I   1292

a) Hugh of Multona and Joan his wife   b) John of Loncastria
c) Henry son of William Scoche [later 'Skot'] of Kaldebeck and...
d) Agnes his wife
e) William Sleche [*?Slethe*] and ... f) Matilda his wife
g) Ralph of Glenredyn

Property: i) all the lands and tenements of a) in Glenredyn in the vill' of Bartone in the county of Westmorland; with all appurts. both in houses and buildings and in demesne lands, meadows, feedings, pastures, woods, commons, waters, fisheries, easements, attachments and hunting rights; in the homage, fealty and service of the free tenants; in enclosures of [*apprizamenti*] the waste; in wards, reliefs, escheats and in all other appurts. whatsoever belonging to the said land
ii) the lands and tenements which a) received by gift from c) with the consent of d) and from e) with the consent of f)

Recites that d), Agnes Scoche, and f), Mathilda Slethe, are sisters and co-heirs of g). Now a) grant property i) to b) and his heirs to hold of themselves and their heirs at 30s. sterling annual rent, payable at Hoff for the next 13 years; after which the annual rent payable to a) shall be increased to £20 sterling; also rendering the chief lords of the fee their usual rents and services. Property ii) is excepted from this transaction.

Warranty: a) transfer to b) the same warranty that c) and e) gave them on the property and not more nor less; and if it should occur that c) and e) do not, or have no power to make that warranty then a) do not now guarantee the transaction either but regard themselves absolved of any warranty to b) and his heirs.

Witnesses:	lord Hugh of Cressingham, William of Ormesby, John Wogayn, John Lovel, William of Mortymer, justices, then itinerant in the county of Westmorland.
Seal:	formerly two, both absent

CW 284 Gift: at Karli'e, Saturday before the conversion of St. Paul, 25 January, 19 Ed. III   **1346**

a) Adam Parnyng, Lord of Blachal b) Lord Richard of Caldecotes, perpetual vicar of Bramptone c) Thomas of Karli'e d) Isabel, widow [*formerly wife of*] lord Robert Parnyng

Property:	i) all the lands and tenements of a) in Glencone in Westmorland with all meadows and the separate [*several'*] pastures pertaining or adjacent ii) lands and tenements, meadow and the several pasture which d) holds as her dower

a) grants i) to b) and c) and their heirs and the reversion of ii) expectant on the death of d); to hold of the chief lords of the fee by the usual services

Witnesses:	lord Thomas of Musgrave, John of Derwentwatir, Thomas of Styrkeland, knights, Henry of Owertone, Robert of Sandford, John Flemyng then mayor of Karli'e, Robert of Tibay
Seal:	absent

CW 285 Indenture of agreement and bond: in the Chancery of the Lord King at St. Edmund, Saturday after St. Edmund the Archbishop, 16 November, at the end of 24 Ed. I   **1296**

a) William of Styrkeland, knight b) Richard of Bernyngham

Property:	the entire [*integer*] manor of Hakethorp and appurts.

By a recognizance made in Chancery the same date as this deed, a) is bound to b) in £100 of silver that he will, before midsummer next, lease the property to b) for a 4-year term commencing 3 May next and give him full and peaceable seisin, or from other lands and tenements, goods and chattels will compensate him to the full value of this bond.

Witnesses: none
Seal: absent

CW 286 Quitclaim: undated   **circa 1285**

a) John of Raygate, perpetual vicar of the Church of Morland
b) William of Stirkeland c) Lord Robin, former Abbot, and the
convent of the church of the blessed Mary of York
d) Michael, a former vicar of the church of Morland
e) Lord Walter of Stirkeland, great grandfather [*proavus*] of b)

Property: rent of 4 lbs. wax which b) pays to a) for a chantry
in his chapel of Stirkeland

Recites an earlier charter between c), d), and e) concerning the
Chantry whereby a) is now entitled to the said rent. However, he
releases it to b) to enable him and his heirs to enjoy it rent-free
for ever

Witnesses: Michael of Herccla, Thomas of Derwentwater, Hugh
of Multon, knights, Robert of Wardwyke, William of
Windisover, William his son, Adam of Haverington
Seal: absent
Preamble is addressed to '*all the sons of the holy mother church*'.

-oOo-

vii. ii Westmorland deeds: Brampton and elsewhere

CW 287 **Quitclaim:** At Collebi, Wednesday [illegible] St. [illegible] 1333

a) William of Brampton b) Lord John of Morland, chaplain, Master John Brey, John chaplain of Castle Barnard.

Property: lands in the vills of Melkanthorpe, Bolton, Meburn, Maude, Great Askeburi, Knokstalkok, Merton, Duftone and Appelby on either side of Eden and Sandford.

a) received the lands by hereditary right after the death of his ancestors, and by various gifts and purchases. He now releases to b) all rights he may have in the lands, their rents and liberties, etc.

Witnesses: Lord Hugh of Louthre, John of Lancastre of Holgille, John of Rossegill, knights, Henry of Warthecoppe, Thomas of Mauchel, Henry of Connerton, John of Collebi and Robert of Crakenthorpe
Seal: absent

CW 288 **Letters of attorney:**
at Brampton, Monday after St. Dunstan,
19 May, 1333

a) William of Brampton b) Thomas of Overton and Robert of Crakanthorppe, c) Sir John of Morlond, Sir John of Chastel Bernard, chaplains and Master John Brey

Property: Manor and lordship of Brampton in Westmorland and the rents of the free tenants there and lands in the same vill'; lands and tenements in Melkanthorp, Colleby, Meburne, Maud, Askeby, Bolton, Merton, Dufton, Knockes and Appleby; the profits of ?the Law Day fair [*Leverdyfete*] in the vill' of Sandford and the rents and services of the free tenants and all the other tenants, as detailed in relevant deeds

a) appoints b) to deliver seisin to c)
Witnesses: none
Seal: small seal with impression
This deed is in Anglo-Norman French. In the property description there is a punctuation mark between Meburn and Maude.

CW 289 **Final Concord:** Michaelmas term, 8 Ed. III   **1334**

a) Master William of Brampton, plaintiff
b) John of Castle Bernard, chaplain, deforciant
c) Nicholas son of Roger of Leyburn   d) Joan, wife of c)
e) John son of Richard of Brampton   f) John son of John of Crofton

Property: four messuages, 16 acres land, 16 acres meadow and 4d. rent with appurts. in Dufton and Sandford and ¼ of the Manor of Melkanthorpe with appurts; the Manor of Brampton except 3 messuages and 4 bovates of land within the manor

b) grants to a) to hold of the chief lords of the fee fo life; remainder after his death to c) and d) and the heirs of the body of d); with contingent remainders, in default of heirs, to e) and f) and their heirs; or reversion to heirs of a) in default of heirs of e) or f).

Witnesses: none
Seal: none

-oOo-

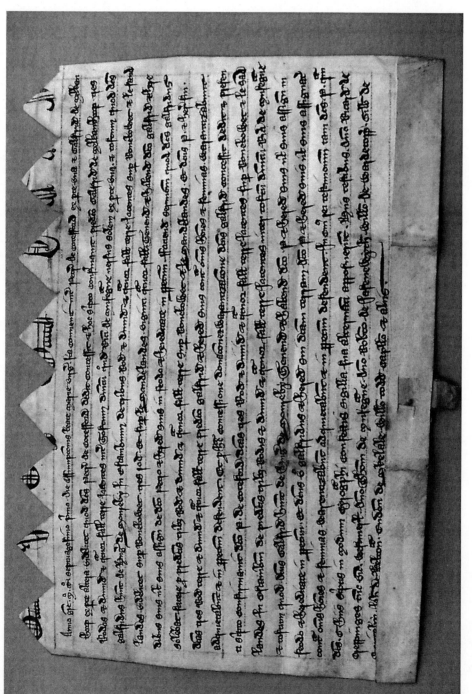

CW 291 This exchange of land in the common fields of Melkinthorpe is of interest for its modern-style date, ...in the year of grace 1271. The more-common method of dating, by regnal year, remained standard until around the close of the 16th century. Also of interest is the heavy lettering across the indenting at the top, a double safeguard against fraud. A single piece of parchment was used for each party's copy of the deed, with a space and lettering in between the text. It was then cut in a zig zag through the lettering. Only those with a true legal claim to the land would possess two halves that matched up.

vii. iii Westmorland deeds: Melkinthorpe

CW 291 **Indenture of exchange:** annunciation of the Blessed Virgin Mary, 25 March, in the year of grace   **1271**

a) Peter of Cotesford   b) Geoffrey of Melkanthorpe

Property: i) 3½ roods of land and 4 poles [*pall'*] lying between the demesne toft of Richard of Musgrave on the south and the toft which b) held of Hugh of Soureby
ii) 3½ roods and 4 poles of land lying upon Rouebowet and le Sandlandes viz. 3 roods on Roubowet and on le Sandelandes 24 poles [presumably in Melkanthorpe]

a) owns i) and b) owns ii) and they freely exchange to hold to themselves and their heirs in fee for ever.

Witnesses: lord Richard of Crepinges then sheriff of Westmorland [*Westmerl'*] lord Thomas of Musgrave, lord Robert of Jafenewythe, William of Wardecoppe, Gilbert of Quiteby, John of Heltona, Hudd [*Eudo*] of Skelale, William Todde the chaplain

Seal: absent

CW 292 **Gift:**   undated   **circa 1275**

a) Adam son of William of Cotesford
b) Hugh son of Adam of Soureby

Property: all the land of a) in the vill' of Melkanthorpe viz. one whole quarter of the entire vill', with appurts. and one quarter part of the mill and [all] the suit of the mill within the vill' and without

In return for his homage and service, a) grants to b) and his heirs to hold at 2s. sterling annual rent, to hold freely, without suit of court; but liable to the amount of foreign service as pertains to that land

Witnesses: lord Robert of Askeby, lord William son of John, lord Robert of Javenewit, Thomas of Musgrave, then sheriff of Westmerlande, Thomas of Noubighing, Peter of Cotesforde

Seal: impression and legend

CW 293 Grant: undated   **circa 1285**

a) Robert son of William le Engleys   b) Hugh son of Adam of Soureby   c) Eve, daughter of Geoffrey of Cotesford   d) Adam of Cotesford

Property: all the land and appurts. which Geoffrey of Cotesford once held of the ancestors of a) in the vill' of Melcantorp

In return for his homage and service, a) grants to b) and guarantees the property against all claims including that c); but excluding that of d) and his heirs

Witnesses: lord Richard of Creppinges then sheriff, lord J. of Morville, lord R. of Askiby, H. his brother, W. of Tylia, Richard of Colleby, clerk

Seal: absent

CW 294 Grant: at Soureby, Tuesday after Ss. Marcellinus and Peter, 2 June, 26 Ed. I   **1298**

a) Hugh son of Adam of Soureby   b) John of Ulram
c) Adam of Cotesford, father of b)

Property: i) all land of a) in Melkenthorpe with all appurts withing the vill' and without, in woods, plains, marshes, pastures, waters and mills
ii) 3 roods of land in Melkenthorpe

a) holds property i) by grant from c). He now gives it to b) in exchange for one acre already given by b) to a); but he excludes property ii), which a) has since given to Geoffrey of Melkenthorpe. An annual rent of 2 shillings is payable to the chief lords and 1d. to a) each Christmas for such foreign service to which he or his heirs may be liable in respect of that amount of land.

Witnesses: lord Hugh of Multon, William of Stirkeland, Robert of Askeby, knights, Lord Nicholas of Tilya then sheriff of Westmerl', Adam of Baverington, William

of Wyndesover, John le Frauncays of Cliburne, Nicholas
of Grindon.

Seal: faint impression

CW 295   **Indenture of gift:** at Appelby, Monday after St. Nicholas,
6 December, 32 Ed. I   **1303**

a) John of Ulram son of Adam of Cotesforde   b) Master William
of Brampton and William his brother   c) Hugh of Soureby

Property: capital messuage of a) and all his lands and tenements
and all his wood and ¼ part of his mill; with suit of the
same by villagers and outsiders [*secta eidem intrinseca
et forinseca*] in the vill' and territory of Melkanthorpe;
and with all appurts., common of pasture, liberties
and easements within the vill' of Melkanthorpe and
without

Reciting that he received the premises by gift from c), a) grants to
b) and his heirs to hold of the chief lords of the fee by the usual
services and rendering to himself one pair of gloves at the feast
of St. Laurence the martyr (10 August) for 12 years from the date
of this deed, after which a) shall pay b) and his heirs 100s. sterling
each year; with power for a) and his heirs to distrain for arrears

Witnesses: John Mauchel, Robert of Neubigging, John Franceys
of Clyborne, Henry of Warthecoppe, John of
Cotesforde
Seal: absent

CW 296   **Grant and quitclaim:** at Askeby, Thursday after the translation of
St. Thomas the Martyr, 7 July, 33 Ed. I   **1305**

a) John of Ulram son of Adam of Cotesforde
b) Master William of Brampton and William his brother

Property: as in CW 286 above

a) grants to b) to hold of the chief lords of the fee by the services
that pertain; releasing all his rights in the property to them and
their heirs

Witnesses: Henry of Warthecoppe, Gilbert of Querton, John
Maukael, Robert of Loncastre, John of Cotesforde,
John of Riblis, Hudd of Cotesford
Seal: absent

CW 297   **Quitclaim:**   at York, Saturday St. Vincent the Martyr, 22 January, 16 Ed. II   **1323**

a) Joan [of Ulramm], widow of ... b) John of Ulramm
c) Master William son of Simon the elder of Brampton.

Property: lands and tenements in the vill' of Melkanthorpe

a), who received the property from b) now quitclaims to c)

Witnesses: lords Roger of Somervile and Geoffrey of St. Quintin, knights, Thomas of Mounceux, Robert Tohe of Layset, Robert of Drynghou, Roger of Kendale, clerk.
Seal: absent

CW 298   **Grant for life:** 6 September, 13 Hen. VIII   **1521**

a) Edward Lancastere of Brampton, gentleman   b) William Lancaster, son and heir of Christopher Lancaster of Deppedalle

Property: one tenement in Melkanthorpe in occ. of Robert Culpeper and William Culpeper, tenants at will
a) grants to b) to hold during the lifetime of a)

Witnesses: John Waux the younger, gentleman, John Welkenson, chaplain, Roger Lancaster, gentleman
Seal: rough seal and impression

Livery of seisin: endorsed, in English, 24 September 1521, by a) to b)

Witnesses: John W[ar]thcope of Smardell, farmer, Thomas Walker of Melkenthorpe, William Warkeman of the same and William Wilkinson, husbandmen, John Jacson [?the younger], Roger Lancaster, gentleman

CW 299   **Quitclaim:**   26 September, 13 Hen. VIII   **1521**

a) Joan Lancaster, widow of John Lancaster of Branton [?Brampton]
b) William Lancaster as in CW 289 above

Property: as in CW 289

a) quitclaims to b) all her rights in the property.

Witnesses: Edward Lancaster, gentleman, Roger Lancaster, John
Patenson the elder

Seal: impression

-oOo-

vii. iii Westmorland deeds: Orton and Roundthwaite

CW 301 Gift: 20 September 28 Hen. VI   **1449**

> a) John Bland son and heir of ... b) Thomas Bland
> c) Richard Hebiltwayte   c) John of Tibbay, clerk
> e) Thomas Dacre, knight, lord of Dacre and Gillesland

> **Property:**   Moiety of one messuage with all its appurts. in the
>   hamlet of Rounthuayte

> Recites that b) got the property by gift from c) who had got it by
> gift from d). Now a) grants it to e) and his heirs to hold of the
> chief lords of the fee

> **Witnesses:** Richard Musgrave, knight, Roland Waux, Robert
>   Sandeforde, esq., William Birkbeke, vicar of Overton,
>   John Wilson, Addeson of Overton
> **Seal:**   fragment with broken impression

CW 302 Gift: at Overton, 4 November, 4 Ed. IV   **1464**

> a) William Langdale of Overton, in Westmorland   b) John Parr, esq.,
> Thomas Byrkbek, chaplain and John Langdale, natural son of a)

> **Property:**   all the lands and tenements of a) in the vill' of Overton,
>   that is in the village itself and in its fields, with all
>   commodities, profits, feedings, pasture and meadows

> a) grants to b) and their heirs.

> **Witnesses:** Adam Crosseby, William Crosseby.
> **Seal:**   absent

CW 303 Gift: morrow of Epiphany, 6 January, 19 Hen. VII   **1504**

> a) Hugh Langdell of Orton   b) Thomas Salkeld of Rosgill, esq.,

William Langcastre of Sokbred, esq., Reginald Bland of Tybbey, Miles Polson and Edward Thorneburghe

> **Property:** all lands, tenements rents, reversions and services with their appurts. which belong to a) in the vills' and territories of Orton, Langdale, Kelleth and Cotgyll in Westmorland

a) grants to b) and their heirs to hold of the chief lords of the fee by the usual services

> **Witnesses:** lord Robert Hesket, vicar of the church of Orton, Thomas Wharton of Crosby, Edward Whithed, Alexander Thornburghe, John Whithed of Stankbrigg, Alexander Polson, Edmund Polson, Edward Polson
> **Seal:** impression

CW 304 **Quitclaim:** undated   *circa* **1530**

a) Thomas Wharton of Wharton in Westmorland, knight, George Langdale of Langdale in same county, yeoman   b) William Dacre, knight, lord of Dacre and Graistoke

> **Property:** tenement lying within the parish of Overton, called Cotegill, now in the occ. of Thomas Atkynson; with all lands, rents, services, meadows, feedings, woods and pastures and other appurts

Reciting that the property is already in b)'s hands, a) release to b) and his heirs all their rights in it.

> **Witnesses:** none
> **Seal:** none

-oOo-

vii. v Westmorland deeds: Lancaster family premises in Kirkby Thore and elsewhere

CW 305   **Letters of attorney:** 8 March, 4 Hen. V   **1416**

a) John of Lancastre, knight   b) Roger of Crakanthorpe, parson of the parish church of Kirkebythore   c) William of Langtone and William Burhede, chaplains

Property: all lands, tenements and rents of a) in the vill' of Kirkebythore

According to the tenor of a charter previously made by a), he now appoints b) as his attornies to deliver seisin to c)

Witnesses: none
Seal: absent

CW 306   **Gift:**   1 January, 10 Hen. VI   **1432**

a) Hugh Louthere of Ascome   b) Roger Lancastre of Sokbred
c) Christopher Lancastre, brother of a)

Property: all the lands, tenements, rents and services that a) holds in Westmorland.

a) grants to b) and c)

Witnesses: none
Seal: small seal, faint impression.

CW 307   **Letters of attorney:** 25 October, 29 Hen. VI   **1450**

a) William Bix, chaplain   b) Edward Thornburgh, esq.
c) John Lancastire, son of William Lancastire of Yaynewithe

Property: all lands and tenements of a) in the counties of Cumberland, Westmorland and Lancaster.

a), according to the terms of an earlier deed (no details), appoints b) to deliver to seisin to c).

Witnesses: none
Seal: fragment with partial impression

CW 308   **Memorandum:** in the year of Our Lord   1519

a) Richard Robynson, dwelling in London and William Robynson, dwelling in Kyrkhame   b) George [?Con]rweth
c) Master Stephen of [illegible]-ayniby d) Walter Fynson of Kendall

a) acknowledge that they have received £19 12s. 4d. from b) by the hands of c) and d)

Witnesses: ?Parnyll Parker, Margaret Pall, Jene ?Parson
Seal: none
This document, in English, is crumpled and full of small holes

CW 309   **Grant of annuity:** 6 March, 17 Hen. VIII   1526

a) John Warcoppe of Smerdalle, esq.   b) William Lancaster, gent.

Property: all lands and tenements of a) in Smardalle in Westmorland

a) grants b) a rent or annuity of 13s. 4d. out of the property during the life of b), with power to distrain in any year it may be unpaid. a) pays b) one silver penny, parcel of the said rent, as a token of seisin.

Witnesses: none
Seal: signature of a) and small seal with impression

CW 310   **Bond:**   last day of February, 18 Hen. VIII   1527

a) Lancelot Lancaster of Sokebrede, co. Westmorland, esq.
b) Edwin Gilping, gentleman

a) is bound to b) in £40 sterling to fulfil the covenants of a deed of same day's date.

Witnesses: none
Seal: seal; and signature of a)

CW 311   **Award:**   18 August, 23 Hen. VIII   **1531**

a) Ambrose Midilton and Cecily his wife, one of the cousins and heirs of Ambrose Crackenthorppe, esq. deceased
b) William Lancaster of Beth'n', gentleman
c) The Right Noble Henry, Earl of Cumberland
d) Sir William Musgrave, Sir John Lowther, knights, Christopher Aske and Thomas Blenkinsopp, esqs.

Property: three messuages and certain lands and tenements with appurts. in the vill' and field of Kyrkebythore

Recites that a dispute has arisen between a) and b) concerning title to the property; and that they have agreed and have bound themselves in £40 to abide by the judgement of c) and his advisers. c) now therefore, on the advice of d), awards the property to b) together with all appurts., rents and arrears. He orders a) to draw up a deed to this effect, with full warranty, and to hand over to b) all the title deeds that he has to the property. For his part b) shall pay £40 to a) within the next 14 days

Witnesses: none
Seal: signature of c) and seal with impression
This deed is in English

CW 312   **Bond:**   31 August, 23 Hen. VIII   **1531**

a) Henry Barton of Ormished [Ormside] co. Westmorland, gent.
b) William Lancaster of Dappedalle in the same county, gent.

Property: i) a tenement with appurts. in Patrikesdale, co. Westmorland
ii) three tenements with appurts. in Kyrkebythore in the same county

The parties have exchanged land, a) giving i) to b) and b) giving ii) to a) and £6 in money; now a) is bound to b) in £20 that he will pay him £6 if at any time in the future he recovers any part of property ii) against b) or his heirs.

Witnesses: none
Seal: absent

-oOo-

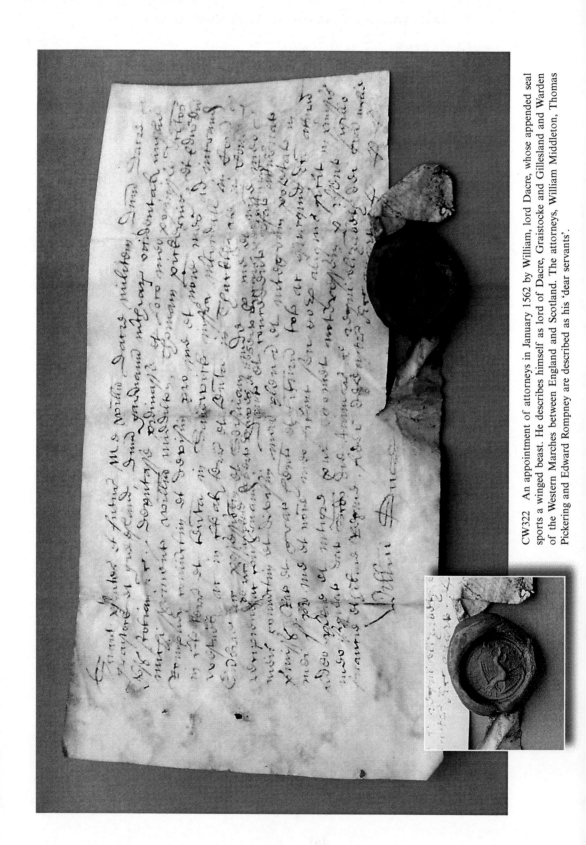

CW322 An appointment of attorneys in January 1562 by William, lord Dacre, whose appended seal sports a winged beast. He describes himself as lord of Dacre, Graistocke and Gillesland and Warden of the Western Marches between England and Scotland. The attorneys, William Middleton, Thomas Pickering and Edward Rompney are described as his 'dear servants'.

vii. vi Westmorland deeds: Dacre purchases and lordship

CW 313 **Mortgage by gift:** at Newby on Thursday after St. James
the Apostle, 25 July, 4 Hen. VII   **1489**

a) John Kirkeby of Hawthorne in the Bishopric of Durham, esq.
b) William Kirkeby, son and heir apparent of a)
c) Mabel [*Mabille*], Lady of Dacre and Gillesland

Property: one tenement in Newby upon the Stones [*Newby super
lez Stanes*], with lands and meadows pertaining and
adjacent, with all appurts.

Whenever [no specific term stated] a) and b) or their heirs repay
the sum of 20 marks to c) this deed of gift will be null and void
and a) and b) will regain full possession of the land

Witnesses: Christopher ?Cannesfeld [?Caunesfeld], rector of the
church of Aykton, Robert Chapman, rector of the
church of Beamount, John Mire, Thomas Beverley,
Alan Walton
Seal: two, with impressions

CW 314 **Appointment of attorneys:** Thursday after St. James the
Apostle, 25 July, 4 Hen. VII   **1489**

a) Mabel Dacre of Dacre and Gillesland   b) Richard Marshall
and Roland Thompson   c) John and William Kirkeby

Property: as in CW 313 above

a) appoints b) as her attorneys to receive seisin from c)

Witnesses: none
Seal: small with indistinct impression

CW 315   **Quitclaim:**   Wednesday before St. Andrew, 30 November,
5 Hen. VII   **1489**

a) John Kyrkeby of Hawthorne in the Bishopric of Durham, esq.
b) Mabel, Lady of Dacre and Gillesland

Property: as in CW 313 above

a) release to b) all the estate and title in the premises that he or
his heirs may enjoy

Witnesses: Roland Ratclif and Robert Skelton, esqs., Thomas
Porter, William Bowman, John Farlam
Seal: small with indistinct impression
This deed has split into two pieces, due to mould and insect
damage.

CW 316   **Sale and Confirmation:** at Penreth, 18 August 36 Hen. VIII   **1544**

a) Thomas Collsell of London, gent.   b) William Dacre, lord of
Dacre, Graystok and Gilleslonde   c) William Lancaster, gent.   d)
Humphrey Radclyff of Bedyngton, co. Surrey, knight   e) William
Pykering, esq. and Thomas Talentire   f) Richard Threlkeld and
Laurence ?Bowman   g) John ?Walker, Michael Herryson, Thomas
Thomson, Gerard ?Lancastre, Richard Thomson, John Lancastre,
William Martendale, Robert Louthere   h) John Boost, Gilbert
[illeg., and another person with illegible name], William Herryson
and John Dauson

Property: all and singular the lordships, manors, messuages, tofts,
gardens, orchards [*ortus pomar'*], lands, tenements,
mills, meadows, feedings, pastures, warrens, fresh water
ponds, rivers, fisheries, woods, underwoods, commons,
rents, reversions, ?ale-rents [*cervic'*], liberties, franchises,
knights' fees, wardships, marriage taxes, reliefs, glebes,
annuities, pensions, portions, advowsons, donations,
presentments and right of presentation of churches,
chapels, chantries and hospitals whatsoever.... in the
vills and fields of Depedalle, Patterdalle, Penreth,
Carleton and Farleton in Westmorland, Lancashire
and Cumberland

Recites that the properties used to belong to c) who has since been
attainted for high treason; that they were late in the tenure of d)
by virtue of letters patent of 11 July last and that a) has since
bought the properties from d).

Now a), in return for a sum (not specified) of money given by b), sells to b) to hold to himself and his heirs; and a) appoints e) as his attornies to enter the premises, to take seisin and to deliver it to b).

Witnesses:	Ambrose Mideltone, esq., Thomas Talentire, John ?Boost, Anthony Heton, George Aresmythe, Robert Mounsey
Seal:	small armorial impression

Endorsement: memorandum that on 30 January 1546 f) received seisin on behalf of b) at Depedalle of properties in Westmorland and it was witnessed by g). Seisin of the properties in Cumberland was received at Carleton on 20 March same year and witnessed by h).

CW 317 Grant and licence: 4 February 36 Hen. VIII   **1545**

a) The King [Henry VIII]   b) Thomas Colsell of London, gentleman and Mary his wife   c) William lord Dacre

In return for a licence fee of £3 13s. 4d. the King grants that c) may recover the properties as in CW 316 above from b) and hold them to himself and his heirs

Seal:	Great Seal with reasonable, slightly crusty image

CW 318 Grant of wardship: 16 October 1 Eliz.   **1559**

a) Rt. Hon. William Dacre, knight, Lord Dacre, Graistocke and Gillesland, Lord Warden of the Western Marches between England and Scotland
b) Nicholas Boaste of Dufton co. Westmorland, gentleman
c) Lancelot Threlkeld of Patterdale co. Westmorland, deceased

Property:	all lands, etc., of c)

a) grants b) the right of wardship and marriage of c) during his minority

Witnesses:	none
Seal:	absent; signature of b)

CW 319 Gift: 6 September 2 Eliz. I   **1560**

a) William Brysbye of Soureby, yeoman
b) Robert Vickars and Robert Daws of Sandwick

Property: all messuages, tenements, rents, reversions, meadows, feedings, woods, underwoods of a) in Sandwick and in the territories of Sandwick, with all commodities, profits and advantages [*advauntagii*] pertaining

In return for a money payment of £30 a) grants to b) and their heirs

Witnesses: - to livery of seisin, endorsed: Thomas Martyndale, John Dawes, Robert Lowder, William Dawes
Seal: impression

CW 320   **Bond:**   6 September, 2 Eliz. I   1560

Parties as in CW 319 above
a) is bound to b) in £100 to stand by the terms of CW 319 above and, within the next three years, to execute another deed such as a fine or recovery to better secure their title and negate his own powers of inheritance

Witnesses: none
Seal: impression

CW 321   **Acquittance:** at Greystoke, 28 March 3 Eliz. I   1561

a) William Brisbye of Castell Sowrebye in Cumberland, yeoman
b) Robert Dawes and Robert Vikers of Sandwike in Westmorland, yeomen
c) Mr John Dacre, clerk, parson of Greystok, Receiver General of William, lord Dacre

Property: property as in 319 above, described as '*a tenement in Sandwike*'

a) acknowledges that he has received £12 from b) by the hands of c), being the *fulle and laste payment* due on a previous *deid of saile* (ie. CW 319 above)

Witnesses: none
Seal: paper encased

CW 322   **Appointment of attorneys:** 2 January 4 Eliz. I   1562

a) William Dacre, knight, lord of Dacre, Graistock and Gillesland, warden of the western marches between England and Scotland
b) William Middilton, Thomas Pickering and Edward Rompney

Property: certain lands and tenements in Sandwick in Martyndale

in Westmorland and other lands and tenements in
Thackthwaite in Cumberland

a) appoints b), his dear servants [*dilecti servientes*], to enter the
properties and to receive seisin on his behalf

Witnesses: none
Seal: signature of William Dacre and seal with good
                 impression

-oOo-

THE DUKE OF NORFOLK'S DEEDS
AT ARUNDEL CASTLE

CATALOGUE 1   PART I

Dacre Estates in Northern Counties

viii

*An estate in Cleator, Hensingham
and Egremont, co. Cumberland*

viii. An estate in Cleator, Hensingham and Egremont, in Cumberland 1503-1553

Early estates in the Egremont area of Cumberland may have come to the Dacre family by one of two routes: firstly from Richard de Lucy of Egremont (fl. mid-13thc.) who was the grandfather of Joan de Multon who was the second wife of Sir Randolph Dacre (d. 1286), Sheriff of Cumberland 1268-1270; and secondly via Lucy de Lucy who was the first wife of William, lord Greystoke (d. 1359). However, neither of these marriages produced the heir to their respective lines. If early title was held in the Egremont area, there is no trace of it in these archives.

The deeds in this section relate firstly to the separation in 1526-1530 of premises in Cleator, Hensingham and Egremont from more extensive estates (see below) in Lancashire, Cumberland and Westmorland held by the Levyns or Lyons family (see CW 331 for details). This is followed by their purchase by Sir Christopher Dacre, in 1538; and further land deals from 1541 to 1553 by William, lord Dacre. It was this William Dacre, the 4th Baron Dacre, who, on his mother's death in 1516, became the first Dacre to inherit the Greystoke lands and title.

It will, of course, be observed that this collection is entirely post-medieval. However, it remains under the 'Medieval deeds' title for reasons that are explained in the introduction, *History of the deeds collections.*

The Levyns family estates mentioned in 331-332 below, but whose title is not followed through in these deeds, were:

Lancashire:	Ulverston in Furness
	Dalton in Furness
	Kirkby Ireleth (*Kirkby in Furness*);
	Kyrbywodlande,
	Netilslake'
Cumberland:	Bootle and Hayton (near Aspatria)
	Corney and Annaside (near Bootle)
	Whitbeck near Broughton in Furness
	Wilton Hale, ?Wilton near Egremont
Westmorland:	Kirkby Kendal (*Kyrby Kendal*)

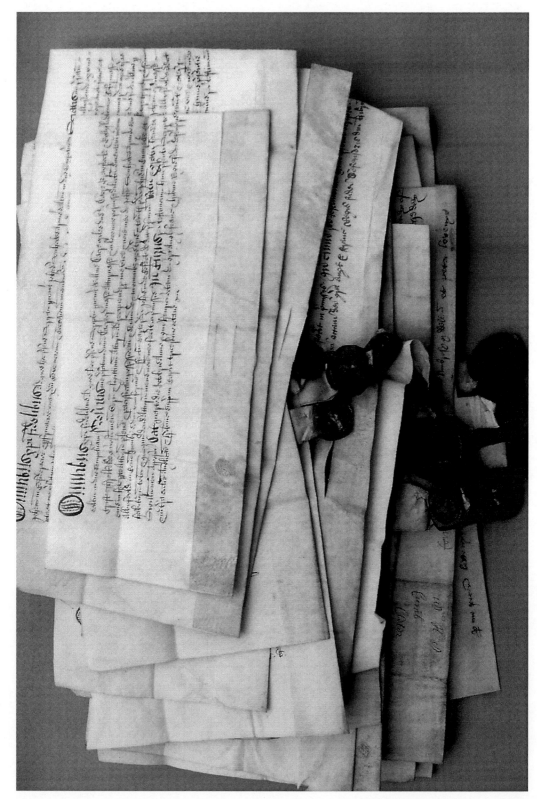

CW331-349   The Cleator and Hensingham deeds after flattening but before repackaging.

viii. An estate in Cleator, Hensingham and Egremont, 1503-1553

CW 331 **Grant in trust and letters of attorney:** 16 August, 18 Hen. VII   **1503**

a) William Levyns of Plompton, co. Lancs
b) Henry Doket, esq., Peter Levyns, Thomas Saunderson and John Newton, chaplain

Property: messuages, tenements, rents, reversions and services, with appurts., in Ulverstone, Fournes, Dalton in Fournes and Netilslake, co. Lancs; the same in Botehill, Heyton, Corney, Annerside, Whytebeke, Hensyngham, Cleeter, Wilton Hale and Egremonde, co. Cumberland; and the same in Kyrby Kendall co. Westmorland

a) grants to b) as feoffees to the uses of his will. He appoints Micheal Miles, clerk of Hudlestone, Thomas Laurence of Kyrby in Kendale, gentleman and John Corker, as his attornies for livery of seisin.

Witnesses: John Priore of Conyngeshede, Henry Kyrby, Christopher Bardesey, esq.
Seal: impression

CW 332 **Gift:**   13 March, 17 Hen. VIII   **1526**

a) Peter Levyns and John Newton, chaplain   b) Thomas Levyns alias Lyons of Enborne co. Berks., gent., son of ...   c) William Levyns late of Plompton co. Lancs. esq., decd.   d) Henry Dokett, esq., Thomas Sanderson, chaplain
Property: as in CW 331 above

a) recite that, together with d) who have since died, they were granted the land by c) to hold to the uses of his will. They now grant it to b) and his heirs

Witnesses: none
Seal: two with impressions, one worn

CW 333 **Bargain and sale and covenants:** 13 March, 17 Hen. VIII **1526**

a) Thomas Levyns alias Lyons of Enborne co. Berks., gentleman
b) John Fodergyll, clerk and Richard Cragg

Property: meses [sic], mills, lands, tenements, woods, waters, rents, reversions, services and appurts. in Cleeter, Hensingham and Egremonde in Cumberland

In return for the purchase money of £100, a) grants to b) and their heirs for ever and he covenants that the net annual value of the premises is £5 4s. 8d; also that he will, before the feast of St. Peter in Chains next (1 August), secure their title by the process of a Common Recovery, the cost of this to be borne by b). He also covenants and binds himself in the sum of £200 to deliver to them the deeds relating to the property by the same date.

Witnesses: Ambrose Middleton, Peter Levenys
Seal: good impression, though somewhat worn

CW 334 **Confirmation and appointment:** 5 April, 17 Hen. VIII **1526**
Parties and property as in CW 333

a) confirms the property to b) and appoints William Corker as his attorney to enter and deliver seisin to b)

Witnesses: Thomas Senose, esq., William Ponssonby, gentleman and William Robynson of Egermount
Seal: as in CW 333 but less worn

CW 335-
336 **Final concord:** Easter Term, 18 Hen. VIII **1526**
Parties as in CW 333-334 above

Property: seven messuages, one mill, 60a. land, 10a. meadow, 7a. pasture with appurts. in Hensyngham, Clotter and Egurmount

Two copies

CW 337 **Gift and appointment:** 8 August, 22 Hen. VII **1530**

a) Richard Crag b) Peter Levyns, clerk
c) Richard Phelepson, chaplain and William Arloshe

Property: all his messuages, mills, lands, tenements, rents, reversions, services, meadows, feedings, pastures, waters, woods and underwoods in the vills and fields of Cleter, Hensyngham and Egremont

a) grants to b) and his heirs and appoints c) as his attorneys to enter the property and to deliver seisin to b)

Witnesses: none
Seal: crude impression of hawk and prey

CW 338 **Quitclaim:** 10 September, 22 Hen. VIII   **1530**

Parties a) and b) and property as in 337 above; a) releases all rights of self and heirs to b) and heirs

Witnesses: none
Seal: as in CW 337

CW 339 **Gift:** 20 December, 30 Hen. VIII   **1538**

a) Peter Levyns, clerk   b) Christopher Dacre, knight

Property: seven messuages, one water mill, etc. (as described in CW 335-6) in Hensingham, Clotter alias Cleter and Egremownt, with all rents and services, etc. pertaining

Recites that a) obtained the premises from Thomas Levyns alias Lyons, son of William Levyns. Now, in return for an unspecified amount of money paid by b) to a), a) now grants to b) and his heirs; and he appoints c) to enter and deliver possesssion to b)

Witnesses: none
Seal: impression

CW 340 **Appointment of attorney:** 20 December, 30 Hen. VIII   **1538**

a) Christopher Dacre, knight
b) William Haryson the younger and Edward Romney

Pursuant to CW 339 above a) appoints b) as his attorneys to take livery of seisin of the property.
Witnesses: none
Seal: a blob with worn impression

CW 341 **Bond for performance of covenants:**

16 November, 33 Hen. VIII   **1541**

a) John Ribton the elder, of Ribton, gentleman
b) Elizabeth, wife of a)   c) John Ribton the younger, late of the same place, son and heir of a)   d) William Dacre, knight, Lord of Dacre, Gillesland and Graystoke

a) and b) are bound in £110 sterling, to perform the covenants of a deed made the same day as this by parties a) c) and d)

Witnesses: none
Seal: two with vague impressions, one broken

CW 342-
343   **Bargain and Sale:** 16 April, 37 Hen. VIII   **1546**

a) The Rt. Hon. William Dacre, knight, lord Dacre, Graystoke, Gilleslonde   b) Thomas Stagge of Walle of Gilleslonde in Cumberland, husbandman

Property: all his 'meses, lands, tenements, medoes, pastures, woddes and underwoddes', and appurts., in Cleter

In return for a money payment of £20 sterling, b) sells the premises to a) and his heirs and promises to hand over all documents [*evydences, escriptes and mynymentes*] re. the property and to take all further steps to secure the title at law, at the costs and charges of a)

Witnesses: none
Seal: impression
2 copies, one indented, the other being the 'chirograph' of b)

CW 344 **Quitclaim:** 21 April, 37 Hen. VIII   **1546**
Parties and property as in 342-343

a) releases all his rights in the property and those of his heirs to b) and his heirs

Witnesses: none
Seal: impression

CW 345 **Quitclaim:** 4 October, 38 Hen. VIII   **1546**

a) William Dacre, knight, lord of Dacre and Graystocke and Gyllyslonde   b) John Senhows, esq.

Property: premises in Hensingham, Cleter and Egremonte, as in CW 333-339 above, except one messuage and all appurts. and 20s. rent in the occ. of William Grayson

Recites deed made between the same parties 24 Sept. 1546. Now a) releases to b) and his heirs all rights of self and heirs in the premises.

Witnesses: none
Seal: absent

CW 346 Quitclaim: 4 October, 38 Hen. VIII   1546

On the same transaction as CW 345 above, a) now promises b) and his heirs that no actions concerning the property will be brought against him by b) or his heirs.

Witnesses: none
Seal: absent

CW 347 Appointment of attorneys: 4 October, 38 Hen. VIII   1546

a) John Senhows, esq.
b) Richard Newton of Glassenbye in Cumberland, yeoman and John Dyxson of Albyseylde in Cumberland, husbandman

In pursuance of covenants etc. of CW 345-346, a) appoints b) to enter and take possession and deliver seisin to William lord Dacre.

Witnesses: none
Seal: absent

CW 348 Appointment of attorneys: 4 October, 38 Hen. VIII   1546

a) William Dacre, knight, lord of Graystock and Gyllyslond
b) Christopher Threlkelde, gentleman

Citing as in CW 345-347, a) appoints b) to receive seisin in his stead
Witnesses: none
Seal: absent

CW 349 **Agreement:** 24 December, 1 Mary   **1553**

a) Rt. Hon. William Dacre, knight, lord Dacre, Graystok and Gylleslonde and Lord Warden of *the west and myddell marches of Englonde for agenst Scotlande*
b) John Senhows, squyer

Property: one mese and tenement with appurts. in Hensingham, of the clear yearly rent of 20s., now or late in the occ. of William Grayson, parcel of mill lands estate in Hensingham, Cleter and Eggremounte.

Reciting that a dispute has arisen between the parties, it is now agreed that a) shall hold the messuage in Hensingham until b) can provide him with an estate of equivalent value elsewhere in Cumberland or Westmorland. The remainder of the mill lands estate in the three parishes shall be held by b) and his heirs. Further covenants concerning delivery of title deeds, etc.

Witnesses: none
Seal: winged horse; and signature, 'William Dacre'

-oOo-

THE DUKE OF NORFOLK'S DEEDS
AT ARUNDEL CASTLE

CATALOGUE 1   PART I

Dacre Estates in Northern Counties

ix

Casterton in Westmorland

ix Premises in Casterton, Westmorland

It is unclear why this deed is in the Duke of Norfolk's archives. St Philip Howard, heir to the Greystoke estate in right of his wife Anne, was imprisoned in the Tower of London at the time. He could not, therefore, have been serving as a Justice of the Peace for Westmorland, to whom the matter is addressed.

CW 351 **Letters patent:** at Westminster, 3 July 35 Eliz.   **1593**

> a) The Queen [Elizabeth I]   b) The justices of Assize for the county of Westmorland   c) William Midleton, Richard Aplegarth, Edmund Garnett, John Lyndesey, Francis Stith, John Hogeson, Gilbert Dodgeson, John Jackson   d) Thomas Cansfeild, gentleman
>
> **Property:**   the house and chattels of d), together with certain lands and tenements in Casterton, Westmorland, all being property of the Crown
>
> The Queen orders b) to hold an inquiry at Appelby on 16 August next to establish whether c) broke forcibly into the property and harrassed d) who is the farmer.
>
> **Witnesses:** none
> **Seal:**   part of Great Seal

-oOo-

The old packaging

CW 361 **The old packaging:**   **1 bundle**
The deeds now numbered as CW 1-151 above were found encased in good quality wrapping paper, often very dirty, with (now obsolete) lists of contents written in ink on the outside, ?by Charles Kent, the 15th Duke's archivist. This packaging has mostly been destroyed but the lists themselves have been cut out and kept under the reference CW 361, for their antiquarian interest. Also in this bundle are some old lists of parts of these deeds (?prepared by Frederick Wood of Ockley Manor in Keymer in the 1920s); and the old card envelopes in which those of the deeds listed by the HMC which have been incorporated into this catalogue were formerly stored.

THE DUKE OF NORFOLK'S DEEDS AT ARUNDEL CASTLE

CATALOGUE 1   PART I

Dacre Estates in Northern Counties

x

North and East Yorkshire

x. Fauconberg and Meynell estates in North and East Yorkshire

Introduction

The 'Yorkshire Deeds' formed a substantial part of the 'Medieval Deeds' collection at Arundel. They were labelled simply as *Yorkshire deeds* in the old Norfolk House archives. Cataloguing them in 1992, I allocated the prefix YK/-, as part of the County series, without further reference to content. All the Yorkshire deeds were found in five packets, one arranged alphabetically by place, the other four chronologically. In the latter scheme the same groups of parishes were found in all periods, and each of the four chronological packets had deeds relating to places found in the alphabetical packet. I therefore decided to re-sort them all by place.

This method eventually allowed the true provenances of the Yorkshire deeds to reassert themselves. Firstly, a clear series related to Sheffield and its satellite settlements in south Yorkshire. Together with other deeds in north Nottinghamshire and north Derbyshire, these formed part of the Earls of Shrewsbury's properties. They relate to the Worksop estate which later became the Dukes of Norfolk's chief seat following the marriage of the Shrewsbury heiress, Alatheia Talbot with the 14th Earl of Arundel in 1606. None of these are included in the present *Deeds Catalogue 1*.

The second series, which comprise section *x* of the present catalogue, relate principally to the North and East Riding of Yorkshire. The provenances within it are more mixed but they substantially relate to two early lordships, Fauconberg and Meynell.* The former had a seat at Rise in Holderness (east of Hull) and another, Skelton Castle, in Cleveland (north of the North Yorks Moors). The Meynell lordship was centred on Whorlton Castle in Cleveland. In 1344/5 the Meynell heiress, Elizabeth, married John, Lord Darcy. At her death in 1368 the 'hereditary Barony' of Meynell became united with Darcy. The Fauconberg estates descended with the family name until the lifetime of Joan Fauconberg who was born in 1406 at Skelton. She married William Neville, 8th son of the Earl of Westmorland and, at his death in 1462, the Fauconberg barony fell into abeyance.

It is with the Strangways family that the various strands in this North Yorkshire collection seem to come together. Sir James Strangways and his son Sir Richard, in the 15th century, united half of the Meynell and half of the Fauconberg inheritance into a single line of descent. For Sir James had married Elizabeth, a Darcy (Meynell) heiress, while his son married Elizabeth, a Neville (Fauconberg) heiress. In 1472 the next Strangways heir, Sir James, married Alice, daughter of Thomas, Lord Scrope

---

* This and subsequent introductions within the Yorkshire Deeds section of the catalogue are based upon the deeds themselves, on Henry Howard's Memorials of the Howard Family (cited above), upon the Meynell, Fauconberg, Darcy and Scrope sections of the *Complete Peerage*, or as specifically referenced.

of Masham, heiress to half the barony of Scrope of Masham. By the space of a further generation a Dacre interest had entered the pool, with the marriage of Sir Thomas Strangways and Anne, daughter of Humphrey, lord Dacre. In 1541, on the death of their son Sir James Strangways, his estates were claimed by lord Dacre of Greystoke. The relevant 'fine', or 'final concord', in Court at Westminster lists all the parishes or manors involved, many of which are found in this catalogue.* His claim was upheld in Chancery in 1543 and he thus gained the Castle and manor of Whorlton and eighteen further manors and other land.

While this Strangways / Scrope alliance presumably provided the route through which the deeds in section x. vii below (YK 91-94) came into Dacre possession, there was in fact an earlier link between the Scropes and the Dacres. John le Scrope of Masham died in 1455 and was succeeded by his eldest son and heir, John who married Margaret, daughter of Thomas, 6th lord of Gilsland. The marriage was childless and his brother Thomas inherited his estates. This Thomas, acceding in 1455 as 5th Lord Scrope, married Elizabeth, daughter of Ralph of Greystoke, 5th Lord Greystoke.

None of the deeds in this collection relate to the Fauconberg/ Meynell lands when the Dacres held them. They are all earlier, generally very much earlier. As with other medieval deeds collections in the Duke of Norfolk's archives, there is no continuity of title through from the Meynell/Darcy era to post-medieval collections. The principles of selection on antiquarian merit were presumably used here, as elsewhere, to ensure retention of the early items while the later deeds passed out of the family with the estates. One deed relating to Nocton in Lincolnshire (YK 81 below) survives among the Darcy collection, formerly wrongly catalogued as 'Notton' in Yorkshire.

Two 14thc. deeds, YK 101-102, while part of a varied group of North and East Yorkshire deeds whose provenance is unclear, have been treated separately. This is because they relate to the Stapleton family from whom the late Duke (died June 2002) descended in his maternal line and it therefore seemed worth identifying them. These deeds came into the Howard family collections from long before his mother's lifetime and they seem to reflect early connections by marriage between the Stapletons and the Fauconbergs (as discussed in x. ix below (introduction to YK 101-102).

The Dacre family's Greystoke inheritance in Yorkshire is not represented in this collection but in the first part of the Cumberland catalogue, above and in Part II, below. The chief Yorkshire seats of the early Greystoke lords were at Sheriff Hutton, north east of York, and the manor of Henderskelf a little further on, towards Malton. These did not descend through Anne Dacre to the Howard family but were inherited by her sister Elizabeth. Henderskelf became 'Castle Howard', in possession of the Earls of Carlisle. It is possible that some stray deeds in the final section of this catalogue (section x. xi) may relate to that estate.

---

* Yorkshire Fines I (Yorks. Arch. Assoc., Record Series, vol.II, 1887), pp. 300-301.

x. *Fauconberg and Meynell family estates in North and East Yorkshire c. 1225-1493*

YK4 Undated, *circa* 1225: a fine early script and knightly seal of Walter of Fauconberg - in which he grants to his son Andrew 48 carucates of land in Catwick, representing a knight's fee. The tenant of the land is one William of Lula. Excepted from the grant is a carucate of land which Fauconberg had already given to Nunkeeling Priory for the soul of his brother Philip.

x. i Yorkshire: Fauconberg properties
in Holderness, East Riding

The properties in this group are in the following parishes/places: Arnold, Bilton, Catwick, *East Hatfield, Lambethorpe*, Rise and North Skirlaugh. The eleven deeds (YK 1-11) are presented in alphabetical order of parish.

ARNOLD IN HOLDERNESS

YK 1   **Quitclaim** : undated   **circa 1250**

a) Peter of Faukenberge, then rector of the house of Swina and the free men of Norhkirlae [North Skirlaugh] and of Ru't' [Rowton], viz. Philip of Norhkirlae, Laurence of Ru't' and Simon Foleb't b) Sibilla, prioress of Swina d) The nuns of Swina [Swine]

Property: Lands called Milnehole and Cornuwra [also spelt *cornewra*] and in the meadow adjoining, in the territory of Harnaal'; so that the nuns will be permitted to enclose the said lands with a ditch [*fossatum*] and sew it each year and improve it if they wish; and to have the said meadow and its crop to their own uses without and contradiction or impediment

a) release all rights (i.e. rights of common) in the land to b) and c); they also grant the nuns right of way with their carts and animals across their own lands in order for the nuns to get to their land and cart away grain and hay from the land and meadow; and if damage is done to either parties' crops it shall be sorted out by an arbitrator elected by each party; and Peter of Fauconberg for himself, and b) for herself promise the men of Norhkirlae and Ru't' that they will take their animals off the pasture of the said lands when the crops are growing and out of the meadow in the fenced season

Witnesses: Lord Sayer of Sutt' [?Sutton], William of Herma, Andrew of Faukenberge, Peter of West', knights , William then steward of Rise, P. the parson of Rise,

191

John of F'bois, Richard of Ullingham, Thomas of
Sict' Henry Coleman
Seal: absent

YK 2   **Grant:**   at Ryse, St. Nicholas, 6 December, 3 Ed. II   **1309**

a) William of Grymmesby and Agnes his wife b) Lord Walter of
Fauconberg of Skelton c) John of Lenna, father of Agnes
d) Margaret his wife, mother of Agnes e) Hugh of Arnale
[Arnold]

Property: one bovate of land with appurts. in the vill' and territory
of Arnale in Holdernesse

Recites that the land was formerly held by c) who had it from e)
on his marriage to d); a) now grants to b).

Witnesses: lord Herbert of St. Quentin, lord Henry of Faucumberg,
knights, Stephen Hautayn, Ralph of Merton, William
son of John of Wythornwyke, Walter Northinby of
Ryse
Seal: formerly two; one remains with blurred impression

BILTON IN HOLDERNESS

YK 3   **Lease:**   at Rise, Thurs. St. Peter in Cathedra,
22 February, 15 Ed. III   **1341**

a) Lord John of Faucumberg, Lord of Skelton
b) Lord Walter of Faucumberg of Biltoun

Property: one plot of meadow in Biltoun called Riseland in
Holdernes, with all appurts.

a) grants to b) to hold for 14 years commencing from the day of
this deed at annual rent of one gillyflower clove at Christmas if
demanded

Witnesses: none
Seal: shield impression, somewhat indistinct

CATWICK

YK 4   **Gift:**   undated   **circa 1225**

a) Walter of Faucumberge b) Andrew his son c) William of
Lula d) the Monks of Killinge [?Nunkeeling Priory]

Property: all the land of a) in Kattinwic which is held of him by c) except one bovate which a) gave to d) for the soul of Philip, brother of a); 48 carucates of the whole being one knight's fee.

With the agreement of his heirs a) grants to b) and the heirs of his body. If he should die without such heirs the property shall revert to a) and his heirs.

Witnesses: John of Oketune, William Foliot, Robert of Wascande, William of ?Bouinter, William of Areines, Serle of Haithfeld, Richard of Frismareis, Richard of Arnhale, Ingram of Bouinter

Seal: fine seal, 6cm. diameter; impression of mounted rider and legend

YK 5   **Gift:**   undated   **circa 1280**

a) William son of Simon of Setone   b) Walter of Facumberge, Lord of Rise   c) Margaret of Arnestorpe

Property: one messuage, two perches in width, in the vill' of Cattewik and all its appurts. lying between the toft of Henry of Sigelistornum [Sigglesthorne] and the toft of Thomas the miller

The premises were formerly held by c) from a). The latter now grants to b) and his heirs to hold of him at the annual rent of one ginger root in lieu of all services

Witnesses: Henry of Facumberge, Simon of Phittibye, knights William of Phittibye, William of Levene, Henry of Neyle, Robert Nortiby of Rise, Robert le Vavasur [ie., *the lessee*]

Seal: absent

YK 6   **Gift:**   at Ryse, Sunday the vigil of St. John of Beverlake, 7 May   **1283**

a) Walter of Fauconberge, son of lord Peter of Fauconberg
b) Franco, son of a)   c) Laderina formerly wife of Walter of Apeltone   d) Simon son of Titty

Property: i) 40 s. annual rent in the vill' of Catwick from: one messuage and one croft called Le Westcroft and four bovates of land and appurts; ii) two bovates of land and appurts.

Recites that c) formerly held i) at 32 shillings rent and d) held ii) at 8 s. rent. a) now grants both rents to b), to hold for the term of his life, at a rent of one red rose at Midsummer in lieu of all secular dues.

Witnesses: lords Herbert of Quentin, William of Fauconberge and John of Carletone, knights, William of Wytick, Simon of Wytick, Alan of Weyle of Catwyck, William Barn of Brandeburtone, William of Brustwyck, Alexander the clerk.

Seal: shield impression and legend

EAST HATFIELD

YK 7   Agreement: in the year of grace   **1264**

a) Walter of Faucumberg, lord of Rise   b) William, son of Gilbert of Munceaus   c) John of Munceaus   d) Lucy, mother of the sons and heirs of c)   e) Lord James of Mora, Bernard of Araines, John son of Walter of Witorwic, Hugh at Hall   f) The Lady countess Albemarle [*Alba Marlia*]

Property: all the lands of the sons and heirs of c) in Est Hatfeld, with the mill and the villeins and their services, dues and customs

It is agreed between a) and b) that b) shall have the wardship of the property for a period of 10 years with liberty and he shall enjoy a full 10 years' crops, in return for an annual rent of 9 marks of "*good and legal pence*" 3 shillings and a penny; reserving to a) the third of the property which belongs to d); and if a) should sell or give away the land during the 10-year term b) will still be entitled to the full amount of crops and can reclaim any expense he may incur because of the sale; b) shall also have the house in which his mother once lived for the 10 years and one further year on payment of 4s. a year to a) or his assigns; and b) finds e) as his faithful guarantors and pledges to pay 40s. to f) if he defaults on this agreement.

Witnesses: lord Henry of Fauconberge, lord Simon Withik, knights, lord William of Caverle, Peter of Fauconberge, Walter of Fauconberge of Apeltun, William of Withik, Stephen of Haborp, Peter the marshal, John the clerk

Seal: formerly five, all absent

LAMBETHORPE

(?Lamwath near Sutton on Hull)

YK 8 **Lease:** undated 1278

a) Walter of Faukenberge, knight   b) Firma [?*Farina*] the Prioress of Swinar and the convent of the same place

Property: one croft in the territory of Lambethorpe with all appurts.

a) grants to b) for 10 years beginning at the feast of St. Martin (11 November) 1278 to hold at annual rent of 11 shillings silver.

Witnesses: John of Surdeval, Armand of Luda, Richard Marescal of ?Swinar, Simon son of Hugh of the same, William the cook of the same.

Seal: none

RISE

YK 9 **Sale:** undated **circa 1280**

a) Robert le Vavassur [*the lessee*] of Ryse
b) Walter of Faukenberge

Property: one bovate of land with all appurts. and easements in the territory of Ryse, extending in length and breadth throuout the whole territory of Ryse, with free entry and exit in its feedings, meadows, ways, paths and dykes [*fossata*]

Citing that the property had been held by his mother as her dower a) sells [*vendidi*] to b) for 5 marks of sterling, to hold at the annual rent of one rose at midsummer; and if a) dies [*should go the way of all flesh*] before his wife, he wills that his heirs provide her dower out of this property

Witnesses: lords William Constable, Sayer' of Suttone, Henry of Fauconberg, knights Robert of Hylton, Herbert of St. Quintin, John of Surdeval, Roger of Dol, William of Witheton, Richard Marscall

Seal: fragment of an oval seal with *Robert* legible

NORTH SKIRLAUGH

YK 10   **Gift and quitclaim:** undated   **circa 1280**

a) Robert Bealsieu   b) Walter of Faucumberge once son of Lord Peter of Faucumberge

Property: all the land of a) in Norh Scyrelaye, viz. i) one croft, 5 selions lying between the croft of Peter le Huner one one side and the croft of Robert known as the lay brother [*Robertus dictus frater conversus*] on the other; ii) 8 selions outside the close, lying between the land of Robert the lay brother and the close that Augustine once held of Philip of Scyrlaye, in length alongside i) from the common way of Scyrlaye as far as the water course of Rutona; with all appurts. and lands pertaining

Recites that a) once held the land from b) in fee. He now grants it to b) to hold as his own fee

Witnesses: lord Simon of Wytike, lord Anselm of Harphaym, knights, John of Surdvale, Walter of Appeltona, Roger of Dole, Matthew of Rutona, Robert the lay brother of Scyrlaye, Nicholas Sicling of the same

Seal: absent

YK 11   **Gift:**   at Ryse, Tuesday after St. Augustine, 26 May,   **1283**

a) Robert le Frerbroyer of Northskirlaw and Margery his wife Walter son of Lord Walter of Fauconberge   c) Alice, daughter of Nicholas Sicling and Matilda and Agnes her sisters

Property: a certain toft and croft in Northskirlaw which lie between the toft of Roger the miller on the north and Le Uttegangland on the south

Citing that c) occupy the property a) grants to b) the annual rent of 2s. payable by c); for which b) must pay a) a rose at midsummer in lieu of all secular services and dues.

Witnesses: lords Walter of Fauconberge, John of Carletone, William of Fauconberge, John Palmer, knights, Robert Hildyard, William of Wytick, Walter of Apeltone, Walter Northyby of Ryse

Seal: fragment of one; one absent

x. ii Yorkshire: Fauconberg properties: various

The premises mentioned in the deeds in this section are in the parishes of Hunmanby near Filey, Kettlewell (presumably the Kettlewell in Swaledale), Roston (presumably Ruston Parva near Driffield) and Raisthorpe, near Sledmere (between Driffield and Malton).

HUNMANBY

YK 12 **Gift:** undated **?circa 1225**

a) Gilbert of Gant b) Peter of Lestane

Property: i) Four carucates of land in Hundemanebi with all appurts. in that vill' in meadows, feedings, waters, paths and easements: whose tenants are as follows: Ralph of Nitherafne 3 bovates, Ralph son of Walter 2, John of the Hill [*del hyl*] 2, William son of Walter 1, Robert Danz 2, Gerard Child 2, Simon Danz 2, John son of Authen 2, Everard of the Fount 1, Hugh son of Godwin 1, Richard son of Walter 1, Walter Nout 1, Albert son of Authen 2, Agnes the widow 1, William son of Authen 1, Ralph son of Gosse 2, Stephen son of Dune 2, Thomas the smith 1, Geoffrey the carpenter 1. Henry son of Ray 1, Stephen of the Well [*del fonte*] 1, Richard Noel 1, Geoffrey of the Moor [*de la more*] 1, Walter son of Arnold a half, with the tofts and crofts that pertain to them. ii) tofts which the following formerly held: Ralph of Nitherafne 1, Ralph son of Walter 1, John of the Hill 3, Henry Peper 1 , Arnald the parker 1, Simon Danz 1, Robert Reinbute [?Rembute] 1, Freissant 1, Anna 1, William Trittling 1, Sigerithe 1, Hosegot 1, Richard the smith 1, Geoffrey the butler 1, Geoffrey son of Authen 1, Huelina the widow 1, Robert Charles 1, Gerard son of Ingolf 1, William the tailor 1, Ormer 1, Albert Bray 1, one where Gilda ?Sel-[illegible], Alger' 1, and Walter ?of the manger [*mangeri*] 1

a) grants to b) in return for the service of one third part of a knight's fee

Witnesses: Ellis [*Eliseus*] the Prior of Bridligtona, Stephen of Gant, Reginald of Gant, John of Melsa, Peter of Melsa, Henry of Folketona, Ralph of Novilla, Walter of St. Laud, Roger son of Malger

Seal: absent; a long tag of woven cloth survives

KETTLEWELL

YK 13   **Grant and quitclaim:** Undated   **?circa 1285**

a) Walter of Faucumberge   b) Peter of Faucumberge, brother of a)   c) Walter of Faucumberge, father of a)

Property: moiety of the vill' of Keteleswelle and moiety of the advowson of the church there; including the demesnes (of the manor), the rents and services both of the free men and of the customary tenants; and all the goods of the latter wherever they are, , in the wood, the plain, the meadows, the feedings, ponds, mills, moors, marshes and turbaries; with all liberties belonging to the said land within the vill' and without.

Citing that a) received the property from c), a) now grants and quitclaims to b); he also pledges that if his wife (not named) should claim right of dower on any of the said land, he or his heirs will grant b) an equivalent amount of land elsewhere in England in compensation during her dotage. He also promises, by the Holy Apostles, (*tactis sacrosanctis Ewangeliis*) that he will deliver to b) the deeds relating to the land on pain of 1000 penances for himself and his heirs if he fails so to do.

Witnesses: Robert of Kokefeld, Andrew of Faucumberge, Ralph son of William, Nicholas Ward, Robert of Stapeltone, Richard of Goudesburge, William Martel, William of Widindon, Adam of Stanel, Henry ?Walin, Reginald of Stawa

Seal:

fragment of large seal with floral impression

RAISTHORPE

YK 14   **Gift:**   undated   **circa 1285**

a) John Wybbe   b) William of Hertelay
c) Henry Wybbe, father of a)   d) Thomas son of Thomas

Property: a certain toft with its buildings and a plot of land adjoining in the vill' of Raynaldthorpe lyiing, in length and width, in Gamelcroft and abutting on the highway

Reciting that he obtained it by hereditary right from c), a) now grants the property to b) and his heirs to hold of d) at 2 ½d. silver annual rent, payable to d), in lieu of all services, suits of court etc.

Witnesses: Henry of Hertelay, Richard of Bernis, Richard of Huccbrig', Robert of Birlay, John son of William of Raynaldthorp, John son of Peter of the same.

Seal: damaged; partial impression and legend

YK 15   **Gift:**   undated   **circa 1285**

a) Peter del Hil of Raynaldthorp   b) William of Hertlay

Property: ½ acre of land lying in Gameliscroft next to le Dickbecke its W. head abutting on the toft of a) and its east head on land of John del Lye, with all commons, liberties and easements in all places pertaining to the sd. ½ acre.

a) grants to b) and his heirs to hold at ½d. annual rent in lieu of all secular services and customs etc. Warranty covers the half acre *in all its length and width without any diminution*

Witnesses: Henry of Hertlay, Richard of Bernis, Richard of Huccybrig, John son of William of the Hall, Peter of Crosselay, John son of Nicholas of Raynaldethorp, Hugh the clerk

Seal: ecclesiastical; perhaps of Hugh the clerk.

YK 16   **Gift:**   undated   **circa 1290**

a) Peter del Hylle of Raynaldethorp   b) William of Hertelay

Property: 2½ acres lying in Gamelcroft in the field of Raynaldthorp in length and breadth between land once of Thomas Thirs which he held of the Hospital, on the west, and land of William the fuller on the east, its north head abutting on the vill' of Raynaldthorp and its south head on the assart of Hugh of Langeleye; with all liberties, commons and easements in all places pertaining to the premises.

199

In return for a money payment a) now grants to b) and his heirs to hold at 2d. annual rent.

Witnesses:	Henry of Hertelay, John son of Wiliam of the Hall, John son of Henry Wibbe [looks more like *Wilbe*], Richard del Bernis, Richard of Huchtibrig, Peter of Crosselay, John del Bernes, William the clerk.
Seal:	ecclesiastical; impression and legend, slightly damaged; perhaps of William the clerk.

YK 17 **Gift:** Monday before St. Lawrence the Martyr, 10 August **1290**

a) Henry Wibbe of Raynaldthorp b) William of Hertelay

Property:	i) 3 roods of land as the lie in length and breadth called Selenge under Stubbinggrene in the field of Raynaldthorp, the north head abutting on land of John Crukhorn, the south head on land of b) ii) one acre of land called Dikhaker as it lies in length and breadth in Gamelscrofte between le Munkenge and Spinkeswelleflat, with all appurts. as in YK/16 above.

In return for a money payment a) grants to b) and his heirs to hold at ½d. of silver as annual rent in lieu of all secular services etc.

Witnesses:	Henry of Hertelay, Peter del Hylle of Raynaldthorp, John son of William of the Hall of the same, Richard del Bernes, John del Bernes, Richard of Hucytibrig, John son of Nicholas Crukhorn, William of Roderham, clerk
Seal:	none

YK 18 **Gift:** at Raynaldtorp, Sunday after St. Peter in chains, 1 August, **1315**

a) Thomas of Hertelay b) Henry of Hertelay, father of a)

Property:	land, meadow and wood in the vill' and territory of Raynaldtorp, with all easements pertaining.

Cites that a) received the land from b). He now returns it to him and to his heirs.

Witnesses:	Ralph of Waddeslay, John of Houselay, Peter of Crosselay, John of Birlay, Richard of Birlay.
Seal:	none

"ROSTON", ?RUSTON PARVA

YK 19   **Grant and Quitclaim:** undated   **circa 1280**

a) Robert son of William Drenge of Rostone, born of [*genitus*]
Margaret wife of the same William   b) Alan Suthiby of Roston
and Alice his wife   c) Alan the clerk of Rostone

Property: toft with appurts. in Rostone lying between the toft
which b) holds by gift of Robert his father and the toft
which Thomas son of Roger holds of the Provost of
Beverlac [Beverley], in length from the common way
in Roston as far as the field

Recites that a)'s father bought the land from c); a) now grants it
to b) and their heirs.

Witnesses: Lord William of St. Quintin, Richard of Torny, Richard
of Anlagheby, Walter of Kelk, Robert Drenge the elder,
William his son, William of Hammerton
Seal: wrapped and formless

-oOo-

x. iii *Fauconberg premises in Cleveland, North Yorks*

Walter of Fauconberg (d. 1304) whose family estates are the subject of YK 1-19 above, married Agnes of Brus [or Bruce]. She was the eldest of four sisters, daughters of Robert of Brus (lord of Annandale - see *Complete Peerage*). Their brother, Peter, was lord of Skelton and Danby in Cleveland, but, on his death, his sisters each took her share of his possessions. Agnes and Walter Fauconberg got Skelton Castle, while the youngest sister, Laderayne of Brus, who had received various Yorkshire manors including Carlton (near Drax), brought that share of the Brus inheritance into the Stapleton family, from whom the present Duke of Norfolk is sprung (see YK 101-102 Introduction, on p. 236 below). Although nominally a Brus inheritance, the North Yorkshire estate had in fact descended from the girls' mother who had been a co-heir of Sir William of Lancastre, lord of Kendal.

The Fauconberg lordship in Cleveland descended with Skelton Castle as its feudal centre for five more generations to Sir Thomas of Fauconberg (b.1345, d.1407), until his treachery against the King in 1370 caused the forfeiture of all his estates. Twenty years later they were granted to trustees, two brothers by name of Robert and John Conyers. By 1405, Fauconberg's insanity caused another transfer of the estates, to his father in law Sir Thomas Brownflete, and Sir Robert Hilton. His son and heir apparent was beheaded in 1405 and Sir Thomas himself died in 1407, leaving a daughter Joan, an idiot since her birth in 1406, as heir. Despite her lunacy, in 1422 she married William Neville, 8th son of the Earl of Westmorland. The Barony of Fauconberg fell into abeyance but, through the three daughters of the marriage, the Skelton estates passed on into the Strangways and the Conyers families.

Four deeds, YK 81-84 on pp. 228-229 below, relate to the 15th-century descent of the Skelton lordship. The greater part of this group are earlier, relating firstly to premises in the parish of Skelton, secondly to premises in the nearby parish of Marske by the Sea, and finally to various other parishes and places in the locality. True to the nature of the collection, overall, they generally relate to insignificant holdings within the lordship.

YK42 This interesting indenture dated the Friday before Midsummer's Day 1338, was drawn up in Guisborough Priory between lord John Fauconberg and the Prior. Fauconberg grants the Prior rights of common and timber rights in a wood in Guisborough but he reserves to himself full hunting rights there.

x iii. Yorkshire: Fauconberg properties in Cleveland, North Yorks

This section of the catalogue has been arranged as follows:

YK 21-28   Premises in Skelton
YK 31-36   Premises in Marske by the Sea
YK 37-46   Premises in various parishes, viz.
            Appleton le Moors, 'Grenerig' (?in Liverton),
            Guisborough, Linthorpe, Redcar and Upleatham,
            Wyte' (?Whitby), Whitby

SKELTON IN CLEVELAND

YK 21   **Gift:**   undated   **circa 1275**

a) Richard Bretun of Sceltona   b) Guy [*Wido*) of Roucestra
c) Lord Peter of Br' (Brus)

Property: 3½ acres of land in the field of Sceltone in Karlecroft;
all the land of a) at Buttes which stretches out on
Brakinhoued; three acres at the Buttes of Salemantros
nearby; half an acre which William of Witeby held of
a); one acre in Lag-[*missing*]-es; ½ acre in Wanlaus;
one rood in Buerholm; with all appurts., liberties and
easements within the vill' and without

In return for his homage and service a) grants the properties to
b) and his heirs to hold of himself and his heirs at ann. rent of
one penny payable at Christmas. The grant includes liberty of the
mills belonging to c), who is a)'s Lord, viz. he may grind ?every
16th measure [*ad sextumdecimum vas*) of the corn which grows on
his own land and every 20th measure of the corn which he has
bought; and ?this must go in to the hopper after his own corn
comes to the mill [*et statum post bladum quod s' in tramallo qu'
bladum suum venit ad molendinum*]

Witnesses: Alan the clerk, John of Thocotes, William of Layrton,

William Pickwastel, Alexander Costard, William of Wyteby, Goce Costard, Robert of Wpliu', Clement of Beverlac, Richard Cornard

Seal: absent

YK 22   **Quitclaim:**   undated   **circa 1275**

a) Alice daughter of William Mareschal   b) Lord Peter of Brus

Property: a toft and croft in Sceltone viz. one acre and one third of an acre lying near the toft of the wife of Richard Le Wayte on the N.

Reciting that she received the land from her father [not named], a) releases to b) who is her Lord any claim that she or her heirs may have to it; and she ratifies the deed by an oath sworn on the holy bible [*tactis sacrosanctis ewangeliis jura*] in front of the parishioners of the church of Sceltone

Witnesses: Simon of Brus, John of Thocotes, Robert Buscel, William Pick-[*was*]-tel, Hugh Haubeg', Goce Costard, Adam Scot, Reginald of Burgate, Ralph le Brazur, Robert of Uplium

Seal: absent

YK 23   **Gift:**   undated   **?circa 1300**

a) Godfrey [*illegible*] of Sceltone in Clyveland
b) Richard son of William of Foxholes

Property: one bovate of land with a meadow adjoining and all appurts. in the vill'of Skeltone in Clyveland, 15 acres in all, of which: 1½a. lie at Le Clyf between the land of Odenell of Manfeld on the E. and the land of Peter son of Elyas on the W; 1r. lies at Stachau, 1a. at Berehyllyth, 1a. at Westgrenwal, 1a. at Estgrenwal, 1r. at Biglandes, ½r. at grenwalendes, 1r. at Claphauholme, 1r. at Foghou, 1½a. at Langelandes in two places, 1r. at Thorpdale, ½a. at Halholm, 1½r. at [?Over]-holm, ½a. at Laulandses, ½a. at Spedmenwra, ½r. at Wandaltes, 1a. at Langacres, 1a. and ½r. at Falfen, 1 r. at Littalayrlandes; 1r. at the head of the vill' on the E. of the house of Hugh Pickewastel; 1r. on the N. beneath the croft of [illegible]-endal, 1½r. at Byman Roshache; ½a. at Thyrnoue below the meadow of the said vill' on the N.; 1r. at Wanlaus-[*illegible*] at Le

Brocis; ½a. at Grauteng [or ?*Graneeng*] on the E.; ½a. of meadow between the meadow of the said Odenell on the E. and the meadow of the said Peter on the W; 1r. of meadow in the same place between the meadows of the same persons; with all liberties and easements in moors, meadows, feedings, and pastures

a) grants to b) and his heirs to hold of himself and his heirs at ann. rent of [*illegible*], payable at Christmas

Witnesses: lord Laurence then chaplain to the parish of Skelton, Matthew of Glapheu, [*illegible*] del Auneye, Michael of Tokotes, Nicholas the Hauberger, Hugh Pickwastel, John [*illegible*], William the baker, William Cru-[*illegible*], [*illegible*] Play

Seal: fragment of ecclesiastical seal

This deed is illegible through staining in several places

YK 24 **Lease for life:** at Skelton, Thursday in the Vigil of
St. James the Apostle, 25 July **1337**

a) John of Faucomberge, Lord of Skeltone, knight
b) Thomas of Restone

Property: one toft, built upon, with appurts. in the vill' of Skeltone lying between the toft of a) on one side and Le Westbekes on the other, with all commodities within the vill' and without that pertain to that toft

a) grants to b) for the duration of his life; to hold of a) and his heirs at 2s. annual rent and by suit of a)'s Court at Skelton twice a year at the next courts held after Michaelmas and after Easter each year

Witnesses: Richard of Wyresdale, John of Biltona, William of Hay, Peter Grauntes, Cuthbert Scot

Seal: small but decorative

YK 25 **Lease for life:** at Skelton in the vigil of Pentecost **1350**

a) Walter of Fauconberge, Lord of Skelton   b) Peter the weaver [or possibly 'thatcher', *textor*] of Skelton

Property: all that close with its buildings in Skeltone called Cadicroft

a) grants to b) to hold for the duration of his life from a) and his heirs at 3s. annual rent and he must attend a)'s courts, that is, the next courts after Michaelmas and Easter each year and he must grind his corn at a)'s mill

Witnesses: none
Seal: impression and legend

YK 26 **Lease for life:** At Skelton, Wednesday in the feast of St. Andrew, 30 November, 30 Edward III   1356

a) Walter son of John of Faucomberge, knight, Lord of Skelton in Clyveland   b) Henry le Goldbeter and Alice his wife

Property: i) one messuage and three acres of land in the vill' and territory of Skeltone and common of pasture for 12 cows and their calves ?up to 3 years old [*sequela sua trium annorum*] and 40 ewes in all the lands and tenements of a) in the vill' of Skelton; common of pasture for 4 oxen or cows in the park of a) called Westpark, common of pasture for one heifer with her young up to 3 years old in the park called Maugrepark; and in a place called La Haye common turbary rights in all the moors and marshes of a) in Skeltone, that is, b) may dig and cut 12 cartloads of turf each year of their life and, as housebote and haybote may cut 12 cartloads of wood each year in the woods of a)
ii) an annual rent of a quarter of salt to be taken at Michaelmas each year throughout the whole of a)'s manor of Skeltone
iii) licence to cut 40 packs [*sarcina*] of heather in all of a)'s moors in Skeltone and to take a certain annual rent of two cartloads of straw at Michaelmas each year from the whole of a)'s manor of Skeltone; with licence to carry all these commodities to b)'s house and licence and to grind each 30th measure of their corn at all of his mills within the demesne of Skeltone, after the first corn has been put into the hoppers of the same mills
iv) annual rent of £20 to be taken from manors of a) in Merske in Clyveland and Wyththornewyke in Holderness

a) grants i), ii) and iii) to b) for the duration of their lives; and recites a deed whereby property iv) was previously granted to them for life by a); but now, in return for all the rights granted in i) - iii) above, a) will in future pay only £10 sterling to b), in lieu of the former rent or £20 as specified in iv).

Witnesses: none
Seal: two seals with shield impressions and faint legends

YK 27 **Quitclaim:** at Skeltone, 16 May 36 Edward III   1362

a) Walter son of John of Faucomberghe of Skeltone in Cliveland
b) John of Whetteley the elder, of Thornton in Craven, residing in Skeltone   c) Beatrix of Laysingby, sister and heir of ... d) John who was brother and heir of ... e) Adam of Skeltone f) William of Kyllom, chaplain

Property: annual rent of 15s. 4d. to be taken in the vill' of Skelton in Clyveland

Reciting that the rent was quitclaimed by c) to a)'s father; and that it had also been held by f) for the term of his life, by gift of d) and e) [presumably prior to the grant by Beatrix of Lasingby to Fauconberg]. a) now releases to b) all his entitlement to this rent.

Witnesses: lord John of Derlyngtone, Prior of Giseburne [Guisborough], Thomas son of Marmaduke of Thweng, James of Thoucotes, Thomas son of Walter of Faucomberghe of Biltone
Seal:
damaged but (?Fauconberg) shield remains clearly impressed.

YK 28 **Exchange** **20 June**   1396

a) Robert of Grenekeld   b) John Faucomeberge   c) Cuthbert of Langwathe

Property: i) One burgage with a croft next to Poterowe and four acre of land upon les Wandelles in the vill' and territory of Skeltone, lying on the N. side of land of Adam Milner in the same place
ii) One croft in Estgate

a) grants property i) to b) and his heirs in exchange for property ii). Recites that c) formerly held ii)

Witnesses: Robert of Neuland, chaplain, Richard of Merske, chaplain, Adam Milnere, Hugh Walker, John of Thorpe
Seal: faint impression of arms

MARSKE

See also YK 85 below

YK 31   **Gift for lives:** undated   **circa 1280**

a) Walter of Fauconberge, Lord of Skeltona
b) Henry Marescalle and Beatrix his wife, of Merske

Property: one acre of land lying in the place called Gyldehuseflatte,
                immediately south of the tenement that William son
                of John holds of a) by deed [*scriptum*] in the vill' of
                Merske; with all liberties and easements pertaining to
                the said land within and without the vill' of Merske

a) grants to b) for the life of the longest liver of them to hold
of himself at annual rent of 8s. a year and 16 autumn works
[*operaciones*] when required by the ?reeve [*per p'pm* {presum. for
per prepositum}] of Merske

Witnesses: John of Fountains, then steward, Cuthbert Capun,
                Matthew of Aunay, Hugh Pykwastel of Skeltona,
                William son of John of Mersk
Seal: formerly two, both absent

YK 32   **Gift:**   at Mersk, Sunday within the feast of Christmas   **1331**

a) William Brindboys of Merske
b) Hugh son of Richard of Tholesun

Property: three and a half acres of land with appurts. in Merske,
                one and a half of which lie in Over Catteflatte and
                one and a half in Neyer Catteflatte and half an acre
                at Ryehille in le Slak

a) grants to b) and his heirs to hold of the chief Lords of the fee
by the services due

Witnesses: Lord Robert Capoun, knight, Matthew Daunay,
                Nicholas of Hoptone, John of Fountains the younger,
                William Skotte of Merske
Seal: absent

YK 33   **Gift:**   At Mersk, Monday before St. Thomas the Martyr,
                                29 December, 35 Ed. III   **1361**

a) Walter of Faucomberge, Lord of Skeltone   b) Lord Richard
Bewner, chaplain   c) William son of Roger of Redcar d) John
of Funtayns

Property: one bovate of land with appurts. in Merske and all its
                liberties and easements

Reciting that c) acquired the land from d), who are both neifs of
a), a) now grants it to b) and his heirs to hold of the chief lords
of the fee

Witnesses: John of Fulthorpe, John of Toucotes, James of Towcotes,
                 Nicholas Rosele, Thomas Benes of Ootun [or could
                 be *Cotun*]
Seal: good shield impression in decorative border

YK 34   **Grant and confirmation:** at Mersk, Saturday before St. George
                        the martyr, 12 March, 43 Ed. III   **1369**

a) Roger of Faucomberge, son of Lord Walter of Faucomberge,
lord of Skeltone in Clyveland   b) Lord Thomas of Faucomberge
and ... d) Constance his wife   e) Roger Lascelles, knight

Property: all lands and tenements which he has received by gift
                from e) in the vill' and territory of Mersk

a) grants to b) and c) and the heirs of b) to hold of the chief
Lords of the fee by the services due and by 40s. silver annual rent
payable half annually to a); power for a) to distrain for arrears,
and to enter and repossess the lands for the whole of the life of
a) if the rent is 15 days overdue

Witnesses: John of Hurworthe then Prior of Gysebourne, John of
                 Fulthorpe, John Gower of Faiceby, James of Toucotes,
                 John Capon
Seal: damaged but fine decorative impression remains

YK 35   **Grant and confirmation:** at Skeltone in Cliveland 12 April,
                        43 Ed. III   **1369**

a) Roger Lascels
b) Roger son of ... c) Lord Walter of Faucomberge

Property: all the lands, tenementsand their appurts. in the vill' and territory of Merske which a) received by gift from c)

a) now confirms the property to b) and the legitimate heirs of his body to be procreated; in default of such heirs the property shall remain to the heirs of c)

Witnesses: John Percy of Kyldale, John Gower of Sexhowe, James of Toucotes, William of Lackynby, John Capon
Seal: fragment

YK 36   Appointment of attornies at Skeltone in Cliveland 14 April 43 Ed. III   1369

a) Roger of Faucomberge   b) James of Toucotes and John [missing] c) Roger Lascels, knight   d) Walter of Faucomberge, father of a)

Property: all lands, tenements and appurts of a) in the vill' and territory of Merske in Cliveland

Recites that c) has granted the premises to a) and that c) had them by gift of d). a) now appoints b) his attornies to receive seisin.

Witnesses: none
Seal: tiny; shield impression
This deed is damaged, with parts missing.

VARIOUS PARISHES: Appleton le Moors

YK 37   **Gift:**   at Wodappletone   1318

a) Mabel daughter of Benedict of Wodappeltone   b) Stephen, son of Margery, sister of a)   c) Simon, brother of a)   d) John son of David

Property: i) four acres of land in the vill' and territory of Wodappeltone
ii) one toft which lies between the toft of William son of Benedict on one side and the toft of William son of Jueta [the Jewess] on the other, together with 8 acres lying throughout the whole field of Wodappelton iii) land lying between land of the Abbey of the Blessed Mary of York and a certain toft of ?madder (*sanarici*) in the said vill'
iv) A piece of land which John son of Hervey held, in the territory of Wodappeltone Recites that property i)

will come to a) after the death of c) and that property ii) was given by d) to Richard who was father of a); a) now grants the reversion expectant on the premises to b) together with annual rents of 6d. out of property iii) and 5d. out of property iv)

Witnesses: William son of Benedict, John son of Simon, William son of John, William Laundels, John son of Walter of Wodappelton

Seal: small, indistinct impression

YK 38 **Grant for life:** at Wodappeltone, Wednesday after Corpus Christi, 19 Edward III **1345**

a) John of Faucumberge of Skeltone, knight   b) Simon son of William of Rydale   c) Stephen son of Margery

Property: messuage and 8 acres of land with appurts. in Wodappeltone

Reciting that he got the property from c), a) grants to b) to hold for life, paying 12s. of silver as annual rent; b) is to keep the house in as good a state of repair as when he received it

Witnesses: Stephen son of William son of Benedict, Stephen of Edestone, William Laundel, John son of Isabel, John of Thorne

Seal: small with impression and legend somewhat indistinct

VARIOUS PARISHES: *'Grenerig'*

The next deed, YK 39, was found misappropriated to co. Northumberland, but it has now been relocated with the two subsequent Fauconberg family deeds concerning 'Grenerig'. The location of this vill' is probably within Liverton parish (see *Victoria County History: Yorkshire*). YK 40 is a roughly executed, small, deed with a large hole in it.

YK 39 **Lease agreement:** at Easter, in the year **1311**

a) Lord Walter of Faucumberg, Lord of Skeltone
b) William of Grenekelde and John his brother   c) John Ruscel

Property: all that toft with the croft and two bovates of land in the vill' and territory of Grenrige: the croft lying between the toft of Roger of Walplou on one side and the toft of one Alan Burnet on the other; the 2 bovates lying between the land of John son of William Bennet on one side and land of Alan Burnet on the other

Reciting that c) previously leased the property a) and b) agree that a) shall lease it to b) for a term of 16 years at annual rent of 10s. of silver; and b) shall grind every 20th measure [*ad vicesimum vas*] of the corn growing on the property at a)'s mill; and every 24th measure of corn that they have purchased shall be ground there [?or does this mean they get every 20th and 24th turn at the mill]

Witnesses: Cuthbert Capon, John of Funtaynes, Hugh Picwastel, Thomas of Brune, John the clerk

Seal: two; one a fragment, one with impression and legend

YK 40 **Grant:** at Scheltone, Monday before the feast of St. Austin, 26 May, 1338

a) John of Faucumberge, Lord of Schelton b) Roger of Wulfdale
c) Robert of Boineton

Property: one tenement in Grenerig, with all commodities and easements in the vill' of Grenerig

Reciting that the property was once held by c), a) grants to b) for life at 5s. annual rent in lieu of all services (?and) suit of court at Skelton.

Witnesses: William of Boinetone, William of Lelhom, Richard of Wrddesdale, Cuthbert P[missing], John of Lythe,

Seal: absent

YK 41 **Lease:** 1361

a) Lord Walter Fauconberg, knight, Lord of Skeltone in Cleveland
b) John son of Hugh of Grenerig and his wife (not named)
c) William of Flathowe

Property: messuage and two bovates and their appurts. in the vill' and in the fields of Grenerig

Citing that the messuage is that which c) used to hold a) grants to b) for a term of 20 years beginning at Pentecost 1361, at 8s. annual rent; and he shall not make waste but shall leave it as good as he found it or better

Witnesses:	Roger son of Peter, William son of Sybil, Simon son of Hugh, William of Merske, Roger of Woldale	
Seal:	faint shield impression in poor condition	

VARIOUS PARISHES: Guisborough

YK 42 **Grant:** at Giseburne in Clyveland, Friday before St. John
the Baptist (midsummer) **1338**

a) Lord John of Faucumberge of Skeltone b) Robert the Prior
of Giseburne and the convent of the same place

Property: all the wood growing, or that will in future grow, in
the close called Le Swaytiheued in Giseburne, as the
said wood is enclosed with a ditch and a stream called
Swynstibek

a) grants to b) for ever the power to lop [*amputare*] and to fell
[*succidere*] all or part of the wood and to cart the cut wood away;
he also grants b) the right of common of pasture for their animals
of all kinds and promises that neither he nor his heirs will depasture
their animals there in future, or if they do, b) may impound them
and sue for any loss or expense incurred, unless they have got in
because there are holes in the enclosure; and b) are empowered to
make and repair the ditches and hedges as often as is necessary;
provided that the (small) game belonging to a) can get in and out
at the base of the enclosure; and reserving the right to hunt (large)
game [*venatio ferarum*] to a) and his heirs

Witnesses: this deed was drawn up by a) in front of all of b)
Seal: absent

VARIOUS PARISHES: Linthorpe

The next was originally catalogued as Leventhorpe in the West Riding
of Yorkshire. However, the text makes it obvious that it relates to
the area of the river Leven, or a tributary, in the vicinity of Skelton
in Cleveland.

YK 43 **Lease for life:** at Sceltone, Friday before St. Ambrose the
bishop, 4 April, 16 Ed. II **1323**

a) John of Fawkenberge, Lord of Skeltona
b) William of Gaytregg

Property: one plot of land with half an acre pertaining to that
plot in the vill' and territory of Levigthorpe together

with the fishery of the water of Geys opposite that place called Le Fawkenbergnese; with all easements and commodities pertaining to the said land and fishery, both near and far.

a) grants to b) to hold for life, rendering him and his heirs one salmon in Lent

| Witnesses: | Robert of Steynesby, Robert of Martona, Robert of Clipland, Robert of Waxsand, Robert of Thorinotby, Robert the clerk |
| Seal: | impression and legend |

VARIOUS PARISHES: Redcar and Upleatham

YK 44   **Exchange:** undated   **circa 1250**

a) Joan daughter of Godfrey of Hoge b) Lord Peter of Brus

| Property: | i) all the land in Redker which a) holds by gift from Godfrey her father, with all its appurts. |
| | ii) twelve and a half acres and half a rood in Huplyn' |

a), acting in her *free power and virginity*, gives i) to b) and he in exchange gives ii) to her

| Witnesses: | lord Walter of the Park, lord Robert Engram, lord Berard of Fotiby, lord Robert of Muncell', lord William Engram, Alan the clerk, Alan of the Park, Robert of Thorinodebi, John of Tofecost |
| Seal: | absent |

VARIOUS PARISHES: Whitby

[The following deed is assumed to be Whitby, but local knowledge may suggest otherwise]

YK 45   **Lease for lives:** at Wyte' Saturday after St. Denis,
9 October   **1308**

a) Walter of Faucumberge, knight, Lord [of Skelton]
b) Peter le Mariays of [missing] and Beatrix his wife

| Property: | one toft in the vill' of Wyte' with all the buildings on it, lying between the toft of Matilda Coti and the toft of Simon Capelle, extending in length from the common way of the vill' as far as the toft of John at Hall and Simon Bue; with all liberties and easements, viz. ways, paths, waters, meadows, feedings, and pastures |

a) grants to b) for the life of whichever of them lives longest, they paying him 5s. annual rent.

Witnesses: Simon Bigot, Thomas of Kintone, John Mariais, Adam of Aytebi, staying in Wyte', Robert Frauncenant of Halto', Amelin of the same

Seal: absent

Parts of this deed are missing

YK 46 **Quitclaim:** at Whiteby, feast of St. Peter in chains, 1 August   **1410**

a) John Suthwyk and Alice his wife   b) Roger Peche

Property: one messuage in Whiteby in a street called Grapcinctlane

a) and their heirs release all their rights in the property to b) and his heirs

Witnesses: William of the Hall, William Kalwardby, William Hersand, Ralph Gouer, Thomas Hersand

Seal: impression

-oOo-

x. iv Fauconberg dowry in Holderness and Cleveland, 1366

The places mentioned in this deed are Rise, Withernwick, Eastburn, Skelton and Marske by the Sea.

YK 50   **Gift and confirmation:** at Skelton, Wednesday after the nativity
of the Blessed Mary, 8 September,   **1366**

a) Thomas Fauconberge, son and heir of Walter Fauconberge, decd.,
once Lord of Skelton in Clyveland   b) Lady Isabel of Fauconberge
c) Robert son of Juliana, of Hornsebek, neif of a), now living in
Skareburghe

Property: manors of Ryse in Holdernesse, Wythornwyk and
Estbrun with all their appurts; advowson of the church
and chantry of Ryse; one third part of the manors of
Skeltone and Merske in Clyveland

a) grants c) to b) for life, along with all his goods and chattels.
He also confirms to her the rights she has in the properties listed,
as her dower, for life.

Witnesses: lord John Bygote, William of St. Quintin, knights,
Roger of Fulthorpe, John of Malteby, William of
Lackenby
Seal: fine seal of a) with good impression and legend
Deed enrolled in chancery, October 1366

-oOo-

x. v Meynell family holdings in Cleveland

The Meynell family came to England at the time of the Norman conquest and, shortly afterwards, established Whorlton Castle in Cleveland as their seat. The deeds in this section of the catalogue mainly concern small land grants made in the time of Stephen Meynell (the third), who had died by 1269, and by his son and grandson, both called Nicholas. As with the Fauconberg collection, above, the deeds here do not relate to the seat or to the demesnes but to insignificant holdings scattered in neighbouring parishes. This is perhaps to be expected when we know that some of the inheritance descended to the Dacre family, but not the important parts. This does not detract from the great significance of the contents of these deeds to local historians in Cleveland.

Some deeds in this section, YK 55-57 and YK 64, can be singled out for comment because they relate to what was perhaps a difficult time within the family. In around 1305 Nicholas of Meynell (b. 1274) had entered into a relationship with Lucy (b. 1279), daughter of Robert Thweng, despite the fact that she was married to someone else. After her divorce in 1312 Nicholas made various settlements in favour of the illegitimate son they had had together. Some of these are referred to in *Complete Peerage, Meinill*, pp. 628-629 (notes), but YK 55-57 and 62 appear to be further examples. The lordship descended in the legitimate line to Nicholas' younger brother John, but subsequently failed for want of heirs male. Nicholas, the illegitimate son, succeeded to Whorlton Castle as a result of his father's provision and he was created a Baron by writ in 1336. He married Alice, daughter of Lord Ros of Helmsley but the union failed to produce a male heir. Elizabeth, their daughter and heiress, married John Darcy in 1345.

A few stray items relating to premises in Carlton and Potto in the 16th century, owned by Strangways and Dacre families, are in the Duke of Norfolk's archives in Sheffield City Libraries, ref. SD 309-313.

Contents

An early, undated, deed relating to Ingleby. Samson, son of Samuel has paid 4 marks of silver for a bovate of land. The old feudal ties are being watered down in that Samson will hold the land at a money rent and will himself be free of any requirement of service to the grantor. However, if the King were to demand foreign service from the land holder, then Samson would have to perform it. There are no fewer than 27 witnesses, including a Robert the Archbishop (not apparently Canterbury or York, but perhaps a French one).

Inset: seal, in green wax, of the grantor, Roger le Hareng

x. v   Meynell family holdings in Cleveland

BRAWITH IN CLEVELAND

The next three documents were retrieved from among Cumberland deeds where they had been wrongly placed in the old Norfolk House listings. It is assumed that 'Braithwathe' is Brawith in modern spelling, now usually referred to under the name of its neighbour Knayton as 'Knayton cum Brawith'. Here and elsewhere within the Cleveland group of deeds, I originally transcribed the recurring party/witness surname 'Goutone' as 'Gontone', from which it is textually indistinguishable. But 'Goutone' proved to be the proper reading, a local toponymy from nearby township of Cowton. Two of these deeds are dated at Whorlton and one at Stokesley.

YK 51	**Grant and quitclaim:** at Werniltone, Sunday before St. Dunstan,		
		19 May. 30 Ed. I	**1302**

a) Alice, daughter and heir of Robert of Braythewathe
b) lord Richard of Meynille

    Property: lands, tenements, rents, wards, reliefs escheats in the vill' of Braythewathe, and all appurts. of the same vill'

a) grants and releases all her rights that she has, or ever has had, in the property to b) and his heirs

    Witnesses: lord John of Meynille of Midiltone, John of Meynille of Rungetone, Robert Gower, knights, Richard of Scutherskelf, William of Hastinges, Matthew of Semer, Stephen of Goutone, William Gower
    Seal: absent

YK 52	**Lease:**	at Christmas, in the year of Our Lord	**1302**

a) Lord Nicholas of Meynille   b) John son of John of Goutone

    Property: the farm [of the manor] of Braythwathe and 8 bovates of land with a meadow pertaining in the territory of

Braythwathe; with all appurts., liberties, easements that rightfully belong to it, whether near or far

a) leases to b) for 10 years to hold of himself and his heirs at 9 marks annual rent

Witnesses:	lord Robert Gower, knight, Mathew of Semer, Richard of Scutherskelf, William Hasting, Robert of Pothowe, William Gower
Seal:	fragment of impression and legend

YK 53 **Gift:** At Werniltone, Wednesday after Michaelmas **1305**

a) Nicholas of Meynille, son and heir of Nicholas of Meynill
b) Lord John of Bartone of Oswaldkrike and Joan his wife

Property:	the whole manor of Braytwath with 9 tofts and crofts, 8 bovates of land, 11 acres of meadow and pasture for all (the owner's beasts in the moor of Semer; and with all appurts., liberties, commodities and easements)

a) grants to b) and the legitimate heirs of their bodies.

Witnesses:	lord Arnald of Percy, Lord Robert of Furneus, Lord Robert of Colville, Lord Robert Gower, knights, Matthew of Semer, Richard of Scotherskelf, William Gouer
Seal:	absent

YK 54 **Gift:** at Stokeslay, Wednesday after Easter **1350**

a) Nicholas Gower of Sexhow, John Gower his brother, William Gower of Ingelby and John of Mydiltone upon Leven b) John son of Stephen of Bartone c) John of Bartone, knight and Joan his wife

Property:	all the lands and tenements of a) in Braithwathe in Cliveland which once belonged to c)

a) grant to b) an annual rent of 100s. out of the property, with power for b) to distrain for arrears

Witnesses:	John Sturmy, Robert of the How, John son of Cecily of Stokesley, Robert of Chamber
Seal:	two small seals, one with faint impression the other with shield impression

GREAT BROUGHTON

YK 55 **Regrant:**   undated   **?circa 1315**

a) Richard Bolgan of Mekilbrouhtone and Helen his intended wife [*sponsa sua*]   b) Lord Nicholas of Menille
c) Nicholas the son of Lucy who was daughter of Robert Tweng

Property: all the land of a) in Mekel Broughtone

a) regrant the land to b), who is their lord, for him to hold for life, with remainder to c) and the legitimate heirs of his body. In default of such heirs the property shall revert as a whole to the heirs of b)

Witnesses: William of Moubray, William of Hestinges, John Sturmy, John of Sawiltone
Seal: none
Date: a memorandum has been added by a former Norfolk House archivist dating document as before 1217 (the year of William de Mowbray's death at the Battle of Lincoln. However, the script and Meynell family history (see introduction to this section, above) ensure a date of after 1306.

YK 56 **Quitclaim:**   undated   **circa 1315**

a) Richard of Bolgan and Helen his wife   b) lord Nicholas of Menille   c) Nicholas son of Lucy who was daughter of Robert of Tweng

Property: two tofts and two bovates of land in Great Broughton and all other lands and tenements of a) in the same vill'

a) release to b) all their rights in the land for the duration of his life, with remainders as in YK 55 above.

Witnesses: lord John of Eure, William of Moubrai, William of Hestinges, Geoffrey of ?Rasele [very faint], William of Malteby, Richard of Martone, Robert his brother, William Lane, John of Saltone
Seal: small, indistinct impression

YK 57   **Gift:**   undated   **circa 1315**

a) Hugh, son and heir of Thomas of Fennewik of Great
Broctone
b) Nicholas of Menille, knight   c) Richard of Bolgan
d) Nicholas son of Lucy of Twenge

Property: one toft, one croft and one bovate of land with appurts.
in Great Brochtone: the toft and croft lying between the
toft of the abbot of Ryvaus and the toft which b) holds
from c); 17 acres 1 rood of the bovate lying between
the land of said abbott on one side and land which
John the reeve holds of b); and one rood at ?Oveniam
and one rood at Lynberghflat' between land of John
of Saultone and land of the said John the reeve; with
all appurts. in meadows, feedings and pastures

Citing that he got the property from c), a) grants it to b) for life
with remainder to d) and the heirs of his body, etc. as in YK 55-56
above; and to hold of the chief lords by the usual services due.

Witnesses: William of Hestinges, William Moubrai, Matthew
of Semer, John of Gower of Sexhou, Stephen of
Goutone.
Seal: absent

CARLTON, MIDDLETON and TUNSTALL

YK 58-64 below were found with the Cumberland Carleton deeds
(CW 223-232 above) but their content and, particularly, the names of
the witnesses, demonstrate their provenance as part of the Meynell
family estates in Cleveland, North Yorkshire. One of these deeds is
dated at Whorlton.

YK 58   **Grant and quitclaim:** undated   **?circa 1250**

a) John of Lamare   b) Lord Stephen of Meynil, lord of a)

Property: i) Six bovates of land with appurts. in Mideltone which
lie between the land of a) and land of Gilbert son
of John of Mideltone along the S. [*longius sole*]; and
all the furlong [*cultura*] of a) called Galienesflat with
appurts. in Semer ii) the homage and service, both in
esceates, wards and releifs and in all other services due
on two carucates and six bovates of land of Amice of
Tunstall; with appurts. in Tunstall

iii) the homage and service of Reginald Sclipertop for two bovates of land in the same vill'; iv) the homage and service of Walter le Bret for 2 bovates of land with appurts. in Carletone

Recites that b) has paid a) 24 marks of silver in his great need [*in mea maxima necessitate*] and that a) formerly held property i) more successfully from b) [*sicut ego aliquo tempore eam melius et plenius tenui de eodem Stephano*]. Now a) grants to b) all the land and the homage etc. as specified and releases to him all his rights in them.

Witnesses: John of Bulemer, Ralph son of William, Robert of Stutevile, Adam of Hilton, William of Malteby, William Loreng, Richard Waulanc of Stentone, John of Stutevile, Robert of Meynil of Rungetone, Robert Goer, Gilbert of Maltebi, Stephen of Goutone, John of Goulle, Roger of Semer, Robert of Scutherscelf

Seal: absent

YK 59   **Gift:**   undated   **circa 1260**

a) John De la Mare   b) Lord William Fugerest

Property: two bovates in the vill' of Mideltona, that is, the bovates that William son of Richard holds; and two tofts, with two crofts pertaining, which John and Thomas, sons of Mathilda held; with all appurts. within the vill' and without

In return for his homage and service, a) grants to b) and his heirs in fee, to hold of a) and his heirs in fee and by hereditary right without any reservations; with freedom to alienate [sell] to all but religious orders or to Jews, and free of all service except the foreign service that pertains to 2 bovates, on the basis that ten carucates equal a knight's fee [*faciendo omnium forinsecum servicium quantum pertinet ad duas bovatas terre unde decem carucate terre faciunt feudum militis*].

Witnesses: Lord Stephen of Meinil, Adam of Hiltona, William Loringe, Robert of Pothau, William of Lavingtona, Robert of Meinone, Robert Guer, William son of Gilbert, Wala of Mideltona, Gilbert son of John, Simon of Hedleye, Aunsell of Levingtona, William, Arnald, Robert the chaplain

Seal: absent

YK 60   **Gift:**   undated   **?circa 1265**

a) Ralph, son of William Pateman of Bukeby
b) Nicholas of Menille   c) William the Dean

Property: one toft and one croft in the vill' of Karletone, lying between the toft of Robert Gouer of Fayceby and the toft formerly of Simon son of Michael; and all appurts., liberties and easements within the vill' and without Reciting that the property used to belong to c), a) now grants it to b) and his heirs, to hold of a) and his heirs at the annual rent of a pound of cummin, payable at Christmas, in lieu of all other secular services.

Witnesses: lord William of Fougers, lord William of Moubray of ?Camptona, lord Robert of Rungetone, Robert Gouer of Fayceby, Roger Esturmi, William son of Hugh of Fayceby, Robert Bret of Karleton, John of Thorup
Seal: absent

YK 61   **Grant:**   undated   **circa 1265**

a) Robert le Bret of Carleton
b) William son of the priest of Carletone

Property: one toft and croft with appurts. in the territory of Carletona lying next to b)'s own croft towards the S.

a) grants to b) and his heirs and assigns, except men of the Church or Jews, to hold of a) and his heirs free of all secular services anywhere

Witnesses: Robert Guer of Faycesby, Roger Esturmi of the same, John of Torenny of Buskeby, Stephen of Goutone, Geoffrey le Bret of Carletona, Simon his brother of the same, Richard his brother, William ?Dune of Carletone, Henry of Hayckehoued of Buskeby, Adam son of Hugh of Faicesby, John and William his brothers.
Seal: absent

YK 62   **Gift:**   undated   **circa 1300**

a) Simon Breth of Karletune, son of c)   b) Nicholas of Meynyl son of Stephen of Meynyl   c) Geoffrey Breth of Karletune

Property: all the inheritance of a) in Karletune which he received from c) or his forbears, with all homages, esceats, wards, neifs and land pertaining within the vill' of Carletune and without; ½ carucate of land in the territory of Karletune, with all appurts., held by gift from c)

a) grants the properties to b) and his heirs who are to perform foreign service for the Lord of the fee, pro rata for the amount of land held, on the basis that 10 carucates of land equal a knight's fee

Witnesses: lord Peter of Brus, lord William of Percy, lord Robert of Stuteville, lord Adam of ?Myltone, lord William of Feugers, lord Hugh of Eure, lord Robert of Pothow, Robert of Meynyl of Rungetone, Stephen of Gowton, Roger Sturmy, William son of Hugh of Fayceby, Robert Gouer of the same, William of Hastinges of Buskeby

Seal: absent

YK 63 **Grant for life:** at Carleton, Thursday before St. Gregory, 12 March 1 Ed. II 1308

a) Nicholas of Menille b) John son of William the cook c) John son of Juliana of Carletone d) Lord John of Menille of Mideltone

Property: a toft and croft with appurts. in Carletone, with all liberties and easements within the vill' of Carletone and without, near and far

Reciting that a) obtained the land from c), a) now grants it to b) for him to hold for life as a)'s servant; b) shall pay an annual rent of 12d. to d) and he shall perform as much foreign service, should the need arise, as pertains to that amount of land. After the death of b) the land shall revert to a) and his heirs

Witnesses: Robert of Pothowe, Richard of Skutherskelf, Stephen of Goutone, William of Braddefordale of Wherneltone

Seal: absent

YK 64 **Grant:** at Wherletone, 18 April 11 Ed. II 1318

a) Nicholas of Menill, lord of Wherletone b) Robert son of Robert of Midiltone c) Lady Juliana, late wife of Lord John of Menile of Midiltone d) Nicholas son of Lucy of Tweng

Property: one toft and croft in Midiltone

Reciting that c) held the property as her dower, a) grants to b) to hold of a) while a) is alive; and after his death to hold of d) and his heirs; or in default of any heirs of d)'s body, to hold of the rightful heirs of a); and paying an annual rent of 3s. of silver to a), or after his death, to d) and heirs as already specified.

Witnesses: William Hunter, Thomas of Salcok, Thomas of Balleby
Seal: absent

HUTTON [Hutton Rudby]

YK 65   **Agreement:** in the county of York, before noon on 1st March in the 40th week of 32 Henry II   **1186**

a) Reiner the steward of Rannulf of Glanville, sheriff
b) Ernold son of Robert   c) Gilbert of Hottun

Property: i) 20a. of land in the fields of Hotton and of the common of Hara of Hotton, co. York
ii) 7a. of land in Hotton, 4a. next to the bridge on the north and 3a. next to the virgate of b) on the east
iii) a small meadow lying at the head of b)'s land in Faldwarthie
iv) the land of Brigelai

A dispute between b) and c) is heard before a) concerning property i). It is now agreed as follows: b) quitclaims to c) all of property ii). In return c) gives to b) property iii). He also allows b) swine pasture (or mast) for all his own pigs in the vill' of Hotton and wood for his fire to be taken from fallen wood [*de iacente bosco*] in the said Hara of Hotton. Moreover all the demesne animals whatsoever of b), and those of b)'s men, may feed wherever the animals of c)'s men feed. and b) agrees to make a mill next to his house just as there was in the time of c)'s ancestors. Property iv) is granted by b) to c), land over which b) had issued a writ of assize against c), claiming it was common pasture; but now b) and c) may each manure and assart what they wish to take of the common pasture that pertains to their tenements in the vill' of Hotton.

Witnesses: Master Robert of ?Terberge, Master Peter brother of lord Renier, Roger of Bavent, Alan of ?Sinderby, Richard Malevissa, Henry le Noriais, Richard of Hungefort, Ralph of Vado, Thomas son of Thomas, Richard of Wassa, Walter son of Hugh, Walter of Benet [or ?*Bente*] Henry of ?Quornebi, Guy of Lugvilers, William his brother, William the steward, Robert his son, Adam son of Peter, Thomas his brother, Ralph of Beftun, Jordan of the Isle, Samson son of Hugh, Henry son of Dolfin, Robert his brother, Richard of Hudlifte.

Seal: absent

YK 66   **Gift:**   at Hotone, Sunday the octave of Holy Trinity,
15 Ed. II   **1322**

a) William son of Alexander of Hotone   b) Adam of Neuby le Kue and Alice his wife   c) Isabel, mother of a)

Property: one bovate of land and its appurts. in the vill' and territory of Hotone

Citing that the premises were held by c) by right of dower, a) grants to b) and his heirs to hold of the chief lords of the fee. He also grants them an annual rent of 30d. arising from his [other] lands in Hotone [not specified], this to revert to a) if b) both die without heirs of their bodies.

Witnesses: William of Malteby, William of Goutone, John of Pothou, William of Huthewatthe
Seal: tiny fragment

YK 67   **Quitclaim:**   Monday after the Octave of Trinity   **1332**

Parties and property as in YK 66 above.
c) quitclaims to b) her rights in the property

Witnesses: John atte Bek, Alexander Loringe, Reginald Homet [?Honiet]
Seal: none
YK 67 is attached to YK 66

INGLEBY

YK 68   **Gift:**   undated   **circa 1250**

a) Roger lo [sic, ?*le*] Hareng of Engelbi
b) Samson son of Samuel   c) Walter son of Merevin

Property: one bovate of land in Engelbi with its toft and croft and all appurts. belonging to the same land within the vill' and without
Recites that c) used to hold the property from a) for 4 shillings

annual rent. Now, in return for a payment of 4 marks of silver, and for b)'s service, grants the property to b) and his heirs, together with its 4s. annual rent; to hold of a) and his heirs in fee, free from all the services that pertain to a) but with liability to foreign service; six carucates of which make half a knight's fee; and b) is at liberty to sell the land, together with the 4s. annual rent to whoever he wants, clergy or laity, along with its liability to foreign service

Witnesses:	Robert of Maltebi, Walter of Stainesbi, Richard of Hiltone, Roger of Hiltone, Thomas Eggesclif, Roger of Schutherschelf, Ralph of Vade, William of Braidewat, Ylger of Kiltona, Alan of Wiltona, Stephen of Rosel, Robert of Hormanbi, Richard Lofte, Roger of Stainesbi, William of Stainesbi, Raven of Engelbi, Wada of Engelbi, John of Rungtone, William son of Brictun of Jarum, William le ?Waider, Simon Joie, Walter son of Herbert of York, Robert the archbishop, William of Lundon, Stephen Engelram, Robert Pothau, Walter Pothou
Seal:	large seal with animal impression

NEWBY (near Stokesley)

YK 69	**Gift:**	At Neuby, Sunday before St. Margaret the virgin, 20 July, 11 Edward III

1337

a) Silla, formerly wife of William Pother   b) John son of Adam le Keu of Neuby   c) Alice, daughter of a)   d) Thomas du Boys

Property:	two bovates of land and the moiety of one messuage and croft adjoining and all its meadow towards the south of Skelton Kerre, with appurts. in Neuby

Reciting that the property, along with its other moiety of the messuage and two further bovates of land, used to belong to d), a) now grants it to b) and c) and the heirs of their bodies, they paying 26s. to a) as annual rent for her life; and in default of their joint heirs then the property shall remain to the heirs of c) at a rent of 21s; or in default of any heirs of c)'s body, it shall revert to a) and her heirs. Power for a) to distrain for arrears.

Witnesses:	Robert of the How, Thomas Sturmy, Roger of Neuby, Thomas son of Roger
Seal:	faint impression

YK 70   **Gift:**   8 November, 16 Henry VI   **1437**

a) Roger Cotoun and Richard Utley of Gyseburn in Clyveland, co. York   b) Joan late wife of ... c) John Langwathe   d) Thomas Atkynson; Nicholas his brother; Alice wife of John Nykson, their sister

Property: one tenement and two bovates of land in Neuby in Clyveland in the occ. of John Cornford

a) grants to b) to hold for life from the chief lords of the fee; remainders after her death to each of d) and their heirs in turn should the previous one die without heirs, or, in default of any heirs at all, to the rightful heirs of c)

Witnesses: John Dentone, John Boyntone, Richard Wurseley, John Thweyng, esqs., Thomas Gravesone, Robert of the Hall
Seal: fragment with part impression

POTTO

YK 71   **Gift:** undated   **circa 1300**

a) Alice once wife of Hugh *Apesaeger'* [?the beekeeper] of Wernilton, widow   b) Agnes her daughter

Property: one bovate of land in the vill' of Pothou which lies near the ground [*solum*] of two more bovates which a) holds by hereditary right in the same vill' and is next to the land of Robert of Pothou, with all its liberties and easements within the vill' and without, both far and near, in meadows, feedings, pastures, ways, paths, moors and marshes

a) grants to b) and her heirs to hold of herself at the annual rent of 6d.

Witnesses: lord Robert of Meynile, lord John of the sea [*De La Mare*], Alan of Pothou, Robert his brother, John of Goutone, Robert Guer, Robert of Schothereskelf, Alan his brother, Roger Sturmi, Stephen ?the smith, Roger of Pothou, Robert son of Wimme, Hugh of Pothou
Seal: absent

YK 72   **Grant and quitclaim:** undated   **circa 1300**

a) Richard [*missing*]-ard of Pothowe
b) Lord Nicholas of Meynille, Lord of [Whor-]rlton

Property: one toft with the croft and half a bovate of arable land
in the vill' and territory of Pothowe with all liberties
[and easements] within the vill' of Pothowe and without;
the toft and croft lie in length and in breadth between
the toft and croft of John of P-[missing] on one side
and the capital messuage of a) on the other; the half
bovate lies in length and breadth throughout the whole
field of Pothowe between the land of Robert of the
Howe on one side and the land of Emma Levedy
mother of a) on the other

a) releases all his rights in the land to b)

Witnesses: lord John of Meynille of Rungtone, lord Robert
Gower, lord Robert of Scotherskelf, knights, Stephen
of Gowtone, Geoffrey Leuedyman [? same name as
Emma Levedy in property description, ie? Law day
man] Thomas of [?*H*]othaythe]
Seal: absent
There is much surface damage on this deed

YK 73   **Gift:**   undated   **circa 1300**

a) Nicholas of Menylle   b) Robert of Pothowe
c) Stephen Lauerd of Pothowe

Property: meadow called Littelerenge in the territory of Pothowe,
containing five and a half acres, one rood

Reciting that he got the land from c), a) now grants it to b) and
his heirs to hold of himself and his heirs at 1d. rent payable each
Christmas

Witnesses: lord John of Menylle of Rungetone, lord William of
Rasell, lord Robert of Scotherskelf, knights, John of
Menyle of Mideltone, Robert Gouer of Feyceby, Hugh
of Hiltone, Thomas of Semer
Seal: good shield impression and legend, slightly defaced

SEXHOW

YK 74 **Transfer of lordship:** at York, in the feast of St. Martin, 11 November **1288**

a) John of Gouton son of Stephen of Gouton b) William Gouer of Sexhou c) lord Nicholas of Menil

Property: tenements of a) in the vill' of Sexhou

b) has formerly held the property from a) and his ancestors; but a) now now proclaims that, from henceforth, b) shall hold it from c) and shall render to c) whatever services are due, absolved from any dues to a) and his heirs

Witnesses: William of Rosels, John of Menil of Rungeton, knights, Thomas of Semer, Robert of Lelhom, Gilbert of Tunstal, Stephen son of Wymme of Gouton, Geoffrey Levediman

Seal: oval seal, slightly damaged

WHORLTON

YK 75 **Exchange:** undated **circa 1300**
a) Geoffrey Levedyman b) Lord Nicholas of Meynill

Property: i) 2½a. in the field of Wernelton, towards the south, viz. towards Herehow and Suythum, in three furlongs [*cultura*] called Langelandes, Scalestedes and Repedalle; 1½a. and 1r. of land in the field of Wernelton, towards the north, viz., in the park: with all easements and liberties, etc.
ii) 2½a. in the field of Wernelton, towards the south, viz. towards Suythum and Herehou in five furlongs called Hexildsamflat, Thomasflat, Petrusflat, Valays, Roberdbosseflat and Rayschayth; 1½a. and 1r. in the field of Wernelton twards the south viz. towards Moregate in one furlong called Bosseflat: with all easements and liberties etc.

a) grants i) to b) in exchange for ii) from him

Witnesses: John of Meynille, John of Meynille of Hilton, John of Meynill of Rungetone, Thomas of Semer, Roger Sturmy, of Faiceby, Robert of Pothow, John of Gowton

Seal: absent

-oOo-

x. vi Fauconberg lordship: Neville family (and Strangways), 1427-1473

This section and the following section x. vii, contain incomplete snippets of the story that united the Fauconberg dynasty at Skelton and that of the Meynell family at Whorlton during the 15th century.

YK 81   **Quitclaim:** 1 August, 5 Henry VI   **1427**

a) Edmund Hastynges, esq. b) William Nevyll esq., lord of Faucomberg

Property: all those lands and tenements in Merske, Ridker and Uplethome in Cliveland called Downayland

a) releases all rights in the land to b)

Witnesses: Christopher Boyntone, Robert Lambtone, James Toucotes, John Dentone, Thomas Wharrome, William Fulthorpe
Seal: small, with impression

YK 82   **Quitclaim:** 30 January 25 Henry VI   **1447**

a) Katherine late wife of ... b) Lord Robert Playce
c) Lord William Nevylle, Lord of Faucomberge

Property: one messuage with appurts and four bovates of land with appurts. in Skeltone

Citing that the property formerly belonged to b), a) now releases any rights she may have in it to c) and his heirs

Witnesses: none
Seal: absent

YK 83   **Gift:**   12 April 35 Henry VI   **1457**

a) Christopher Conyers of Hornby   b) John Pygott of Ripone

237

c) John Pygott, father of b)   d) William Nevylle, Lord of Fawkenberge

Property: all lands and tenements of a) and b) in Skeltone in Clevelande

Reciting that the premises used to belong to c), a) and b) now grant them to d) and his heirs

Witnesses: Laurence Berwyk, James Towcotes, esq., Robert Wilkynson, Robert del Hill
Seal: two, small, with impressions

YK 84   **Declaration of receipt:** 20 August 12 Edward IV   1473

a) John Berwyk, esq. ... b) Joan, now deceased, formerly wife of a) c) James Strangways, knight

Property: farm of the castle, manor and demesne of Skeltone and all its lands, tenements and rents

Recites that the property belonged to b) by hereditary right and that a) leased it to c) for the term of her life; a) now declares that he has received £10, on top of £30 previously received from c) in payment of the rent owing for the stated term

Witnesses: none
Seal: fragment in two pieces

-oOo-

x. vi Meynell lordship: Darcy family (and Strangways), 1385-1493

NOCTON, co. LINCS.

Though formerly listed as Notton in (West Riding, co Yorks.), from dating evidence and from knowledge of Darcy holdings, I judge it to be Nocton in co. Lincs. Textually, a 'ct' rather than 'tt' is marginally more probable.

YK 85   **Lease for life:** at Knaythe on Christmas Day 9 Richard II   **1385**

a) Lord Philip Darcy, Lord of Menylle
b) John Maunsel and Joan his wife

Property: one messuage and one bovate of land with appurts.
in Nocton which William Forester formerly held
a) grants to b) for the duration of their lives to hold from a) and his heirs according to the customs of the manor and the services due there and by the annual rent of 8s. 6d; b) are liable to keep the messuage in good repair
Witnesses: none   clear impression
The text of part of this deed is damaged by staining

AISLABY (in Whitby)

YK 86   **Lease of woods:** *"En le fest de Nowell"* 14 Richard II   **1390**

a) Mons. Philip Darcy of Menylle   b) Piers (Peter) del Launde
c) John Nikson of Asilby, Thomas *"othe"* Hall of the same and John Yunge of the same

Property: all the wood belonging to a) ?formerly [or ?now] in the tenure of b) and *"le Ragarth"* of Asilby, that is Blapot, le Oldeparke and Symfeld except [*"forpris"*] all the borders of Halhylle and the border of the Oldeparke and the border of Blapot
a) leases to b) and c) at an annual payment of £10 of silver.
Clause re. *"wayveres"* [*?wayneres*], to be taken under supervision of the parker; and *"holyns"* to be left alone; they may enclose the woods at their own cost for 10 years from the feast of the Invention of the Holy Cross next [3 May] but may not cut in the spring period.

239

Witnesses: none
Seal: none
Endorsement: ?concerning the purchase by b) of *tot le spryng [i.e. new shoots, coppice or pollard] ?in the park at Whitby for 3 years beginning Michaelmas 1390*
This deed is in Anglo-Norman French

YEDINGHAM, HESLERTON

YK 87   **Quitclaim:**   Thursday after St. Luke the evangelist,
18 Oct, [*illegible*] ?Richard II   **circa 1377-1399**

a) Joan, ?formerly wife of Thomas of Potthow b) Lord Philip Darcy of Menyll c) Lord Nicholas of Menylle, Lord of Wherltone

Property: lands and tenements in the vill's of [West] Heslerton and Yedyngham

Reciting that she received the property by gift of c) a) now releases all her rights in it to b)
Witnesses: none
Seal: impression

YK 88   **Gift:**   St. Peter in chains, 1 August, 22 Richard II   **1398**

a) Philip Darcy, Lord of Menylle b) John Darcy his son

Property: lands, tenements, rents and services in the vills of Heslerton and Yedingham
a) grants to b) for life to hold of the chief lords of the fee
Witnesses: Richard Darcy, John Gunthorpe, Hugh of Mitforth, Walter Toppecliffe, Geoffrey of Waltone
Seal: plaited parchment rim and deeply recessed impression
NB. YK 87-88 are badly water stained

YK 89   **Gift:**   8 July 8 Hen VII   **1493**

a) James Strangwais, knight, Thomas Darell, James Strangwais of Snetone, Richard Aclom, Thomas Suertes, esqs., Robert Marshalle, gentleman Henry Traham, chaplain and William Hille, yeoman
b) Richard Strangwais, second son of the said James the knight

Property: annual rent of £10 out of the manor of Whorltone and all its lands and tenements in Whorltone in co. York
a) grant to b) for life with power to distrain for arrears
Witnesses: none
Seal: five: three tiny fragments; two with impressions

-oOo-

This neat deed, referred to by the donor as *this indented script*, confers land at Little Silton to Sir Geoffrey Scrope. It is dated at York, on a Sunday in April, on the Feast of St Mark the Evangelist 1333, and is an example of how local business was not always carried out locally. People often used Sundays and feast days in market towns and cathedral cities as natural opportunities to meet up with others and to get things done. Ref. YK91.

x. vii Deeds of the Scrope family of Masham

SILTON

YK 91 **Lease:**   at York, Sunday the feast of St. Mark, 25 April,
7 Edward III   **1333**

a) Oliver son of William of Little Silton
b) Geoffrey le Scrop, knight

Property: one bovate of land and meadow with appurts. in Little
Siltone, with all easements, etc. pertaining

In return for a money payment a) grants to b) for a period of 12
years starting at Michaelmas next

Witnesses: John of Hiltone, Ralph of Siltone, Henry son of Henry
of the same, William his son, Reginald of Collesby.

Seal: impression and legend

FEARBY

YK 92 **Gift:**   at Fegherby, Saturday after St. William, bishop and
confessor, 8 June, 2 ?Ed. III   **? 1329**

a) John [missing-]beke of Fegherby
b) William Papioy of Helay

Property: one toft lying [missing] of Fegherby between land of
the lord of Newyll on the east and ?the sapling toft
[*toftum caprone*] on the west; and one [missing, ?*acre*]
of land in the north field of Fegherby between land
of the lord of Nevell on either side

a) grants the property with all its appurts. to b) and his heirs to
hold of the chief lords of the fee

Witnesses: Ranulf [missing], knight, Alan of Staflay, Geoffrey
Bucktroyte, John of Burghe of Suttone, Stephen
Marchall of Fegherby, Thomas [missing] of the
same

Seal: fine decorative impression

Large parts of this document are missing

UPSALL, SOUTH KILVINGTON AND THIRSK

YK 93 **Agreement:** at Sandhall, Tuesday before St. Denis,
9 October, 3 Edward III   1329

a) Monsieur Geoffrey Scrope
b) Monsieur Geoffrey of Upsale

Property: i) the manor and the woods of Upsale
ii) the woods of Loftscoughe, Gildensdale, Orberghrane
iii) the woods and coppices [les coupiz] which are within Le Conyngger of Upsale called Clivelandgate
iv) the lands of South Kylvyngtone and Tresk'

Recites that actions of waste and trespass have been brought in the King's courts by a) against b) cutting woods in property i), which b) holds for life but which a) stands to inherit. It is now agreed between the parties that a) shall have properties ii), iii) and iv), all of which are parcel of property i). In return a) will drop all actions against b). Moreover, a) shall have the property free of any claims from b)'s heirs and he shall be at liberty to fell what wood he wants, to make enclosures and to cut the coppices when they are 10 years old
Witnesses: none
Seal: fine impression of arms, in decorative surround
This deed is in Anglo-Norman French

AINDERBY STEEPLE

YK 94 **Grant of advowson:** in the Abbot's Chapter House,
8 Jan. 14 Ed. IV   1475

a) William Par, abbot of the Monastery of St. Mary of Jervaux and the Convent of the same
b) Thomas of Scrop, Lord of Scrop of Masham, knight

Property: advowson of the vicarage of the church of Aynderby, with its belfry

a) grants to b) with the addendum that b) shall nominate a suitable parson for the church whenever the living becomes vacant; the heirs of b) to continue making nominations after his death, to a) or his successors.

Witnesses: none
Seal: none
This document was originally catalogued with Westmorland deeds.

-oOo-

YK101 Though it doesn't look much, this deed is of great significance to the present dukedom because it relates to the estate at Carlton Towers in Yorkshire where Miles, father of the present Duke of Norfolk, grew up. As a declaration of receipt of deeds, it catalogues all the charters that pertained to the estate in 1311. Many of these are now lost, so the information contained in this deed is of great value to historians.

x. viii Stapleton family deeds

Nicholas of Stapleton, party to the deed YK 101 below, was a direct ancestor of Edward, the 18th and present Duke of Norfolk and owner of these archives, through the lineage of his paternal grandmother, Mona Stapleton, 11th Baroness Beaumont. This deed was executed in 1311 during the lifetime of Nicholas' father, Miles, who was killed at the battle of Bannockburn in 1314. The lands that are the subject of the deed relate to his inheritance from Laderayne de Brus, his maternal grandmother. One of the manors, Eastburn, had previously come into the possession of Walter of Fauconberg, lord of Rise and Withernwick in Holderness, through his marriage to Agnes de Brus. It was that marriage that brought the Cleveland estates of Skelton and elsewhere (see YK 21-46 above) into the Fauconberg lordship.

Although this whole collection of North and East Yorkshire deeds arrived in the archives of the Duke of Norfolk by a route through the Dacre family, it is nevertheless clear from this deed that there is an earlier, direct link between the Stapleton and Fauconberg families and this must explain the presence of these two deeds in the collection.

Miles, late Duke of Norfolk, was not descended from Lord Miles Stapleton, party to deed YK 102, but from a younger brother. Of the various places mentioned in YK 101, Carlton and Camblesforth descended in the Stapleton/Beaumont line. Carlton hall developed to become Carlton Towers and the late Duke's childhood home.

The places mentioned in this deed are: Thorp Arch and Wilstrop in the West Riding; Easton near Bridlington; Tibthorpe and Eastburn near Driffield; Appleton le Moors (near Pickering); Carlton and Camblesforth near Selby; Walton [?Walton in Ainsty] and the chantry of Tockwith [*Scokirk*].

YK 101   **Declaration as to receipt of deeds:** at Euerwik [presum. York], Tuesday the feast of St. William, 8 June, 4 Edward II   **1311**

   a) Nicholas of Stapelton, one of the heirs of "Laderayne" of Brus
   b) Alan of Folyfayt, attorney to Sir Ducher fitz Henry and Joan his wife   c) Dame Isabel, formerly wife of Sir John of Belewe

Property: an indenture between Peter de Brus the third and the prior of Parkes re 20a. land in Thorpe; a quitclaim of William of Percy re. two marks in rent of the mill of Thorpe; a charter of Stephen son of Roger of Warneby re. 1½a. land in Camelsford; a quitclaim of 'Rabot' son of Walter of Bonyngton re. two bovates of land in Tibthorpe; a deed [*escrit*] of the prior of St. Osewald re. the chantry of Scokirk; a quitclaim of Joan ?late

247

[*iadis*] wife of Richard of Wilesthorpe re. 10 marks of rent in Wilsthorpe; a deed of Roger of Smytheton of 'petit cathal' and a deed of William of Hedonre re two bovates of land in Walton; a quitclaim of Wymer ?late wife of William le Mouner of Thorpe and a quitclaim by Robert le Vavasour to Jowette of Arche; a deed of William Fairfax to Sir Peter of Brus re. land in Walton; a deed of Richard of Wymondthorp made with Sir John of Belewe re. lands in Estbronne [Eastburn]; a deed of Peter of Fontaygnes made with Hugh of ?Colluns re. 40 shillings rent in Carlton and Camelsford; a charter of Robert Alafilie made with Peter the son of Sir Peter of Brus re. a bovate of land in Tibthorpe; an indenture of Walter of Faucomberge re. services in Appleton; a quitclaim of Peter of Fountaygnes to Sir Peter of Brus for 40 shillings rent [place not stated]; a charter of Gerard of Camelsford re. one toft in Camelsford; a charter of Giles, brother of Gerard of Fontaignes re. 1a. land in Camelsford; a quitclaim of Thomas of Beleby to Sir Peter of Brus re. 20 shillings rent in Camelsford; a deed of Richard of Langthuayt made with Sir Peter of Brus re. land in Camelford; one indenture between Sir Peter of Brus and Joan of Cliveland re. tenements in Carlton; a quitclain by Rabot son of Walter to Peter of Brus re. one bovate of land in Tibthorpe; letters patent of Peter of Brus to Henry of Leyrton; an indenture between the Abbot of Selby and Sir Peter of Brus re. one acre of land in Carlton; a charter of Gregory of Skelton and Thomas of Heiton re. tenements in Camelsford; a charter of William of Aton and Thomas of Heiton re. one serf and ½ bovate of land in Camelsford; a deed between Robert, son of Richard of Wilesthorpe and Master Richard of Arnale re. the manor of Wilsthorpe and other tenements; and another indenture between the said Robert and Richard re. the same manor; a deed between Sir Peter of Brus and the Prior of '*la Trante Deverwyk*' [?Holy trinity, York] re. the manor of Wilesthorpe; a quitclaim of Alan of Arches to Adam of Brus re. three '*charies*' of land in Walton; a deed of Peter of Brus; a deed between Sir John of Bellewe and Laurence, son of Thomas of Lancastre re. the manor of Estone; an indenture between Peter of Brus and Richard of Colthorp re. one bovate of land and one toft in Thorpe; an assignment by Sir Peter of Brus to William of Lairton of 100 shillings in rent [place not stated]; a charter of Robert of Tolby and William of Hedon re. two bovates of land in Walton; a quitclaim of Thomas of [illegible] to Sir Peter of Brus re. tenements in Camelsford; a deed of Henry son of

William son of Thomas and Sir Peter of Brus re 2½a.
land in Thorpe; a charter of William of Sansey and
Sir Peter of Brus re. 12 bovates of land in Thorpe; a
quitclaim of Theodore [rendered as *Terry*] of Ribrok
and Sir Peter of Brus re. 73a. and 2 tofts in Thorpe
'Arches; and indenture between Sir Peter of Brus and
the prior of St Oswald re. a chantry at Scokirk; a
charter of the King [Edward I] ?re. the warren of
Carlton [*une chartre le Roy de la gareyne de Carlton*];
an indenture beteen sir John of Bellewe and William
son of Alexander of Walton

a) and b) testify that they have received 43 deeds relating to the
various properties from c), as detailed above. The transactions of
these deeds are not noted.

Witnesses: Sir Robert of Plumptone, Sir John of Walkingham, Sir
Randolf of Blawmusters, Walter of Osgotby, Ralph of
Scottone
Seal: fragment of shield impression

The following deed was one of those catalogued by the *HMC* in
1909 who assumed the place *Westh'* to be West Haddesley (one
of the seats of the Stapleton family). The *HMC* reference was
Box X, 79.

YK 102   Exchange: undated   **?circa 1350**

a) Roger of Wridelesford
b) lord Miles Stapleton, chief lord of a)

Property: i) 14 perches of land in Suallai, with appurts., in Westh';
ii) 14 perches of land in Gillepighel, in the same vill';
iii) all the lands of b) in Suallai, Asshelay, Suallacker
and le Holme in the same vill'

a) grants i) to b) in exchange for ii). He also states that neither
he nor his heirs will claim any rights, including rights of common
on any part of iii) which would prevent b) from holding the land
as a separate close, from putting up permanent fences, and ?from
getting rid of a)'s cattle and effects there.

Witnesses: lords Adam Deveringham and Richard of Berlay,
knights, John of Lasci of Gaitford, Walter Basset and
John of Birne
Seal: absent

-oOo-

x. ix Various parishes

The following five deeds demonstrate no clear link with any of the previous categories. It is hoped that those with local knowledge may be able to suggest a provenance.

CEDDRICH [?Catterick]

YK 103   **Quitclaim:** at Erdcleye, Sunday after St. Edmund the martyr, 20 November, 5 Ed. II   **1311**

a) Peter Marck of Ceddriche
b) Walter of Colingham

    Property: all that pightle (*phittelum*) called Doullemad phittel in the vill' of Ceddrich

Citing a deed previously made, a) now quitclaims to b)

    Witnesses: John of La More, John of ?Everele, William of Cameseford, Walter of Mandreffe, John Ede
    Seal: none

AMPLEFORTH

YK 104   **Grant and quitclaim:** at Oswaldekirke, Saturday after St. Gregory, 12 March,   **1326**

a) Alice, once wife of Hugh of Nonewick, widow
b) Geoffrey of Fyngale   c) Geoffrey of the Bekes
d) Adam of London of Ampleford

    Property: i) all the assart of Clarice in the field of Ampleford
               ii) all of another assart in the field of Ampleford; the two together being 23 acres of arable

Recites that a) held i) by demise from c) and that ii) once belonged to d); and that b) held both of them by demise from Hugh, former husband of a); a) now grants both properties to b) and quitclaims to him all her rights in them, for him to hold for ?both their lives [*ad totam vitam nostram*], rendering a) one rose in season [*tempore rosarum*].

Witnesses: Thomas of Ectone [or ?Ettone], Richard of Pykering, William Starre, John of Neutone, Robert of Outone
Seal: slightly damaged at rim: bird impression in decorative border

YK 105   **Grant and quitclaim:** at York, Wednesday the Annunciation, 25 March, 1 Ed. III   1327

Parties as in YK 104
Property: all assarts of Clarice in the field of Ampleford on the soil of Oswaldekirk

a) grants to b) and his assigns

Witnesses: Richard of Huntynton, William of Horneby of York, John of ?Heres
Seal: absent

GREAT HABTON
[near Castle Howard]

YK 106   **Quitclaim:** at Great Abytone, Wednesday after Christmas 42 Ed. III   1369

a) Juliana Lote of Great Abytone
b) John of Abytone son of Roger of Abytone

Property: 28 acres of arable land and a certain vacant place with liberty of one fold for 100 sheep in the vill' and field of Great Abitone

a) quitclaims to b)

Witnesses: Edmund of Abytone, Walter Crisp, Robert Crisp, Nicholas Beverreche [?*Benerreche*] Robert Trumpe
Seal: small, damaged; stag impression

CATTON

YK 107   **Order for release of goods:** at Chester, 18 January 14 Henry IV   1413
a) The King   b) Thomas Wyllesthorpe, Robert of Wheldale, William Hatterberythe, James Buk, Robert Danyson, Walter Hatterberythe,

William Habley   c) Robert Jackson of Fangfosse,   d) Thomas of Meysham and John of Huxley of co. Chester,   e) William Fulthorpe, esq., Richard Norton, Robert Rudstan, John Gledhowe, John Clerk, King's bailiffs,   f) Ven. father in Christ, Thomas Langley, Bishop of Durham, Thomas Erpyngham, esq., Richard Norton, master John Rykyhnhale and Thomas Petlyng, clerks   g) Louis [*Ludovic*] del Pantre of Pocklyngton, John Crosseby, marshall, Richard Carlell, William Wharrom and Robert of Langton of Pocklyngton

Property: manor of Catton co. York, held of the Palatinate of Chester

In a dispute between between b) and c) concerning the property, the latter has been detained at Chester by d), on bail for forty days with e) and f) being his pledges, to appear on next Tuesday fortnight. It is judged, however, that goods of c) have been unjustly detained by b) and, ?at the complaint of g), the King now therefore orders b) to deliver them to c)

Witnesses: none
Seal: none

-oOo-

THE DUKE OF NORFOLK'S DEEDS
AT ARUNDEL CASTLE

CATALOGUE 1   PART II

THE POST-MEDIEVAL SERIES OF DEEDS

Dacre Estates in Northern Counties

Contents: Part II

1. *A general introduction to the post-medieval deeds*

The context of the post-medieval deeds at Arundel Castle has been explained under *The deeds collections and their previous catalogues* in the general introductions to this publication. Here I am attempting to explain the post-medieval deeds in more detail and to discuss some of the strategies for dealing with them. Although only the deeds relating to the Dacre family inheritance are presented in this catalogue, the collection is being tackled as a whole. The listing of material for other counties is ongoing and will be published in due course.

Amounting to approximately 8,500 documents and relating to 19 different counties, the post-medieval deeds were hand-listed by Dr. Steer under the prefix **D/-** and **STD/-** during his work at Arundel Castle. These lists remained in manuscript at the Castle where they have provided an invaluable source for answering research enquiries. But without being typed up, or published in any way, the source has been under-used. Researchers planning a trip to Arundel have been inconvenienced by not being able to assess the potential of the material in advance and have had to rely on our personal knowledge of the collections in suggesting relevant items.

The handlists of the **D/-** and **STD/-** collections were mainly composed from the information contained on the old bundle labels. The format for each entry is that of a bundle list: covering refs., general description, no. of docs., covering dates. Some items were investigated individually by Dr. Steer, with details such as field names being given, but this is patchy, due, I imagine, to the magnitude of the task. Back in the 1960s and 1970s when the lists were compiled, the 8,500 post-medieval deeds were a mere element of the entire Arundel archive in which other, more important, papers were prioritised for the published catalogues.

The bundles in the **D/-** series existed when the archive was at Norfolk House where they were locatable by shelf reference. One suspects that many bundles were haphazard creations whose mysterious origins had become too sacrosanct to question. Once I had crossed this threshold myself, it became clear that there were many inconsistencies within bundles. Contents did not always tie up with labels. Deeds which clearly belonged together, as different parts of the same conveyance, could be found in two or more different bundles. Many of the bundles contained diverse and unrelated material which simply could not be covered by a brief catalogue entry. I have tackled these problems as follows.

Where a bundle consists of unrelated material I have created new itemised catalogue entries, enabling the piece to be slotted in at a sensible place in the catalogue. Bundles with early deeds which merit an individual entry have been treated in the same way. To avoid confusion where research in the collections has already been published, the previous reference numbers have generally not been altered. Additionally, I have retained Dr. Steer's style of presentation, even where the entry now relates to a single document rather than to a bundle. However, as the overall cataloguing progresses, different strategies have seemed appropriate for different groups of deeds. For some, an expanded form of bundle listing will suffice. For others, itemisation is better. For the Dacre/Howard family deeds listed here it was possible to make itemised entries because the collection is so small.

Cleaning, re-packaging and re-boxing the post-medieval collections has gone hand in hand with the cataloguing. Whereas the **STD/-** deeds had received some basic cleaning and re-packaging before I came to Arundel, the far larger **D/-** collection had not. I am therefore doing this as I go along, splitting unwieldy bundles and flattening items where appropriate. While this might slow down the cataloguing results a little, it is an absolutely unavoidable process. The outer dirt on the bundles was so loose that we could not produce the deeds to researchers without cleaning them. I was perplexed by the amount of sooty dirt on these archives until I discoverd that lighting fires to keep out the damp in the muniment room was considered an essential part of the proper care of the ducal archives in the mid-19th century. But at least the archivist was advised to put the fire out before he went home at night!*

As with the medieval deeds series, the spellings of all places mentioned in the property description are rendered in the catalogue as found in the original. A gazetteer *Introduction 4*, below, helps identify the modern locations, where known. Spellings of the home parishes of parties to deeds are rendered into modern form after 1650. Keeping Dr. Steer's numbering means that the deeds cannot be presented in numerical order, but to assist research, a concordance, relating deeds numbers to pages in the catalogue, follows in *Introduction 3* below.

Finally, as observed in the general introductions at the start of this publication, the distinction between '*medieval*' and '*post-medieval*' deeds is imprecise. It reflects the overall impression of original bundles. Inevitably, a few medieval and Tudor deeds have been found in the post-medieval bundles. They have been kept with their bundles, with the result that the 'post-medieval' series in fact runs from 1486 and includes Dacre family as well as Howard family deeds.

It remains to say, of course, that much more could be done, both in cleaning and conservation, and in cataloguing. But like Dr. Steer before me, I am anxious to get some sort of list in print before I pass on. Additions and refinements can wait for my successors.

Heather Warne, June 2005

---

* Arundel Castle Archives FC132

2. *The Greystoke Estate in Howard family hands*

These deeds relate to properties inherited by the Howard family from estates formerly belonging to the Dacres, lords of Greystock. Commencing in 1486, they dovetail in with and follow on from the medieval and Tudor titles in Catalogue 1, part I above. They mainly relate to the chief holdings of the de Greystoke, Dacre and Howard families in Cumberland and Westmorland. Lesser properties within the estates occur towards the end of the catalogue in relation to sales and leases. As with other collections within the Duke of Norfolk's archives, these deeds were, at some time in the past, artificially severed from others in their true category. There is therefore some anomalous overlap with Catalogue 1, part 1 above.

The Dacre family estates in Cumbria were centred on their two lordships, Greystoke and Gilsland; in Northumberland at Morpeth and in North Yorkshire at Hinderskelf (Castle Howard). After the death of their brother, George Dacre, in 1569 the estates were partitioned between three sisters Anne (b. 1557), Mary (b. 1564) and Elizabeth Dacre (b. 1565). All three women were contracted to marry Howard brothers, but Mary's death before her age of consent caused a reshuffle of the partition between Anne and Elizabeth. The lordship of Gilsland around Naworth Castle, together with Morpeth and the Yorkshire estates, came to Elizabeth. Her marriage to William Howard, a younger son of the 4th Duke of Norfolk, founded the dynasties of the Earls of Carlisle at Naworth and Castle Howard and the Howards at Corby Castle. The archives, including title deeds, of these estates are in the keeping of the Earls of Carlisle at Castle Howard, at Durham University Library and at Cumbria Record Office.[*]

The Greystoke barony came to Anne Dacre and, by her marriage to Philip Howard in 1571, descended to her great-grandson Thomas who was restored to the Norfolk Dukedom in 1660 as 5th Duke.[†] Following his death in 1677 the ownership of the estate was contested between his brother Henry, who became 6th Duke, and a younger brother Charles. The latter cited a settlement made in Charles' favour in 1647 by his grandfather. The estate was awarded to him by chancery decree in 1682 but this decision was reversed in 1683. Finally, in 1685 it was reversed again and Charles Howard's future at Greystoke was secured.[†] These difficulties arose, not from personal greed on the part of the 6th Duke, but from his (successful) quest to restore the finances of the Dukedom following many years of attainder and overspending. Deeds and

---

[*] For the Earls of Carlisles' archives see: Guides to sources for British History, 10, Principal family and estate collections: family names A-K, pp 90-91. For the Howard of Corby archives, see Cumbria (Carlisle) Record Office Catalogues, ref. D/HC.

[†] Litigation papers re. the estate in this period are at Arundel Castle, ref. MD1090 and GL Boxes 6 and 7 (uncatalogued but accessible).

settlements relating to the dispute are on pp. 278-279 of this catalogue. The estate remained with Charles Howard's descendants until after the 11th Duke's death in 1815, after which they were passed to a cadet branch of the family.

Many of the deeds catalogued here are internal family settlements and they are supplemented by further material in the *Family deeds catalogue* (see *Introduction 2 ii*, to Part I above). In such a high status family as that of the Duke of Norfolk there were many circumstances when it was decided to package together a parcel of estates for a marriage settlement, or for securing a debt, and so on. This means that the Greystoke estates get mentioned frequently in such packages - but there are no new property descriptions. It is often a difficult decision as to whether an item properly belongs with the 'Family' series or with a county series and there is inevitably some overlap. The diligent researcher wanting more information about *The family deeds catalogue* may apply in writing to the Archivist at Arundel Castle.

---

* G. Brenan and E.P. Statham, The House of Howard, Vol II (1907), pp 584-6.

Introduction 3

A NUMERICAL CONCORDANCE

A numerical concordance is provided for this part of the catalogue because it is not possible to alter the numbering system allocated by Dr. Steer. His catalogue was not presented in numerical sequence and my system of presentation of the material has mixed this up even more.

Ref.	Page	Ref.	Page	Ref.	Page
D4585-4588	286				
D6688-6689	286	D7116-7118	277	D7136	282
D6966-6989	268	D7119-7120	279	D7137	278
D7021	279	D7121-7122	273		
D7077	281	D7123-7124	274	D7138-7139	284
D7078	275	D7125-7126	283	D7140-7142	285-6
D7079	283	D7127-7128	275	D7174	272
D7111-7112/1	269	D7129-7130	276		
D7112/2-7113	270	D7131	279		
D7114	272	D7132	280	**STD** 69/4-6	277
D7115	281	D7133	278	**STD** 170	270

Introduction 4

The places mentioned in this gazetteer should be compared with those for the gazetteers for the baronies of Greystoke and Burgh in Part I above. Spellings are rendered in modern form where location is certain and in italics where in doubt. Italics follow in brackets where original spellings are very different from the modern.

A BRIEF GAZETTEER

Cumberland:

Aikton
Ainstable
Array /Arey Parks
   (?near Gowbarrow)
Beaumont
Berrier
Biglands
Blakhall (in St. Cuthbert
   without)
Bleatarn in Irthington
   (*Blaterne*)
Bowness on Solway
Boustead Hill
Brunskathe (near Burgh
   by Sands)
Burgh by Sands
Cardurnock
Carlisle
Carlton
Cleator
Crosby
Cumcatch (in Brampton)
Dalston
Downehull (?in Aikton)
Drumburgh
Drumleaning
Dykesfield
Easton
Etterby

Cumberland cont.

Fingland and
   Finglandrigg
Gamelsby
Gowbarrow
Glasson
Great Blencow
Greystoke
Grisedale (and forest:
   W. of Keswick)
Gill
Gillcambon
High Ireby (*High Jerby*)
Johnby
Kirkandrews on Eden,
   (*Kirkanders*)
Kirklinton (*Kirklevington*)
Kirkoswald
Lancroft (?clerk's error
   for Lanercost)
Langrigg
Laverickstone
   (near Oughterby)
Laithes
Longburgh (near Burgh)
Matterdale
Melmerby
Moorhouse
Motherby

Cumberland cont.

Murrah
Newbiggin
Newlands
Parton
Penrith
Renwick (*Ramwicke*)
Rockliffe and its castle
Scalehouses
Skelton
Stockdalewath
   (*Stokelwath Magna*)
Sowerby Row
Sparket (*Sparkhead*)
Stainton
Staffield
Talkin
Tallentire
Thistlewood
   (*Thistlethwaite*)
Thornby and
   Thornby Moor
Thursby
Ulton (?Oulton)
Ullesby
Wampool
Whitrigg and Whitrigglees
Wiggonby

Lancashire: (p.270-72)

Hutton
Roose

Northumbs:

Benridge (p.269)
Morpeth (p.272)
Ulgham (p.272)

Notts:

Worksop (p.283)

Salop: (p.271-3)

Aston
Cotton
Dyches/Diches
Edstaston
Hanwood

Salop cont.

Hinstock
Horton
Loppington
Lowe
Overley

Salop cont.

Slaype
Standbroke/Stanbroke
Steyll
Tilley
Wem

Westmorland:

Appleby
Barton
Drybeck
Dufton
Deepdale

Westmorland cont.

Farleton
Farleton Knot
Glencoyne
Hoff

Westmorland cont.

Orton
Patterdale
Sandwick
Ullswater

Yorkshire:

Amotherby
Belby
Benton
Blesthroppe
Brounom/
  Burnholme
Butterwick
Bysydefalde
Calottes
Croft In Teesdale
  (*Croftethwaite*)
Denton
Dringhoe
Duggleby
Etton
Fangfoss
Faram (?Fairholme
  in Swine)
Flixton
Folkton (*Folton* -
  near Scarborough)

Yorkshire cont.

Ganthorpe
?Gowerdale in Dale Town
  (*Gobedalle*)
Grimston (*Northgrimston*)
Grimthorpe
Howgate Parva
Howike
Henderskelf
Hyngham
Low Hutton (*Hutton upon*
  Darwen)
Malton
Millington
Meltonby
Molescroft near Beverley
Morton upon Swale
Nidd
Nunburneholm (*Brounom/*
  Burnholme)
Osmotherley
  (*Osmonderley*)
Raisthorpe (*Raystrop*)
Rillington (*Relyngton*)

Yorkshire cont.

Rotherham (p.278)
Scagglethorpe
  (*Skargilthorpe*)
Scampston
Sherburn
  (nr. Scarborough)
Sledmere
Slingsby
Staxton
Terrington
Thrintoft (*Thirntoft*)
Thornton le Moor
Thorpe Bassett
  (alias *Thornepassett*)
Waplington
Wharram le Street
?Welburn (*Welbury*)*
Wigganthorpe
Yapham
Youlthorpe

---

* re. Welbury: Dr. Christopher Ridgway, archivist at Castle Howard, to which many of these deeds relate, informs me that the deeds in his keeping mention a Welburn as well as Welbury and he therefore assumes that Welburn near Malton and Welbury near Northallerton were both part of their former estates.

STD 69/1 Anne Dacre and her sister Elizabeth were joint heiresses of all the family estates. By her marriage to Philip, 13th Earl of Arundel, she brought her half, including Greystoke Castle itself, into the Howard family and, after the restoration of their full titles, to the Norfolk dukedom. As a widow in 1611 she drew up several deeds to secure the future of her estates, in which this rare example of her signature was found. D7174 in this catalogue is a part of the overall transactions of that date. The settlements themselves are in the Family Deeds catalogue because Greystoke was only one element of her overall possessions.

i. Chief family properties

D 7111   Exemplification of a Common Recovery by Robert Bothe, clerk, William Roukeshawe, clerk, Alex Rokeby, clerk and William Wellys, clerk against Sir Ralph Greystok of Greystok, of:

> Manors of Croftethwayte and Morton upon Swale, co. York; manors of Hilderskelf and Gaunthorpe, co. York; the manor of Nyde, co. York; ten messuages in Benrygge, co. Northumbs; manor of Dufton and two messuages in Appleby, co. Westmorland.

Great seal formerly appended, but absent.

1 doc., July 1486

D 7112/1   Grant, at Carlisle, by a) Sir Thomas Dacre, knight, lord of Dacre and of Graystok and Elizabeth his wife, cousin and heir of Ralph Graystok, lord of Graystok to

b) Christopher Dacre, esq., Cuthbert Conyers, doctor of decrees of Karliol' Archdeaconry and William Husband, master of the College of Graystok, of:

> Manors of Westlevynton, Brunskathe, Drumburghe, Fyndlane, Eston and Bownes together with the advowson of the church of Bownes and the third part of the manor of Beamount; and the manors of Etterby, Blatern', Cumcatche, Talkyn, Crosby and Blakhall in Cumberland; and all other his tenements and appurtenants in the same place.

a) grant the premises to b) to hold as trustees of the will appended below, specifically with regard to the chief lordships and their customary services owed. They appoint Thomas Bendeley and William Skelton as their attornies to deliver seisin

Witnesses: Simon Senofe, prior of the cathedral church of the Blessed Mary of Karliol', John Legh, constable of the castle of Karliol', John Myres, Robert Share and Richard Blackburn; and **signature** of Thomas Dacre.

1 doc., 22 August 1513.

D 7112/2 Original Will of Sir Thomas Dacre, appended to **D7112/1** above.
Clauses include:

> a canon to say mass in St. George's aisle of Lanercost
> Priory at Lord Dacre's death, with prayers for his
> Dacre ancestors who founded the priory, etc. (details)
> and 8 marks annually to be levied out of Bowness
> and Cardrunnock manors to pay for the same and
> from lands and tenements in Etterby; with provision
> for 'mortifying' these premises [keep them thus bound
> in mortmain] in the case of his sudden death at the
> hand of the Scots, or otherwise; further provision for
> members of Lanercost Priory out of the parsonage of
> Bowness; an annuity of £28 4s. out of the same premises
> for Dame Isabel Harryngton, widow; Christopher
> Dacre, brother of the testator to enjoy his lands and
> tenements in Westlevinton, Brunskath and Blaterne for
> life; Nicholas Harryngton to have 10 marks rent from
> the same; to his son and executor William Dacre, all
> his plate and hangings, especially 'a boke signed with
> myne awne hande', for life, with remainder to the lords
> of Kirkoswald Castle; Christopher Dacre and William
> Husband, master of Graystoke College to look after
> his son William, to provide for his widow Elizabeth out
> of the revenues of Kirkoswald Castle and to devote
> all the 'Whitmonday farm' [rents] at Kirkoswald to
> the finishing of the 'werkes of Kirkoswald'.

Signature: of Thomas Dacre
1 doc., 22 August 1513

STD 170 Royal grant by King Henry VIII to his dear and faithful servant,
Sir Humfrey Radclyffe:

> Manors, messuages, lands, mills, fisheries, feudal dues,
> [etc.], in the vills and fields of Depedale and Patterdale,
> Penrith, Carleton and Farleton in cos. Westmorland,
> Lancashire and Cumberland.

The premises were formerly the possessions of William Lancaster,
gentleman who had forfeited them by attainder; to hold to Radclyffe
as the 20th part of one knight's fee.
Decorative heading; fragment of Great Seal.
1 doc., 1544.

D 7113 Final concord between Thomas Dacre, lord of Dacre, Gyllesland
and Graistocke, and Elizabeth his wife, plaintiffs, against Thomas
Carus, Serjeant at Law, William Rosewell esq., Solicitor General,
Thomas Preston, esq. and Laurence Banaster, gent, deforciants
of:

i) The Barony and Castle of Hynderskelff alias Hylderskelf with the liberties, franchises and manors of Hynderskelf, Thornepassett alias Thorpebassett, Burnholme, Grymthorpe, Welbury, Thornton in le More, Nydd, Mortone, Thirnetofte, Slyngesby, Hutton uppon Darwen', Skargilthorpe, Burnholme, Butterwike and Fangfosse, with the park of Hynderskelf and 500 messuages, 600 tofts,, 500 cottages, 10 mills, 10 dovecotes, 600 gardens, 400 orchards, 8000a. land, 3000a. meadow, 10,000a. pasture, 3000a. wood, 10,000a. moor, 10,000a. furze and heath and £50 rent in [parishes as above]; and also in Faram, Wygenthorpe, Teryngton, Gaunthrop, Amotherby, Malton, Relyngton, Skamiston, Bysdefalde, Northgrymston, Quarram in le Strete, Dogleby, Shurborne, Staxton, Flyxton, Folton, Benton, Sledmere, Drynghowe, Mollescrofte without Beverley, Etton, Bylby, Waplyngton, Millington, Youlthrop, Meltingby, Yapham, Raystrop, Howgate Parva, Gobedalle, Unkelby, Hyngham, Grymston, Blesthroppe, Osmonderley, Calottes, Croftwhaite and Howewike and the advowson of the churches of Thorpebassett and Folton, all in co. York; and one messuage and garden in the City of York

ii) The Barony and Castle of Graystocke and the manors of Graystocke, Skelton and Laythes and the forests or free chases of Flastowarde and Grysdall with their liberties; and the feedings of Gowberra with apurts; and 300 messuages, 300 cottages, 12 mills, 400 gardens, 300 orchards, 5000a. land, 3000a. meadow, 6000a. pasture, 8000a. wood, 10,000a. furze and heath, and 20 free rents in Graystocke, Skelton, Laythes, Eyilcambon' [or -bouer], Newbyggyn, Gyll, Grysedall, Berear, Sowerby, Newlands, Stokelwathe Magna, Staneton, Motherbye, Matterdale, Wethermealock and Sparkehed; and the avowsons, gifts, etc. of the churches of Graystocke and Skelton in co. Cumberland.

iii) the Barony of Dufton with its liberties and franchises and the manor of Dufton with its appurts. and 40 messuages, 20 cottages, 2 mills, 40 gardens, 30 orchards, 1000a. land, 500a. meadow, 2000a. pasture, 1500a. wood, 2000a. moor, 2000a. furze and heath, 3 free rents and rent of a pound of pepper, with appurts. in Dufton and Appleby, and advowson of the church of Dufton in co. Westmorland

iv) The manors of Weme, Loppington and Hynstocke with their appurts and 300 messuages, 400 cottages, 5 mills, 8 dovecotes, 300 gardens, 200 orchards, 1500a. land, 1000a. meadow, 2000a. pasture, 1000a. wood,

> 1000a. moor, 1000a. furze and heath and 100 marks in rent, with appurts. in Weme, Tyllula alias Tylley, Aston, Edstaston, Cotton, Standbroke, Horton Lowe and Dythes Newton, Oberley, Steyll, ?Slape, Hanwood and Loppington, and the advowson of the church of Weme in co. Salop

The deforciants acknowledge that all the various baronies, manors and other premises above are the right and inheritance of the plaintiffs and they release and quitclaim them to the plaintiffs; who immediately transfer them all to the deforciants to hold during the life of Elizabeth Dacre.

1 doc., Hilary term 1565

D7114   Final concord between John of Olebury, parson of the church of Eure and Walter of Lancaster, clerk, plaintiffs, and William of Craystock, knight, deforciant, of:

> The manor of Brounom with appurts in co. York; the manors of Morpath and Ulgham with appurts in co. Northumberland;

It being agreed that the deforciants hold 'two parts of two parts' [a sixth each] of the manors of Craystock, Brounom and Morpath by gift from the plaintiff, they grant them to him and his heirs; they also acknowledge a third part of the same manors, which Elizabeth the former wife of Ralph fitz Rauf held as her dowry, and another third part which Alesia, former wife of Ralph of Neville held as her dowry, which devolve to the deforciants after the deaths of Elizabeth and Alesia, are the hereditaments of the plaintiff. Contingent remainders are detailed should the plaintiff die without heirs male.

1 doc., 12 Feb 1574

For a grant of free warren in Cumberland and Westmorland in 1558 by the Crown to Thomas, earl of Arundel and Surrey , see **D7011** in *Catalogue 6, Family deeds and settlements* (in preparation)

D7174   Exemplification of a fine by Sir Edward Carrill, John Holland, esq. and Robert Cansfield, esq., plaintiffs *v* Thomas Calston, esq. and Mary, his wife, deforciants, of:

> 24 messuages, 10 cottages, 24 tofts, 100a. land, 100a. meadow, 50a. pasture, 20a. wood, 300a. furze and heath, 1000a. moor, 100a. marsh, and £11.10s.4d. rent in Hutton and Roose [co. Lancs.], and in Alton and Sowerbie [Soweby], cos. Cumberland and Westmorland.

1 doc., 9 October 1611.

NB. Several Family trusts were made around this time, many of which include Cumberland and Westmorland premises, see *Catalogue 6: Family deeds and settlements* (in preparation); and see illustration on page 268.

**D7121-
7122**

Release, and counterpart, and covenant to levy a fine by Randall Dacre, son and heir of Francis Dacre, decd., who was youngest son of the late Rt. Hon. William Dacre of Graistocke and Gilsland to The Rt. Hon. Thomas, Earl of Arundel and Surrey, Earl Marshall of England, one of His Majesty's Hon. Privy Council:

i) The barony or lordship of Brough alias Burgh upon Sands; and manors of or lands and tenements in, Burgh, Longburgh, Dikesfield, Bowstedhill, Murhouse, Ayckton, Wyginby, Thorneby, Thorneby Moore, Parton, Downehull, Dromlening alias Dromlyning, Biglands, Gamelsby, Laythes, Wampoole, Lavereckstone, Etterby, Thursby alias Thurisby, Bemond alias Bemont, Kirkanders, Rowcliffe and the Castle of Rowcliffe, Westlyvington alias Westlevinton alias Westlenton, Fingland, Finglanrigg, Cardronock, Drumbrugh alias Drombugh and its castle, Bownes alias Bowlenes, Glasson alias Glassen, Whittrigg, Whittriglees, Easton alias Eston, and the City of Carlisle, all in Cumberland

ii) The barony or lordship of Graistocke alias Craistock with its castle and with all its rights and members; and manors of, or lands and tenements in Graistocke, Motherby, Stainton, Skelton, Matterdale alias Madirdale, Grisdale, Wethermelock alias Wethermelott, Sparkhead, Berrier, Newbiggin, Thistlethwate alias Thistlethwayte, Melmorby, Penrith alias Pearith, Carleton, Ullesby, Staffull, Kirkoswold alias Keyrkeiswald, Glassonby alias Glassenby, Ramwicke, Skalehouses and Ainstableth, all in Cumberland

iii) Manors, lands, tenements and hereditaments in Hoffe, Dribeck, Orton, Glencoine, Barton, Dufton, Patterdale alias Patrikdale, Depedale, Farleton, Farleton Knott, Barton, Sandwick, Ulleswater, with its fishing, and Appleby, all in Westmorland.

iv) Barony or lordship of Wem with all its rights, members and appurts in the County of Salop with manors, lands, tenements and hereditaments in Hoppington [sic, should be 'Loppington'], Hinstock, Tillula alias Tilly, Asten, Edstaston, Cotton, Stanbroke, Horton, Lowe and Diches, Newton, Overly, Steyll, Slaype and Hawood, all in Salop

Dacre agrees that the fine shall be levied to the use of Thomas, earl of Arundel and his heirs [thereby ratifying the Howard family claim to these estates resulting from the marriage of Ann Dacre and St. Philip Howard]

One counterpart is signed *Ranulphe Dacre* and the other *Arundell Surrey*, each with the personal seal of the signatory.

2 docs., 4 Feb 1633/4

[Ranulphe died later the same year, aged 26 and unmarried, the last of his line. He was buried at Greystoke on 27 December 1634, having been conveyed there from London at the Earl of Arundel's expense.]

D7123   Lease for ten months, from previous Michaelmas, by Henry Frederick, earl of Arundel and Surrey to John Lightfoot of Grays Inn, Middx., esq. of:

> i) Baronies of Greystock and Burgh with the castles of Greystock, Drombrough and Rowcliffe and manors of Burgh, Beamond, Kirkanders, Westlevington, Bownisse, Drombrough, Whiterigg anad Whiteriggleas, Lancroft, Aynithorne, Cardronnock, Glasson, Easton, Fingland, Rowcliffe, Etterby, Ayketon, Thursby, Graystock, Motherby, Stainton, Waterdale [*sic*: Matterdale], Grisedale, Wethermelock, Sparkehead, Berryar and Newbiggin; and the forests of Matterdale and Grisedale with their rights, members and appurts; all in the above places and in Gouborow, Array, Murray, Thistlewaite, Penrith and Gill in Cumberland

> ii) Manor of Dufton and advowsons of the churches of Dufton and Orton and lands, etc., in Dufton, Orton, Glenconie, Barton, Patterdale, Deepedale, Sandwick, Ullswick and Ullswater in Westmorland; with free fishing in the water of Ullswater in Westmorland

[This deed is a preliminary to D7124 below and not a true lease]

1 doc., 20 March 1647

D7124   Limitation and declaration of trusts by Henry Frederick, Earl of Arundel and Surrey, with trustees James Stewart, duke of Richmond and Lennox, earl of March, Henry, earl of Kingston upon Hull and marquess of Dorchester, Edward, lord Howard, baron Escrick and Sir Thomas Hatton of Long Stanton, co. Cambs.

Properties as in D7123 above

Reciting another deed of the same date [**not present**] it is agreed that the trustees shall hold the properties for 200 years in trust for

Henry Frederick, earl of Arundel and Surrey, for life with various remainders (specified) to secure the inheritance
1 doc., 21 March 1647

D7078   Deed to raise a tenant to the precipe and exemplification of a fine decreed in the court of King's Bench, Trinity Term 1647, between John Lightfoot esq. and John Pollard, gentleman, plaintiffs *v.* Henry Frederick, earl of Arundel and Surrey, deforciant, regarding:

> i) Baronies of Greystoke and Burgh as in D7123 above
> ii) Manor of Dufton, 60 messuages, 100 cottages, 2000a. land, 1000a. meadow, 10,000a. pasture, 1000a. wood, 2000 a. furze and heath, 4000a.; Ullswater fishing rights, and 60s. rent in Glencoyne, Barton, Patterdale, Deepdale, Sandwick, Ullswick and Ullswater

The Earl's previous gift to the plaintiffs and their heirs is acknowledged in consideration of their payment of £1000
2 docs., June-July 1647

**D7127-
7128**   Assignment and declaration by the Hon Charles Howard, esq. of Naworth in Cumberland and Richard Onslow of West Clandon in Surrey

Recites that by the deed [ie the missing one - see D7124 above] of 21 March 1647 the trustees were empowered to raise the sum of £8000 out of the Greystoke estates [as in D7123 above] and pay it to Lady Katherine Howard, eldest daughter of Henry Frederick, Earl of Arundel and Surrey; and that they raised £2850 out of the sale of the manor of Dufton; and a further £852 9s. 8d. has been raised out of the profits of the Barony; and that by deed of 15 July 1656 involving Elizabeth, countess dowager of Arundel, Lady Katherine Howard, Chaloner Chute of Middle Temple, and others, the remainder of the barony lands, except Dufton, were assigned to Charles Howard of Naworth and Richard Onslow for 99 years as security for payment of the remaining £4297 10s 4d; but the sum has been paid by Chaloner Chute. By the present deeds, therefore, Howard and Onslow assign the Greystoke estates, except Dufton, to him and it is declared that Lady Katherine Howard acknowledges the receipt of her full payment.
2 docs., 15-16 July 1647

D6688-
6689　Quitclaims of Francis Howard and Edward Howard, 6th and 5th sons respectively of the late Earl of Arundel to their elder brother Henry [later 6th Duke of Norfolk], second son of the late Earl, in respect of:

>　The Barony of Greystock and other lands (no details) in Cumberland.

2 docs., 1660

D7129　Annuity of £100 by Elizabeth, countess dowager of Arundel and Surrey, with the agreement of the Hon. Charles Howard of 'Darkin' (Dorking) in Surrey, her fourth son, to Philip Howard, esq., her third son, out of:

>　The two parks of Graystocke and Gowbray and their appurtenant lands in the parish of Graystocke in Cumberland

Signature: *Elizabeth Arundell and Surry*

1 doc., March 1668

D7130　Assignment of two lease terms by the Hon Charles Howard of Dorking to John Warham of Benville in Dorset:

>　i) the Castle and site of the Castle of Graystock with all houses, barns, stables and other edifices; mill called Graystock mill, with appurts; the park of Graystock with the lands belonging, viz., 3000a. of land, arable, meadow and pasture; lands called the Demesne lands, Castle Close, the Fitts, Mill Lands and the Haleings; two parks called Gowbrey and Arey Parkes, with appurts; all in the parish of Graystock in Cumberland

>　ii) water corn mill called Grisedale Mill, formerly let to John Robinson at £3 a year; water corn mill called Spence Mill, formerly let to Hugh Robinson at 20s. a year; water corn mill called Knott Mill formerly let to Timothy Fetherston at 2s. a year; water corn mill called Sparkhead Mill formerly let to Thomas Rumney at 2s. a year; cottage with appurts called Smiths Forge, formerly let to William Westry at 1s. a year; parcel of land called Hithering Flatts formerly let to Andrew Wharton at 7s. a year; all the fishings in Ulnesse waters formerly let to various tenants of the manor of Wethermelock at the combined rent of £2 7s; all in Cumberland and parcel of the parish and Barony of Graystocke; and tenement and lands formerly let to John Huetson together with the sheepwalk thereto belonging, in Orton in Westmorland

Recites two previous 21-year leases dated Dec. 1671 from the dowager countess to Charles Howard: the first (property i) at 190 annual rent; the second (property ii) at £16 annual rent. Howard now assigns these leases to Warham as security for the repayment of £260 by June 1679

1 doc., June 1674

D7116-
7118
Bargain and sale and deed to raise a tenant to the *praecipe* [to enable a Common Recovery]

The Rt. Hon. Henry, Earl of Norwich [future 6th Duke of Norfolk], Earl Marshal of England, grants premises as below to Richard Marriott, esq., and Thomas West, gentleman, both of St. Clement Danes in Middlesex, so that Marriott may be the tenant and vouchee from whom the Earl recovers:

> i) The baronies of Graystock and Brough or Burgh, the castles of Graystock, Drombrough and Rowcliffe, the manor and lordships of Brough alias Burgh, Beamond, Kirkanders, Westlevington, Bownsse [sic], Drombrough, Whiterigg, and Whiterigleas, Lancroft, Aynethorne, Cardronocke, Glasson, Easton, Fingland, Rowcliffe, Etterby, Ayketon, Thursby, Graystocke, Motherby, Staynton, Materdale, Grisedale, Wethermelocke, Sparkhead, Berriar and Newbiggin; and the forests of Matterdale and Grisedale with all their rights, members and appurtenants in Cumberland.
>
> ii) The manor of Dufton with its rights, members and appurts in Westmorland and advowson of the churches of Dufton and Orton and free fishing in the water of Ullswater in Westmorland

- with all other castles, forests, parks, warrens, rectories, rents, farms, messuages, houses, mills and lands, etc., in the parishes and places as above, and also in Gowborrow, Array, Murray, Penrith alias Perith and Gill in Cumberland and in Glincoyne, Barton, Patterdale, Deepdale, Sandwicke, Ulleswicke and Ullswater in Westmorland. The Recovery itself is also with these deeds.

3 docs., Oct-Nov 1675

STD
69/4-6
Conveyance by Henry, Duke of Norfolk to Henry, Lord Mowbray, his eldest son and heir, of:

> Baronies of Graystock and Brough and castles of Graystock, Drombrough and Rowclife; and manors of Brough, Beamond, Kirklanders, Westlevington, Bownesse, Drombrough, Whitrigg, Whiterigleas, Lancroft, Aynthorn, Cardronock, Glasson, Easton, Fingland, Rowcliffe, Etterby, Ayketon, Thursby, Graystock, Motherby, Staynton, Waterdale, Grisdale,

Wethermlocke, Sparkhead, Berryer and Newbiggin; Forest of Waterdale [sic, properly, Matterdale] and Grisedale all in co. Cumberland; and the manor of Dufton, with all its rights, in Westmorland.
3 docs., Nov 1680

D7133   Articles of agreement between the Hon. Edward Howard of Norfolk, esq., son of Henry Frederick [15th] Earl of Arundel and [his nephew] the Right Hon. Henry, lord Mowbray, son and heir apparent of the Most Noble lord Henry, [6th] duke of Norfolk, concerning:

> i) an entitlement to part of the baronies of Burgh and Graistocke and lands in Cumberland and Westmorland
> ii) a certain 'cabinett of rarities', part of the estate of Alathea, late Countess of Arundel
> iii) an annuity of £300 from the manor of Rotherham, co. York

Recites that Edward has a financial stake in i); and that he possesses ii) and iii). By the present deed, in return for a payment of £2000, he relinquishes i) and ii), and any of the *reall or personal jewells, cabinetts, Rarities, timber or woodfalls* of the late Countess, to Lord Mowbray; who also promises him annuities amounting to £400 out of i). Edward is also empowered to dedicate iii) to another recipient, if he so wishes.
1 doc., July 1681

D7137   Agreement between Henry, [7th] duke of Norfolk, Earl Marshall of England and Sir John Lowther of Lowther in Westmorland, concerning;

The Barony of Burgh and appurtenant lands in Cumberland.

The Barony of Burgh is to be sold by the Duke of Norfolk to Sir John Lowther for £14,400. It is agreed that Lowther shall withold £2825 of the purchase money against financial claims on the estate that might be made by Philip, Charles, or Esme Howard (brothers of the Duke) or by Elizabeth Theresa, wife of Bartholomew Russell, sister of the Duke. Such claims could arise under the will of their late brother, Francis Howard, desceased.
signature and seal of John Lowther
1 doc., 4 Dec. 1685

D7119   Conveyance for one month by the Rt. Hon. Francis, lord Newport to the Most Noble Henry, duke of Norfolk, knight of the Garter
> Barony and Castle of Greystocke and manors of Greystocke, Motherby, Staynton, Waterdale [sic, properly Matterdale], Grisedale, Wethermelock, Sparkhead, Berryar and New Biggin and the forest of Waterdale [sic] and Grisedale in Cumberland; manor of Dufton (etc., as in D7116-7118, ii,) in Westmorland; with all messuages, etc., in parishes as specified in D7116-7118 above

1 doc., 6 February 1687/8

D7120   Conveyance for one month by John Coggs, citizen and goldsmith of London to Henry, duke of Norfolk, as above:
> Forests of Matterdale and Grisedale, manor of Dufton, advowsons of Dufton and Orton, free fishing of Ullswater, and property in Penreth *alias* Pereth [Penrith], and Gill, Dufton, Orton, Glencoyne, Borton, Patterdale, Deepdale, Sandwith, Ullswick and Ullswater

1 doc, 8 February 1687/8

D7021   Agreement between Henry, duke of Norfolk and his uncle Charles Howard respecting *that there have been and still are severall matters in dispute* between them concerning:
> i) Manor of Dufton and lands in Orton, Ulswick, Sandwick and elsewhere in Westmorland and Cumberland (claimed by b) as part of the Barony of Greystoke)
> ii) arears of rents from the houses in or near Surrey Street near the Strand in Middlesex

The Duke agrees to uphold Charles Howard's claim to the premises cited and they both agree to accept the overall valuation of the Greystoke estate which William, as arbiter and judge appointed on 7 March last, shall decide, the Duke to compensate Charles Howard upon the valuation.

1 doc., 27 April 1693

D7131   Bargain and sale by a) the Most Noble Prince, Henry, duke of Norfolk, Earl Marshall of England to b) the Hon Charles Howard, esq., uncle of a), and to c) Henry Charles Howard, son and heir apparent of b)
> The Barony of Graystock, the manor, lordship and castle of Graystock and all appurtenant rights and liberties, etc. and advowsons, in Cumberland and Westmorland

The Duke grants the premises to c) to hold in trust for the heirs of b).
1 doc., 10 May 1695

D7132   Revocation by parties b) and c) of D7131 above of the terms of a deed of 26-27 March 1700 concerning the Barony of Greystoke as above; and declaration that they hold the premises to the use of c) and his heirs.
I doc., Nov. 1707

-oOo-

ii Sales from the estate

D7077   Bargain and sale for £245 6s. 8d. by Philip, Earl of Arundel, and Ann, his wife, to Cuthbert Syssom and Edward Harrysoun, both of Barton, co. Westmorland, yeomen, of:

> Capital messuage called Thistlethwaite *alias* Kirkbaroughe in the parish of Barton, with the several messuages and lands pertaining, producing an annual rent of 53s. 4d., viz: capital messuage and lands at Ellerbeck at yearly rent of 13s. 2d; messuage and lands called Thorpe at yearly rent of 15s. 1d; messuage and lands in Sockbreed at yearly rent of 7s. 4d; closes of arable called Momsey Close (1a) and Little Ellerclose (1a.) at yearly rent of 16d; close of meadow and pasture called Skallowe Close (4a.) in Trostormonte, and ½ a. land in Bartons Closes at yearly rent of 3s. 4d; all in Barton. Names of tenants given.

All conveyed with common of pasture, turbary and brakes in various [unspecified] places in Barton.
1 doc., 14 Oct 1583

D 7115   Bargain and sale for £19 by [St.] Philip, [13th] Earl of Arundel and Lady Anne his wife and Francis Lamplughe of Dovanbie in Cumberland

> Messuage and appurts in Tallentyer in Cumberland in the occ. of John Bowes and Elizabeth Bowes, widow, held at 13s. 4d. annual rent; messuage in High Jerbye in the occ. of John Sympsoun, annual rent 7s. 8d; another messuage and appurts in High Jerbye in the occ. of John Fell annual rent 8s. 8d.; another messuage and appurts in High Jerbye in the occ. of John Hutchenson, annual rent 8s. 8d; messuage and appurts. in Cleator in the occ. of Gabriel Williamson, annual rent 10s; another messuage and appurts in Cleator in the occ. of Richard Johnsoun, annual rent 2s. 7d; messuage and appurts in Langrigge in the occ. of Edward Raiper and George Porter, annual rent 10s; all in Cumberland and to be held with all relevant houses, lands, woods, commons [etc.]

Signature of Lamplughe; no seal
1 doc., 14 Oct. 1583

D7136   Bargain and sale by a) Anne, countess dowager of Arundel, Thomas, earl of Arundel and Surrey, the Rt. Hon. lord William Howard of Naward and the Lady Elizabeth, his wife to b) John Holland of Kenninghall in Norfolk, esq., John Cornwallis of Earl Soham in Suffolk, esq., Robert Consfield of London. esq., c) John Dudley of Grays Inn, gentleman and d) Thomas Jackson of Stanicke, yeoman

i) Two messuages each with 12a. arable, meadow and pasture, held at 6s 8d annual rent; 1a. arable, meadow and pasture on the west side of Bocherdgate, held at 20d. annual rent; barn and 1a. and 1½ roods of arable, meadow and pasture at 2s. 9½d. annual rent; barn and 1 rood of arable, meadow and pasture at 3d. annual rent; 1½a. of arable, meadow and pasture in Calvert Close at 2s; each comprising arable, meadow and pasture and held of the manor of Sockage and in the suburbs of the City of Carliell

ii) 1a. at 2s. annual rent, 2a. at 4s., 1a. at 2s. and 1½a. at 3s; each comprising arable, meadow and pasture and each held of the manor of Dalston

iii) House and 1r. at 1s. 4d. annual rent, barkhouse with appurts. in Caldagate at 12d., cottage in Caldagate at 16d. and messuage in Caldagate at 12d., all in the suburbs of the City of Carlisle

iv) Burgage or messuage in Abbey-Gate with 6a. arable, meadow and pasture; barkhouse in the suburbs of the city at 5s. annual rent; messuage or burgage in Fishergate at 9s.; messuage and 1r. arable at 4s. 4d, and messuage and one garth at 6s. 6d., both in Fulkholme

v) 1a. at 4s. annual rent in Weriholme and 2a. arable, meadow and pasture in Wereholme and Brodegarth at 9s., each in Weriholme; barn and a garth in the manor of Sockage in Weriholme at 7½d. annual rent and 1a. of arable, meadow and pasture in Painelands at 2s., also held of the manor of Sockage

vi) One burgage or messuage in Ricardgate in the city of Carliell held at 20s. annual rent; burgage or messuage at Ricardgate within the City with 10a. arable, meadow and pasture held of the manor of Sockage, near the City, at 36s.; burgage or messuage at Ricardgate and 4a. arable, meadow and pasture held of the manor of Sockage at 32s. 4d.; messuage and tenement with

a garth at Ricardgate without the City, at 4s.; parcel
(½r.) without the City in the brode garthes near the
City, at 6d. and 4a. arable, meadow and pasture near
the City of Carliell at 7s. 6d. annual rent

Names of tenants of each separate property are
given.

The Dowager Countess and family (party a), and their family
trustees (party b), sell to c) and d) for an unspecified sum of money.
They agree to secure the purchasers' title by a fine or recovery to
be levied to the use of d), the acutual purchaser, and his heirs.
1 doc., 8 May 1611

D7125-
7126   Bargain and sale for £200 by the Hon Henry Howard, esq. of
Albury in Surrey, second son of Henry [Frederick], late earl of
Arundel and Surrey, decd. and heir apparent to his elder brother
Thomas, now Earl of Arundel and Surrey to the Hon Charles
Howard, esq. of Naworth in Cumberland and his heirs

Moiety of the manor of Aynstaple alias Aynstaplith
alias Aynstapleth [Ainstable] with all rights, members
and appurts; and moiety of all the demesnes, houses,
barns, gardens, etc., mills, lands, pastures, meadows,
feedings, commons, etc. turbaries, mines, quarries,
fisheries, etc.

The second deed expresses Henry Howard's worries that Charles
Howard's title has not yet been properly secured. He therefore
grants him the premises below, to hold until the matter can be
cleared up by a subsequent deed:

messuages, tenements and farmholds of the yearly
value of £18 10s. and £3 6s. (tenants' names given) at
Gaitford within the manor of Worsopp alias Worksopp,
co. Notts,

2 docs., July 1656

NB. *Re. sale of the Barony of Burgh for £14,000 in 1685, see D7137*
on page 261 above.

D7079   Conveyance for £300 by Hon. Charles Howard to Matthew
Humberstone, esq. and Samuel Winder, merchant, both of London,
of a fee simple estate in remainder in:

The manor of Dufton and advowson of the church
of Dufton; with all messuages, cottages, mills, lands,
commons, glebelands, woods, courts, privileges, etc.

Cites another deed of same date; and original lease of 1645 by the
Henry Howard esq., one of the sons of Henry Frederick, earl of

Arundel, to Thomas Hatton and others
1 doc., July 1695.
NB. *This deed is pursuant to D7021 on p.262 above*

D7138-
7139   Conveyance by the Hon. Henry Charles Howard, lord of the Barony
of Greystoke to Thomas Dawson of Great Blencow in the parish
of Dacre, gentleman

> Messuage called Townehead lying in the town and fields
> of Great Blencowe with arable and meadow in the
> Ennam and Bullose Close and in various other places
> in the fields of Great Blencowe (27a.); two closes of
> arable and meadow called Powlett Croft and Crooks
> (4a.), abutting S. on Blencow Common and parcel
> of the former messuage; messuage called Heskett's
> tenement and several parcels within the town fields and
> territories of Great Blencowe (18a.); with other ground
> lying in the territories of Newbiggin in Cumberland,
> viz. ½a. upon the Ings, 3r. on a place called Mirelands,
> 1r. upon Moss Fornes; parcels of land (12a.) known
> as Murrays Tenement; freehold messuage or farmhold
> with appurts. in the fields and territories of Stanton
> and Newbggin; annual tithes of hay arising from the
> north side of Graystock, north from the church to the
> Townhead, which were subject of a former exchange in
> 1549 between Giles Cannon and John Dacre, parson
> of Graystock, exchanged for a close of ground called
> Haybray near Gillfield
> Names of tenants of all holdings are given.

The conveyance was effected by a lease of the premises to Richard
Sare of St Andrew, Holborn, Middlesex, stationer, to hold for 99
years or during Thomas Dawson's life time; and by a lease and
release to George Wilkinson of Penrith, gentleman in trust for
Thomas Dawson. Dawson was to pay the rental value to Charles
Howard for a short lease term, as security for his eventual payment
of the full purchase price of £200. Howard also agrees to levy a
fine to secure Dawson's title. [The property descriptions in these
deeds imply that Dawson, or his father had already acquired the
various pieces of land from previous tenants. This may therefore,
in effect, be a manorial enfranchisement, though it is not stated
as such in the text.]
3 docs., 26-28 March 1717

-oOo-

iii *Leases, and other evidences of title*

D7140   Exemplification of a judgement in Court of Kings Bench in a case of trespass and ejection by William Aldured, by his attorney Richard Aston, plaintiff, *v.* Thomas Jeffrey, defendant, concerning:

> Two messuages, 40a. land, 40a. meadow and 40a. pasture in Thursby in Cumberland

Recites a former lease for 7 years commencing October 1674 by Edward, Lord Howard, baron of Escrick and others, to the plaintiff. Judgement in favour of the plaintiff who is to receive £7 19s 10d costs from the defendant.
1 doc., Oct 1675

D7141   Prospecting lease for 31 years by William Williams of Joneby Hall in Cumberland, gentleman to the Right Hon. Henry [Howard], earl of Norwich and Earl Marshall of England, at annual rent of 340 cart-loads of coal:

> Mines, quarries and seams of coal in or on the various wastes of the manor of Jonesby, co. Cumberland, or in a pasture called Upper Leeshow near Greystoke Park

Liberty for the Earl's workmen to dig, etc. The rent is payable only after coal is found.
1 doc., Jan 1675/6

D7142/1   Lease for 21 years at an annual rent of £18 by Henry, Earl of Arundel, to James Maxwell of Naward, co. Cumberland, gent., of:

> Parcel of ground called Birckmire Boggs, in Kirklevington, in the manor of West Lavington, co. Cumberland

Lease to run from Martinmas next. The premises are already in Maxwell's occupation.
1 doc., Aug 1681

D7142/2 Case heard in the Court of Kings bench in a plea of trespass taken by Charles Howard, esq., plaintiff against Edward Shepherd, yeoman, defendant concerning:

> Rights of estovers in Gowberray Park in the barony of Greystoke

> The defendent had cut grass and bracken, etc., for fire and other necessities at home, which he claimed was part of his right as tenant of an ancient holding of the manor of Wethermealocke, itself parcel of the Barony of Greystoke

Judgement to be made at the forthcoming Michaelmas assizes to be held at Carlisle
1 doc., Trinity term, 1687

**D6966-
6989** Abstracts of title, reciting from 12 January 1707/8 to 24 May 1774, of Charles, Earl of Surrey to the Barony of Greystoke and lands in Cumberland and Westmorland, being:

> Greystoke Castle, manors of Greystoke, Motherby, Stainton, Matterdale, Grisedale, Wethermealock, Sparkhead, Barrier, and Newbiggin, and the forest of Matterdale and Grisedale; Greystoke Park, manor of Deepdale, fishing of Ullswater;

With attested copies of deeds relating to this estate, 1779 -1788.
24 docs., 1707/8 - 1788.

**D4585-
4588** Grants of annuity by Charles, Duke of Norfolk to James Wombwell of Bath, Somerset, esq. on

> (i) Chatterlen Hall (235a.) with Chatterlen Wood Farm (97a.) and wood ground (51a.) all in Newton co Cumberland
> (ii) Deepdale Hall (131a.), Glencoine Farm with Gowberrow West park (810a.), unenclosed ground (1052a.), Glencoine Fishery and Brown How (1a.). Names of tenants given.

The annuities are granted in 1806 and 1812 pursuant to loans originally taken out in 1798. [**See also:** *Surrey title deeds: consolidated ducal estates.*]
4 docs, 1798-1812

-oOo-

THE DUKE OF NORFOLK'S DEEDS
AT ARUNDEL CASTLE

CATALOGUE 1

Dacre Estates in Northern Counties

Index

Introductions to the index

Place names

One of the most time-consuming tasks in compiling this catalogue was to allocate provenance by estate to deeds which had formerly been arranged alphabetically by place. It is hoped therefore that the basic arrangement of the catalogue itself will guide researchers to the places they are looking for. It is advisable, in any case, to look at each section holistically in order to understand the context of any individual deed. The *Contents* on page v of the *General Introduction* and on **page xxv (Part I)** and **page 257 (Part II)** give an overview of the entire catalogue. The more-specific lists of *Contents* are as follows.

The main Greystoke family holdings in Cumbria and several other counties:
Use the gazetteers on pages **3-5** (medieval deeds) and on pages **265-266** (post-medieval deeds).

Contents for individual estates in Part I, Medieval Deeds, are as follows:
Cumbria: Greystoke Barony p. **29**; Barony of Burgh, p.**40-41**; Carlisle, p.**85**; Kirkoswald, Penrith and area, p.**103**; Appleby and area, p.**117**; Westmorland deeds, p.**143**; Cleator and area, p.**173**.
Lancashire: a few references are included in the Cleator deeds, see *Contents*, p. **173**.
Yorkshire: use main *Contents* on p. **189** and subsequent short lists on pp **197, 219, 221, 223** and **247**.

Personal Names

This is a simplified index of surnames only. It is intended as a preliminary guide to local and family historians and, as with place-names, above, it is hoped that they will allow themselves time to look holistically at the entire group of deeds in which a particular name occurs. One person's name is often written in many variant forms. The researcher therefore needs to think laterally.

A large proportion of these deeds originate in an era when surnames of ordinary people were in the process of being formed. A large number of surnames describe where they live, while others reflect an occupation. If a party or a witness is described as *the skinner*, or, *the baker*, there is no absolute guarantee that his descendants became Skinner or Baker, but it is very possible. The same applies to those who are described by reference to their father, as, for example, *William son of John*. Their descendants may well have the surnames John, Johns or Johnson. Indeed, the very fact that their name was recorded in that particular way helped the perpetuation of that form. It would become necessary to refer back and to perpetuate the form as part of the verification of legal title.

For persons cited by a single fore-name, the case is less clear. However, I have included many of them in this index. Parsons lacking their own personal surname have been indexed by the name of their parish and ... *the clerk*, as an occupation, is indexed as *clerk*. Higher ecclesiastical dignitaries can be found under the name of their cathedral, priory or other convent. The noble and landed families whose deeds constitute this catalogue, and other related families, have been indexed generically and not by the names of individuals, except where a distinction has to be drawn, for clarity.

Index of Persons